The Life of
Mr. Thomas Betterton

The Life

OF

Mr. Thomas Betterton,

THE LATE
EMINENT TRAGEDIAN.

BY

Charles Gildon

Routledge
Taylor & Francis Group

First published in 1710 by Frank Cass and Company Limited

This edition first published in 2018 by Routledge
2 Park Square, Milton Park, Abingdon, Oxon, OX14 4RN
and by Routledge
52 Vanderbilt Avenue, New York, NY 10017, USA

Routledge is an imprint of the Taylor & Francis Group, an informa business

© 1710 by New Preface Arthur Freeman

Publisher's Note
The publisher has gone to great lengths to ensure the quality of this reprint but
points out that some imperfections in the original copies may be apparent.

Disclaimer
The publisher has made every effort to trace copyright holders and welcomes
correspondence from those they have been unable to contact.
A Library of Congress record exists under ISBN:

ISBN 13: 978-0-367-17960-1 (hbk)
ISBN 13: 978-0-367-17962-5 (pbk)
ISBN 13: 978-0-429-05866-0 (ebk)

EIGHTEENTH CENTURY SHAKESPEARE

No. 4

General Editor : Professor Arthur Freeman, Boston University

The Life of

Mr. Thomas Betterton

The Life

O F

Mr. Thomas Betterton,

THE LATE

EMINENT TRAGEDIAN.

WHEREIN
The Action and Utterance of the
Stage, *Bar*, and *Pulpit*, are distinctly consider'd.

WITH
The Judgment of the late Ingenious *Monsieur de St. Evremond*,
upon the Italian and French Music and Opera's;
in a Letter to the *Duke of Buckingham*.

BY

Charles Gildon

To which is added,
The AMOROUS WIDOW, or the *WANTON WIFE*.
A Comedy. Written by Mr. Betterton.

FRANK CASS & CO. LTD.

1970

Published by
FRANK CASS AND COMPANY LIMITED
67 Great Russell Street, London W.C.1

Copyright © New Preface   Arthur Freeman

First edition   1710
Reprint of First edition
with a new preface   1970

ISBN 0 7146 2517 5

Printed in Great Britain by Clarke, Doble & Brendon Ltd.
Plymouth and London

Preface

For Charles Gildon, the biographical apology itself—'The Life of Mr. Thomas Betterton'—is little more than a skeleton upon which, as a dramatic critic, he might drape a full consideration of 'the action and utterance of the stage', i.e., the technique of acting and theatrical oratory.

Since 1694 (*Miscellaneous Letters and Essays*), when Rymer's *Short View* focused the interest of contemporaries upon Shakespeare in theory and dramatic practice, Gildon among his miscellaneous works had contributed considerably to the evolution of a critical approach to the stage. Grouped often with Rymer and Dennis for his part in the Shakespearean counterattack upon the former, Gildon went on to 'improve' one of Shakespeare's most difficult and unpopular plays, *Measure for Measure* (1699), and contributed *An Essay on the Art, Rise, and Progress of the Stage in Greece, Rome, and England*, and *Remarks on the Plays of Shakespeare* to Curll's spurious 'Volume Seven' of Shakespeare's *Works* (1709) (Rowe had edited all but the poems in six volumes; Curll cashed in on the popularity of the edition; 'Volume Seven' with its apparatus was republished, then, as a matter of course, in 1714—which Ralli takes unaccountably as the first appearance of *Remarks*—1720, 1725, 1726, 1728, etc.)

PREFACE

Gildon went on to consider the whole aesthetic of poetry, lyrical, narrative, and dramatic, in his *Complete Art of Poetry* (six parts, 1718), which bears on Shakespeare, to an extent, as well. *The Life of Betterton* is not strictly speaking largely Shakespeareana, although most of the instances Gildon chooses for illustration are from Shakespeare; but as a handbook of theatrical methodology it is unique and almost unprecedented. 'I flatter myself', says Gildon, 'that . . . I am (as far as I know) the first who in *English* has attempted this subject.'

There are two states of leaf A5^v, one concluding '*Your Sincere Friend,*/and *Humble Servant,*/ Charles Gildon [in larger type]', and one omitting the name of the author. This has given rise to descriptions of an 'anonymous issue' and even two 'editions', but as it is simply unlikely that anyone intended to publish a dedicatory epistle ending on a comma, the phenomenon might best be treated as one of indifferent variation, the correct version no doubt that with Gildon's name included. Copies of each 'issue' examined (BM 1415.d.15 and 276.i.32, Harvard, three copies) match exactly, to the twenty-nine press marks and broken type, save for the accidental anonymity of the former. The states seem about equally common in commerce and collections.

The present text is printed from an 'anonymous' copy in the possession of the Publishers, dismantled by the General Editor, save for the portrait, which is photographed from BM 276.i.32, and the named variant of A5^v (printed at the

PREFACE

conclusion of our text), photographed from the same copy. The book collates A-M^8 [A1, the engraved portrait, conjugate with A8] A-E^{8}F^4 [F4^v blank; no half-sheet variations in F^4 observed]. There are no cancels or other abnormalities of construction in the copy employed.

April 1969   A. F.

Mr. Thomas Betterton

Totus Mundus Agit Histrionem.

B. Kneller pinx.   R. V. Gucht Sculp.

THE
LIFE
OF

Mr. *Thomas Betterton*,

The late Eminent

TRAGEDIAN.

WHEREIN

The ACTION and UTTERANCE of the *Stage*,
Bar, and *Pulpit*, are diſtinctly conſider'd.

WITH

The JUDGMENT of the late Ingenious *Monſieur
de St. EVREMOND*, upon the *Italian* and
French MUSIC and OPERA's ; in a Letter
to the Duke of *Buckingham*.

To which is added,

The AMOROUS WIDOW, or the *Wanton Wife*.
A Comedy. Written by Mr. BETTERTON.
Now firſt printed from the Original Copy.

Quis Noſtrùm tam animo agreſti, & duro fuit, ut Roſcii *Morte
nuper non commoveretur ? Qui cum eſſet Senex mortuus ;
tamen propter* excellentem Artem *ac Venuſtatem videbatur
omnino mori non debuiſſe.*

Cic. in Orat. pro ARCHIA Poeta.

LONDON:

Printed for ROBERT GOSLING, at the *Mitre*, near the *Inner-
Temple Gate* in *Fleetſtreet*. 1710. Price 3 s. 6 d.

TO

Richard Steele, Efq;

S I R,

THE following Piece was fcarce yet an *Embryo,* when I defign'd its full Growth for your Protection. For tho we Authors generally feem fond

A 3   of

of adorning the Frontispiece of our Books with *pompous Titles,* as if we deriv'd from those not only Security but Fame to our Works: yet I can't but remember, that, among the *Ancients,* the Name of a *learned Friend* was of greater Consideration with the Writer, than the Dignity of a Man of Power ; and that the Greatness of any Man in the *Political State,* according to them, did not raise his Authority in the Common-Wealth of Letters, above his real Merits in the *Arts* and *Sciences,* unless he ennobled it, by giving such Encouragement to them, as they very rarely in our Days meet with from the GREAT ONES.

Being,

Being, therefore, to write on an Art, which has not been much cultivated in our Nation, either in the *Practice* or *Theory*; what I had moſt to wiſh for, on the Publication of this Eſſay, was the Approbation of One, to whom the *Witty* and the *Learned* allow ſome Place in the Politer Studies and Fine Arts. An Addreſs of this Nature is not without the agreeable Vanity of recommending a Man to the World, as a Perſon ſkilful in the Matter, of which he treats; and the Merit of Mr. Steele, in the Kingdom of the *Muſes*, is too well known to the *Beaux Eſprits*, not to ſecure me from the Fear of the Railery of *Aſcyltos* on *Encolpius*,

A 4

pius, in *Petronius Arbiter*───── *Ut foris Cænares Poetam laudaſti;* or of *Manley* on my Lord *Plauſible*──── *That rather than not flatter, he would flatter the Poets of the Age, whom no Body elſe would flatter.*

But I have choſen to addreſs this Diſcourſe to you, becauſe the *Art,* of which it treats, is of your familiar Acquaintance, and the Graces of ACTION and UTTE-RANCE come naturally under the Conſideration of a *Dramatic Wri-ter.* I flatter my ſelf, that, as I am (as far as I know) the firſt, who in *Engliſh* has attempted this Subject, in the Extent of the Diſcourſe before you, ſo I am apt to believe, that I have pretty well

well exhauſted the Matter ; and laid down ſuch *General* and *Par-ticular Rules*, as may raiſe the Stage from the preſent Neglect it lies under, to that Eſteem, which it drew from the moſt polite Na-tion, that ever was in the World, and that, which it will always de-ſerve from Men of Senſe, when under a juſt Regulation, and a-dorn'd, as it ought to be, with GOOD ACTORS and GOOD PLAYS.

The *former* may be rais'd, I hope, from what I have deliver'd in the following Treatiſe, as the *later* from your Example, which may inſpire our Authors with the Knowledge of Nature, and the Art of keeping her al-ways in their View, adorn'd with that

viii *The Epistle Dedicatory.*
that *Harmony,* *Decorum,* and *Order,* which ought perpetually to shine in such PUBLIC REPRESENTATIONS.

I am, *S I R,*

Your Sincere Friend,

and *Humble Servant,*

THE

THE
PREFACE.

I *Should not have troubled the Reader with a Preface to this little Treatise, but to prevent an Objection, which may be made, and that is, that I have been a* Plagiary, *and deliver'd Rules for my own, which are taken out of other Authors. I first allow, that I have borrow'd many of them from the* French, *but then the* French *drew most of them from* Quintilian *and other Authors. Yet the* Frenchman *has improv'd the Ancients in this Particular, by supplying what was lost by the Alteration of Custom,*

with

with *Obſervations more peculiar to the preſent Age.*

Arts *were never brought to Perfection by one Hand, and tho I have made ſeveral Advancements my ſelf upon thoſe, who have gone before me, yet I know not but a diligent Study, and judicious Obſervation, may produce new and more eaſy Rules. If I have lead the Way with any tolerable Succeſs, the Satisfaction will be too great to be leſſen'd by being ſucceeded with a more maſterly Endeavour.*

Being oblig'd to have a Regard to the Action *and* Utterance *of the* Pulpit *and* Bar, *as well as the* Stage, *I was compell'd to bring my Examples from* Oratory *more than from the* Drama. *But if this meets with the Approbation of the Learned, I may perhaps publiſh a Treatiſe for the Stage alone. However, a Player, that is Maſter of thoſe Qualities, which he ought to poſſeſs, by ſtudying with Application this Diſcourſe, may arrive at a Perfection, which this Age has not ſeen.*

E P I.

EPILOGUE

Spoken by Mrs. *BARRY*,

At the Theatre Royal in *Drury-Lane*, *April* the
7th, 1709.

At Her Playing in *Love for Love* ;
With Mrs BRACEGIRDLE.

For the Benefit of Mr. BETTERTON.

Written by N. Rowe, Efq;

S fome brave Knight, who once with
Spear and Shield,

Had fought Renown in many a well
fought Field,

But now no more with Sacred Fame infpir'd,

Was to a Peaceful Hermitage retir'd ;

There

There, if by Chance difaſt'rous Tales he hears,

Of Matrons Wrongs and captive Virgins Tears,

He feels ſoft Pity urge his Gen'rous Breaſt,

And vows once more to ſuccour the Diſtreſs'd.

Buckled in Mail he ſallies on the Plain,

And turns him to the Feats of Arms again.

So we, to former Leagues of Friendſhip true,

Have bid once more our peaceful Homes adieu,

To aid Old THOMAS, and to pleaſure you.

Like Errant Damſels boldly we engage,

Arm'd, as you ſee, for the defenceleſs Stage.

Time was, when this good Man no Help did lack,

And ſcorn'd that any She ſhould hold his Back.

But now, ſo Age and Frailty have ordain'd,

By two at once He's forc'd to be ſuſtain'd.

You

4

EPILOGUE.

You fee, what Failing Nature brings Man to, ⎫
And yet let none Infult, for ought we know, ⎬
She may not wear fo well with fome of you : ⎭

Tho Old, you find his Strength is not clean paft,

But true as Steel, he's Mettle to the laft.

If better he perform'd in Days of Yore, ⎫
Yet now he gives you all that's in his Pow'r; ⎬
What can the youngeft of you all do more? ⎭

(dumb,
What he has been, tho prefent Praife be ⎫
⎬
Shall haply be a *Theme* in Times to come, ⎭

As now we talk of Roscius, and of *Rome*.

Had you with-held your Favours on this Night,

Old Shakespear's Ghoft had ris'n to do him
Right.

With Indignation had you feen him frown

Upon a worthlefs, witlefs, taftelefs Town ;

Griev'd

Griev'd and Repining you had heard him fay,

Why are the *Mufes* Labours caft away ?

Why did I only Write what only he could Play ?

But fince, like Friends to Wit, thus throng'd you
  meet,

Go on and make the Gen'rous Work complete ;

Be true to Merit, and ftill own his Caufe,

Find fomething for him more than bare Applaufe.

In juft Remembrance of your Pleafures paft,

Be kind, and give him a Difcharge at laft.

In Peace and Eafe Life's Remnant let him wear,

And hang his confecrated Bufkin here.

THE

THE
LIFE
OF
Mr. *Thomas Betterton*, &c.

INTRODUCTION.

AS it was said of *Brutus* and *Cassius*, that they were the last of the *Romans*; so it may be said of Mr. BETTERTON, that he was the last of our *Tragedians*. There being, therefore, so much due to his Memory from all Lovers of the Stage; I could not lay aside my Design of conveying his Name with this Discourse at least to a little longer Date, than Nature has given his Body. Nor can I imagine, that it can be look'd on, as injurious to our Reputation, either as Men of Can-

B   dour,

dour, Figure or Senfe, to exprefs a Concern for
the Lofs of a Man fo excellent in an Art
which is now expiring, and for which Antiquity had fo peculiar a Value ; fince it is plain
from the Motto of this Book, that *Cicero* pleading the Caufe of the Poet *Archias*, tells the Judge,
a Man of the firft Quality, that every Body
was concern'd for the Death of *Rofcius* the *Comedian* ; or which is more emphatic, fays he,
*Who of us was of fo brutifh and four a Temper
as not to be mov'd at the late Death of* ROSCIUS?
*Who, though he dy'd old, yet for the Excellence
of his Art, and Beauty in Performance, feem'd
as if he ought to have been exempted entirely from
Death.*

Whether Mr. *Betterton* or *Rofcius* make a
juft Parallel or not in their Merits as Actors, is
difficult to know ; but thus far it is certain,
that let the Excellence of the *Roman* be never fo
great, that of the *Briton* was the greateft we
had : and tho we fhall find, that in *Cicero's*
Time the Decorums of the Stage were more exactly obferv'd, than in ours, yet we may fuppofe Mr. *Betterton*, in his own particular Performance, on a Foot with *Rofcius*, efpecially
when we confider that our Player excelled in
both *Comedy* and *Tragedy*, the *Roman* only in
the former, as far as we can difcover.

To give our *Englifh* Actor yet the Preheini-
nence, I fhall here by writing his Life make
him convey to others fuch Inftructions, that if
they are perfectly underftood, and juftly practis'd,

&ctis'd, will add such Beauties to their Performances, as may render his Loss of less Consequence to the Stage. *Plato* and *Xenophon* introduce *Socrates* in their Discourses, to give the greater Authority to what they say, on those important Points which they would the more forcibly recommend to their Readers I shall, therefore, make the same Use of Mr. *Betterton*, on a Subject in which he may reasonably be thought a very competent Judge.

I know it may be objected, that the Qualifications I make him require, and the Precepts he gives, may seem to render this Art impossible for any other to attain to, as *Cicero* is said in his *Orator*, to do with the Oratorian Art.

I confess that I do make him require Qualifications, of which he was not perhaps Master himself; but I presume that can be no Objection to them provided they are necessary, or at least conducive to the forming a complete Player; for we may daily hear many Painters, or even *Lovers* of the Art, who will tell you what Qualities are necessary to a great Master in History Painting, who yet do not themselves pretend to be possess'd of them. And the same will hold of many other Arts.

But if, indeed, there were any Precepts deliver'd, or any Qualifications requir'd, which would render a Mastery in this Art so difficult, that it could not be attain'd, the Objection would be far more solid, and worthy of our Notice; but I dare affirm, that as the Stages are

now

now in the Hands and Management of the Players, there is not one Qualification fet down,
which is not abfolutely neceffary to do Juftice
to *Art*, in *Judgment* and *Performance*.

Nor can I find that *Cicero*, in his Book *de O-
ratore*, has requir'd any Impoffibility in his Can-
didate for Eloquence ; and it is evident, that has
not fo far difcourag'd others from attempting
that noble Science, but that every Age has produc'd fome eminent in it, tho few or none
have arriv'd to an Equality with him in the
Performance for want of thofe very Qualities
requir'd by him to the forming a *complete Orator*. Thus tho, to be a perfect Mafter, all the
Qualities delivered be neceffary, yet there is
Room for Praife as well as Induftry for others,
who are not capable of attaining the whole.
Such therefore, whofe Genius is not fo exten-
five as to comprehend the whole, ought entirely
to apply themfelves to, and be content with,
the *Performance*, leaving the Office of *Judging*
to thofe, whofe greater Skill and Knowledge better qualify them for Judges.

Having premis'd thefe things by way of Introduction, I fhall now proceed to the Life of
Mr. *Betterton*.

MR. *Thomas Betterton* was born in *Tuttle-
ſtreet, Weſtminſter* ;   his Father being
Under-Cook to King *Charles the Firſt :* And
when he was now come to Years ſufficient, his
Father bound him Apprentice to one Mr. *Rhodes*
a Bookſeller, at the Bible at *Charing-Croſs*, and
he had for his Under-Prentice Mr. *Kynaſton.*

But that which prepar'd Mr. *Betterton* and
his Fellow-Prentice for the Stage, was that his
Maſter *Rhodes* having formerly been *Wardrobe*
Keeper to the King's Company of *Comedians* in
the *Black-Fryars*, on General *Monck*'s March to
London, in 1659. with his Army, got a Licence
from the Powers then in being, to ſet up a
Company of Players in the *Cockpit* in *Drury-
lane*, and ſoon made his Company compleat,
his Apprentices, Mr. *Betterton* for Mens Parts,
and Mr. *Kynaſton* for Womens Parts, being at
the Head of them.

Mr. *Betterton* was now about 22 Years of
Age, when he got a great Applauſe by acting in
the *Loyal Subject*, the *Wildgooſe Chaſe*, the *Spa-
niſh Curate*, and many more.   But while our
young Actor is thus riſing under his Maſter
Rhodes, Sir *William D'Avenant* getting a Patent
of King *Charles* the Second, for erecting a Company under the Name of the Duke of *York*'s
Servants, took Mr. *Betterton* and all that acted
under Mr. *Rhodes* into his Company.   And in
the Year 1662. open'd his Houſe in *Lincolns-Inn
Fields*, with the firſt and ſecond part of the

Siege

Siege of Rhodes, having new Scenes, and Decorations of the Stage, which were then firſt introduc'd into *England*.

Tho this be affirm'd by ſome, others have laid it to the Charge of Mr. *Betterton* as the firſt Innovator on our rude Stage, as a Crime ; nay, as the Deſtruction of good Playing ; but I think with very little Show of Reaſon, and very little Knowledge of the Stages of *Athens* and *Rome*, where, I am apt to believe, was in their flouriſhing times as great Actors as ever play'd here before Curtains. For how that which helps the Repreſentation, by aſſiſting the pleaſing Deluſion of the Mind in regard of the Place, ſhould ſpoil the Acting, I cannot imagine.

The *Athenian* Stage was ſo much adorn'd, that the very Ornaments or Decorations coſt the State more Money, than their Wars againſt the *Perſians* : and the *Romans*, tho their Dramatic Poets were much inferiour to the *Greeks*, (if we may gueſs at thoſe, who are periſhed by thoſe who remain) were yet not behind them in the Magnificence of the Theatre to heighten the Pleaſure of the Repreſentation. If this was Mr. *Betterton*'s Thought, it was very juſt ; ſince the Audience muſt be often puzled to find the Place and Situation of the Scene, which gives great Light to the Play, and helps to deceive us agreeably, while they ſaw nothing before them but ſome *Linſy Woolſy* Curtains, or at beſt ſome piece of old Tapiſtry fill'd with awkerd Figures, that would almoſt fright the Audience.   This,

This, therefore, I muft urge as his Praife, that he endeavour'd to complete that Reprefentation, which before was but imperfect.

Mr. *Betterton* making now the foremoft Figure in Sir *William's* Company among the Men, caft his Eyes on Mrs. *Saunderfon,* who was no lefs excellent among the Female Players, and who being bred in the Houfe of the Patentee, improv'd her felf daily in her Art ; and having by Nature thofe Gifts which were requir'd to make a perfect Actrefs, added to them the Beauty of a virtuous Life, maintaining the Character of a good Woman to her old Age. This Lady therefore Mr. *Betterton* made choice of to receive as his Wife ; and this proceeding from a Value he had for the Merits of her Mind, as well as Perfon, produc'd a Happinefs in the married State nothing elfe could ever have given.

But notwithftanding all the Induftry of the Patentee and Managers, it feems the *King's Houfe* then carry'd the vogue of the Town ; and the *Lincolns-Inn Fields* Houfe being not fo commodious, the Players and other Adventurers built a much more magnificent Theatre in *Dorfet Gardens* ; and fitted it for all the Machines and Decorations the Skill of thofe times could afford. This likewife proving lefs effectual than they hop'd, other Arts were employ'd, and the Political Maxim of *Divide and Govern* being put in Practice, the Feuds and Animofities of the King's Company were fo well improv'd, as to

pro-

produce an Union betwixt the two Patents. To bring this Defign about, the following Agreement was fign'd by the Parties hereafter mention'd.

Memorandum, Octob. 14. 1681.

" IT was then agreed upon between Dr.*Charles*
" *Davenant, Thomas Betterton,* Gent. and
" *William Smith,* Gent. of the one Part, and
" *Charles Hart,* Gent. and *Edward Kynafton,*
" Gent. on the other Part,—— That the faid
" *Charles Davenant, Thomas Betterton,* and
" *William Smith,* do pay, or caufe to be paid,
" out of the Profits of Acting, unto *Charles*
" *Hart* and *Edward Kynafton,* five Shillings a-
" piece for every Day there fhall be any Trage-
" dies, or Comedies, or other Reprefentations
" acted at the *Duke*'s Theatre in *Salisbury Court,*
" or where-ever the Company fhall act during
" the refpective Lives of the faid *Charles Hart,*
" and *Edward Kynafton,* excepting the Days the
" young Men or young Women play for their
" own Profit only ; but this Agreement to ceafe,
" if the faid *Charles Hart* or *Edward Kynafton*
" fhall at any time play among, or effectually
" affift the King's Company of Actors ; and for as
" long as this is pay'd, they both covenant and
" promife not to play at the King's Theatre.

" If Mr. *Kynafton* fhall hereafter be free to act
" at the Duke's Theatre, this Agreement with
" him, as to his Penfion, fhall alfo ceafe.

" In

" In Confideration of this Penfion, Mr. *Hart*
" and Mr. *Kynafton* do promife to make over,
" within a Month after the Sealing of this,
" unto *Charles Davenant, Thomas Betterton*, and
" *William Smith*, all the Right, Title, and
" Claim which they or either of them may
" have to any Plays, Books, Cloaths, and Scenes
" in the King's Play-houfe.

" Mr. *Hart* and Mr. *Kynafton* do both alfo
" promife, within a Month after the Sealing
" hereof, to make over to the faid *Charles Dave-*
" *nant, Thomas Betterton*, and *William Smith*,
" all the Title which they each of them have
" to Six and Three Pence a-piece for every Day
" there fhall be any Playing at the King's
" Theatre.

" Mr. *Hart* and Mr. *Kynafton* do both alfo
" promife to promote with all their Power and
" Intereft an Agreement between both Play-
" houfes ; and Mr. *Kynafton* for himfelf promi-
" fes to endeavour as much as he can to get
" free, that he may act at the *Duke's* Play-houfe,
" but he is not obliged to play unlefs he have
" ten Shillings *per* day allow'd for his Acting,
" and his Penfion then to ceafe.

" Mr. *Hart* and Mr. *Kynafton* promife to go
" to Law with Mr. *Killigrew* to have thefe Ar-
" ticles perform'd, and are to be at the Expence
" of the Suit.

" In Witnefs of this Agreement, all the Par-
" ties have hereunto fet their Hands, this 14th
" of *October*, 1681.

I   I am

I am fenfible, that this private Agreement has been reflected on as Tricking and unfair, but then it is by thofe, who have not fufficiently confider'd the Matter ; for *an dolus, an Virtus quis in Hofte requirit ?* All Stratagems are allow'd betwixt Enemies ; the two Houfes were at War, and Conduct and Action were to decide the Victory ; and whatever the Duke's Company might fall fhort of in Action, it is plain they won the Field by their Conduct. For Mr. *Hart* and Mr. *Kynafton* performed their Promifes fo well, that the Union was effected in 1682. and fo continu'd till the Year 1695. when the Actors under the united Patents, thinking themfelves aggrieved with Mr. *Betterton* at the head of them, got a new Licence to fet up a Play-houfe once more in *Lincolns-Inn Fields.* But when the Succefs of that Company began to give way to the Induftry of the other, and Mr. *Vanbrugh* had built a new Theatre in the *Hay-Market,* Mr. *Betterton,* weary of the Fatigues and Toil of Government, deliver'd his Company over to the new Licence. But they again giving way to the new Mode of *Opera's,* the Companies were once more united in *Drury-Lane,* and the *Opera's* confin'd to the *Hay-Market.* But Revolutions being fo frequent in this *Mimic State,* Mr. *Swinny* got the chief Players over to him and the *Opera* Houfe, among whom was Mr. *Betterton* ; who now being very old, and much afflicted with the Gout, acted but feldom ; and the Year before he dy'd, the Town paid a

par-

particular Deference to him by making his Day worth 500 *l.*

Mr. *Betterton* was fo fenfible of Friendfhip, that tho he loft near 8000 *l.* by the Father, yet he took Care of the Daughter himfelf, till fhe marry'd according to her own Inclinations. Three Plays were written or tranflated by him, and brought on the Stage with Succefs; *The Woman made a Juftice*; *The Amorous Widow, or the Wanton Wife*; and *The Unjuft Judge, or Appius and Virginia.* But he never would fuffer any of them to be printed, tho the *Amorous Widow* from a furreptitiousCopy vifited theWorld after it had been acted almoft 20 Years; but a true Copy will be added to this Book.

Being now feventy five Years of Age, and long troubled with the Stone and Gout, the latter at laft, by repellatory Medicines, was driven into his Stomach, which prov'd fo fatal as in a few Days to put an End to his Life. He was bury'd with great Decency at *Weftminfter-Abby.*

The Year before his Death being at his Country Houfe in *Reading*, my Friend and I travelling that way, according to my Promife, I call'd to fee him; and being Hofpitably receiv'd, one Day after Dinner we retir'd to his Garden, and after a little Walk there, we fell into the Difcourfe of *Acting.* Much was faid by my Friend againft the prefent Players, and in Praife of thofe of his younger Days, for he was an old Man. But being pretty well tired with the Difpute as well as Walk, we fate down in an agreeable Shade,

Shade, and I addrefs'd my felf to Mr. *Betterton* in this manner.

I am fenfible, that my Friend's Tafte of thefe Pleafures was ftronger in his Youth, than at this time, when the *Morofenefs* of Age rebates the Edge of our Appetites in more Pleafures, than one : He would elfe allow that no Woman of his Time excelled Mrs. *Barry*, nor any Man your felf. I mean not to flatter you, (faid I, finding him a little uneafy with my Comple- ment) for it is really my Opinion ; but I muft confefs, I fee but little Profpect, that we have of the Stage's long furviving you two, at leaft, in its moft valuable part, *Tragedy* ; for this excellent Poem lofes Ground every Day in the Efteem of the Town ; nor can I, by any means, attribute this entirely to the Want of Genius in our prefent Poets, fince notwithftanding that we muft al- low, that they are ftill far from Perfection in *Tragedy*, yet we have feen much better Perfor- mances in that kind of late Years, than in the fo much cried up Days of *Charles the Second*, when the Gayety of the Age made ftrange indi- gefted Things, under that Title, go down, in which there was neither *Nature*, nor her Hand- maid ART. But I attribute this Difregard to *Tragedy* chiefly to a Defect in the *Action*, to which we may add the Sowernefs of our Tem- pers under the Preffures of fo long and heavy a War, and laftly to an Abundance of odd Specta- tors, whom the Chance of War have enabled

to

to crowd the Pit and Stage-Boxes, and fway too much by their Thoughtlefs and Arbitrary Cenfure, either to the Advantage or Prejudice of the *Author* and *Player.*

For as War carries abundance of peccant Humours from a State, generated by the Corruptions of a long and luxurious Peace ; fo does it introduce a fort of Libertinifm in our Diverfions, contrary to Decorum and Regularity ; without which no Pleafure can be truly noble. Another ill Effect of Warlike Times, is a Neglect of the politer Sciences of Peace, and a fort of Barbarifm in our Gufto of all the fine Arts. To thefe add, the multiplying the Avenues to Wealth, whofe Number increafing, increafe likewife the Number of thofe, who are drawn into the Purfuit of Riches ; which as it fpreads a mean and private Spirit, of neceffary Confequence makes the Love of the Public more weak and languifhing.

Nor is there any greater Proof of the Virtue or Corruption of the People, than their Pleafures. Thus in the Time of the Vigour of the *Roman* Virtue, *Tragedy* was very much efteem'd, its Dignity kept up, and the Decorum of the Stage fo very nicely obferv'd, that a Player's ftanding out of his Order, or fpeaking a falfe Quantity, was fufficient for him to be hifs'd off the Stage, as *Cicero* affures us in his 3d *Paradox* *.

---

* *Hiftrio fi paulo movit extra Numerum, aut fi Verfus pronunciatus eft Syllabâ una brevior aut longior exfibilatur & exploditur.*

And

And when they gave us the moft noble Examples of Virtue in their real Life, they were moft pleas'd with the Reprefentation of noble Examples on the Stage ; for People are delighted with what bears the greateft Likenefs to the Turn and Temperament of their own Minds. Thus when the *Roman* Virtue decay'd, or indeed was loft with their Liberty, and they fubfifted and fpread their Dominions more by the Merits of their Anceftors, and the *Roman* Name, made terrible by them, than by their own Bravery, then Effeminacy and Folly fpread through the People, which immediately appear'd in their Sports or Spectacles ; *Tragedy* was flighted ; Farce on the one hand, with its *Mimes* and *Pantomimes*; and *Opera* on the other, with its emafculating Sounds, invade and vanquifh the Stage, and drew the Ears and Eyes of the People ; who now care only to laugh, or to fee things extravagant and monftrous.

I wifh this may not be too much our own Cafe. But being unwilling to guefs at a hidden Caufe, when there is an apparent one, I choofe rather to attribute this Decay of *Tragedy* to our want of *Tragedians,* and indeed *Tragic Poets,* than to the Corruption of the People ; which, tho great enough, yet I hope not fo defperate, as what I have mention'd in the *Roman* State.

Tho I am of Opinion, (reply'd Mr. *Betterton*) that the Decay of the Stage is in great meafure owing to the long Continuance of the
War ;

War ; yet, I confefs, I am afraid, that too much
is deriv'd from the Defects of the Stage it felf.
When I was a young Player under Sir *William
Davenant*, we were under a much better Difci-
pline, we were obliged to make our Study our
Bufinefs, which our young Men do not think it
their duty now to do ; for they now fcarce ever
mind a Word of their Parts but only at *Rehearfals*, and come thither too often fcarce recovered
from their laft Night's Debauch ;   when the
Mind is not very capable of confidering fo calmly and judicioufly on what they have to ftudy,
as to enter throughly into the Nature of the
Part, or to confider the Variation of the Voice,
Looks, and Geftures, which fhould give them
their true Beauty, many of them thinking the
making a Noife renders them agreeable to the
Audience, becaufe a few of the Upper-Gallery
clap the loud Efforts of their Lungs, in which
their Underftanding has no fhare.   They think
it a fuperfluous Trouble to ftudy real Excellence,
which might rob them of what they fancy more,
Midnight, or indeed whole Nights Debauches,
and a lazy Remifnefs in their Bufinefs.

Another Obftacle to the Improvement of our
young Players, is, that when they have not been
admitted above a Month or two into the Company, tho their Education and former Bufinefs were never fo foreign to *Acting*, they vain-
ly imagine themfelves Mafters of that *Art*, which
perfectly to attain, requires a ftudious Application of a Man's whole Life. They take it there-

I   fore

fore amifs to have the Author give them any Inftruction ; and tho they know nothing of
the Art of Poetry, will give their Cenfure, and
neglect or mind a Part as they think the Author
and his Part deferves. Tho in this they are
led by Fancy as blind as Ignorance can make it;
and fo wandring without any certain Rule of
Judgment, generally favour the bad, and flight
the good. Whereas it has always been mine
and Mrs. *Barry*'s Practice to confult e'en the moft
indifferent Poet in any Part we have thought fit
to accept of; and I may fay it of her, fhe has
often fo exerted her felf in an indifferent Part,
that her Acting has given Succefs to fuch Plays,
as to read would turn a Man's Stomach ; and
tho I could never pretend to do fo much Service that way as fhe has done, yet I have never
been wanting in my Endeavours. But while
the young Gentlemen will think themfelves Mafters before they underftand any one Point of
their Art, and not give themfelves Leifure and
Time to ftudy the *Graces of* ACTION *and* UT-
TERANCE, it is impoffible that the Stage fhould
flourifh, and advance in Perfection.

I am very fenfible (faid I, finding that he had
done) of the Juftnefs of what you have faid,
Sir, but am apt to believe much of thofe Errors,
which you remark proceed from want of Judgment in the Managers, in admitting People un-
qualified by Nature, and not providing fuch Men
to direct them, who underftand the Art they
fhould be improv'd in. All other Arts People

are

are taught by Mafters skilful in them, but here Ignorance teaches it felf, or rather confirms it felf into the Confidence of Knowledge, by going on without any Rebuke. I have often wifh'd, therefore, that fome Men of good Senfe, and acquainted with the *Graces of Action* and *Speaking*, would lay down fome Rules, by which the young Beginners might direct themfelves to that Perfection, which every body is fenfible is extremely (and perhaps always has been) wanted on our Stage. And tho you have not had the Benefit of fuch an Education in the learned Languages, as fome Men may have had, yet fince you have read much in *French*, and your own Mother Tongue, by the Affiftance of which Languages all Knowledge may now be obtain'd, and have befides a confefs'd Genius, and a long practice in the Art, I wifh I could prevail with you to deliver your Sentiments on this Head, fo that from them we might form a Syftem of *Acting*, which might be a Rule to future Players, and teach them to excel not only themfelves, but thofe who have gone before them.

Were I, Sir, (reply'd he with a graceful Modefty) as capable as you would perfuade me that you think me, I fhould eafily be prevail'd with to communicate my Notions on this Head; but being fenfible of my Incapacity, for the very Reafons you have mention'd, of my Ignorance of the learned Tongues, I muft be excus'd; yet not to difappoint you entirely, I fhall fetch you a Manufcript on this Head, written by a **Friend**

of

of mine, to which I confefs I contributed all, that I was able; which if well perus'd, and through-ly weigh'd, I perfuade my felf our Stage would rife and not fall in Reputation.

On this he went into his Houfe, and after a little Stay return'd to us with fome loofe Papers, which I knew to be his own Hand ; and being feated, after a Glafs of Wine about, he thus began.

Being to treat of the Art of Playing, and the Duty and Qualifications of Actors, I think it will be no improper Method firft to confider, What Regard an Actor ought to have to his Conduct off the Stage, before we treat of what he is to do upon it.

I have not found in all the Clamours againft the Stage, any one that denies the Ufefulnefs of the *Drama*, if juftly manag'd ; nay, Mr. *Collier* the moft formidable Enemy of this Diverfion, (tho his *Proto-Martyr*, Archbifhop *Laud*, contended fo violently for the Book of Sports, and Plays were acted at Court, in the Time of the Royal Martyr, even on *Sundays*) does allow, that the Wit of Man cannot invent any more efficacious means of encouraging Virtue, and deprefling of Vice.

Hence I believe it is evident, that they fuppofe the Moral Leffons, which the Stage prefents, may make the greateft Impreffions on the Minds of the Audience ; becaufe the Inftruction is convey'd with Pleafure, and by the Miniftration of the Paffions, which always have a
ftronger

stronger Remembrance, than the calmer Precepts of Reason.

But then I think there is no manner of doubt but that the Lives and Characters of those Persons, who are the Vehicles, as I may call them, of these Instructions, must contribute very much to the Impression the Fable and Moral will make. For to hear Virtue, Religion, Honour recommended by a Prostitute, an Atheist, or a Rake, makes them a Jest to many People, who would hear the same done with Awe by Persons of known Reputation in those Particulars. Look but into Religion it self, and see how little the Words and Sermons of a known Drunkard, or Debauchee affect his Parishioners; and what an Influence a Divine of a pious and regular Life has on his Congregation, his Virtues preparing them to hear him with Respect, and to believe him as a Man whose Actions call not his Faith into doubt. Tho' the Pulpit must be allow'd to be the more sacred Place, as dispensing the most holy Mysteries of the Christian Religion; yet since the Gospel consists of the *Agenda* as well as *Credenda*, of Practice as well as Belief, and since the Practice is so forcibly recommended from the Stage by a purifying our Passions, and the Conveyance of Delight, the Stage may properly be esteem'd the Handmaid of the Pulpit.

For this Reason, I first recommend to our Players, both Male and Female, the greatest and most nice Care of their Reputation imaginable;

for

for on that their Authority with the People depends and on their Authority in great measure their Influence. They should consider, that the Infamy, that the Profeffion lies under is not deriv'd from the Bufinefs, which is truly valuable and noble; that the Players in *Athens* were honourable, and fo highly efteem'd, that they were fometimes Ambaffadors, and the Mafters to two of the moft noble and glorious Orators that ever *Greece* or *Rome* produc'd ; I mean, *Demofthenes* and *Cicero*, as we fhall immediately fee ; that in *Rome* it felf, where the Stage had a more difadvantageous Rife, than in *Athens*, *Cicero* looks on it as fuch a piece of Ill-breeding and Barbarifm not to grieve for the Death of old *Rofcius*, that he could fuppofe no Noble-man of *Rome* or Commoner could be guilty of. He likewife calls it *an excellent Art.* All which is a fufficient Proof, that the Bufinefs it felf was never infamous in either of thofe two Cities ; nor could be here, if the Profeffors of it by their own loofe Lives, by an open Contempt of Religion, and making Blafphemy and Profanenefs the Marks of their Wit and good Breeding ; by an undifguis'd Debauchery and Drunkennefs, coming on the very Stage, in Contempt of the Audience, when they are fcarce able to fpeak a Word ; by having little Regard to the Ties of Honour and Common Honefty : to fay nothing of the Irregularities of the Ladies, which rob them of that Deference and Refpect, that their Accomplifhments of Perfon would elfe command from
their

their Beholders, efpecially when fet off to fuch an Advantage as the Stage fupplies in the Improvement of the Mind and Perfon.

This is an Evil, which, tho in the Mouths of half the Town, yet to tell thofe, who know themfelves guilty of it, is an Affront never to be forgiven ; fo much more fond are they of defending their Follies, than of removing them, tho to their own Advantage ; and fo much in Love feem they with Infamy more, than a general Refpect and Reputation.   Mr. *Harrington* in his *Oceana,* propofing fomething about a regulated Theatre, would have all Women, who have fuffer'd any Blemifh in their Reputation, excluded the Sight of the Play, by that means to deter Women from Lewdnefs, while by that they loft the Benefit of Public Diverfions.   If this were pufh'd farther, and all Ladies of the Houfe immediately difcarded on the Difcovery of their Follies of that Nature, I dare believe, that they would fooner get Husbands, and the Theatre lofe Abundance of that Scandal it now lies under.

Nor is this fo hard a Task but even our Times, as corrupt as they are, have given us Examples of Virtue in our Stage Ladies.   I fhall not name them, becaufe I would draw no Cenfure on thofe, who are not nam'd.

From what I have faid I believe it is plain, that I wifh fuch a Reformation of the People of the Stage, as would render it more reputable than it is at this Time.   I would have no Man

of

of it a common *Drunkard,* public *Debauchee* ;
nor fo fond of his own Opinion, as to imagine
that a dull Ridicule on things facred will pafs
for Wit with any Man of Senfe or Probity ;
nor would I have him thunder out a Volley of
Oaths and Execrations to fupply the Emptinefs
of his Difcourfe, with a Noife that is offenfive
to all Mens Ears, who are not daily converfant
with the Refufe of Mankind, but acquainted
with good Manners and good Breeding ; nor
to be vain of owing a great Deal , becaufe by Tricks and expenfive Evafions they can
keep a Man from his lawful Debts, tho they
might pay them with half the Money. In
fhort, I would have them keep a handfome Appearance with the World ; to be really virtuous
if they can, if not, at leaft, not to be publickly
abandon'd to Follies and Vices, which render
them contemptible to all ; that they would live
within the Compafs of what their Bufinefs affords them, and then they would have more
Leifure to ftudy their Parts, raife their Reputation, and Salaries the fooner, and meet with
Refpeĉt from all Men of Honefty and Senfe.

The Ladies likewife fhould fet a peculiar
Guard on their Actions, and remember, that
tho it may happen, that their parting with
their Honour, and fetting up for Creatures of
Prey on all that addrefs to them, may bring
them in mercenary Advantages, yet that by
keeping their Reputation entire, they heighten
their Beauties, and would infallibly arrive at
more

more Happinefs (if not Wealth) in Marriages; which they can never find in making themfelves fubject to the Infults of Rakes, and Infirmities of Debauchees, and other Slaveries and Evils not proper to mention, which the Virtuous are free from, admir'd and ador'd by all.

Thus much I thought was proper for me to fay on the Conduct of our Players, Male and Female, off the Stage ; which is a Leffon as well worth their learning as any I fhall deliver.

Tho thefe are Duties which feem abfolutely neceffary to make our *Players* fhine, and draw that Refpect from the People, which now they want, yet are not thefe fufficient to make a good *Actor* ; but there are other Leffons to be learn'd for his Qualifications on the Stage.

From his very Name we may derive his Duty, he is call'd an *Actor*, and his Excellence confifts in *Action* and Speaking : The *Mimes* and *Pantomimes* did all by Gefture, and the Action of Hands, Legs, and Feet, without making ufe of the Tongue in uttering any Sentiments or Sounds; fo that they were fomething like our *dumb Shows*, with this difference, one *Pantomime* expreffed feveral Perfons, and that to the Tunes of Mufical Inftruments ; the dumb Shows made ufe of feveral Perfons to exprefs the Defign of the Play as a filent Action ; and the Nature of this is beft exprefs'd in *Hamlet*, before the Entrance of his Players in the third Act.

Enter a King and a Queen very lovingly, the Queen embracing him ; fhe kneels, and makes

fhew

Love. [*To Phil.*] Pray have a little Patience, Madam, and you'll fee the Event.

Vifc. Lady; I blefs thofe Stars that have directed me to fo happy a Choice; therefore few Words are beft. If you like me as well as I do like you, e'en fend for a Parfon——— *To* Phil.

Lady. Hold, Sir, fure you miftake!

Love. Now——— Now it works. [*Afide to* Phil.

Vifc. What fay you, Lady? Shall we——[*To* Phil.

Lady. I can hold no longer. [*Afide.*
Pray, Sir, are not you the Vifcount *Sans Terre* ?

Vifc. Pretty Creature, I am.

Lady. And come with an Intention———

Vifc. To make this Lady, your Aunt, happy in a Husband, if fhe pleafes.

Lady. I tell you, Sir, I am that Lady you fpeak of; and that is, my Niece *Philadelphia.*

Vifc. Ha, ha, ha; Your Niece, quotha!
Why fure you think to put fome Trick upon me.
This motherly grave Lady your Niece!
No, No; I thank you, Madam, I am not to be perfwaded out of my Reafon.

Lady. He makes me almoft mad. (*Afide.*
I fay again, that I am call'd the Lady *Laycock* ;
And that pert Minx my Niece; who was left in Charge with me till fhe be of Age.

Vifc. 'Sdheart, 'tis impoffible! You look Twenty Years younger than that Lady you call your Niece.

Lady. Oh, dear Sir! That indeed may well be : A great many do allow, I appear to be fomething younger than I altogether am.

Vifc. How could I be fo much miftaken!
Sure, Madam, you but jeft with me.

Lady. Indeed, Sir, thefe Gentlemen know I fpeak Truth.

Cun. 'Tis very true indeed, my Lord.

Vifc.

" Spectator ; then *Venus* blushing, and *Mars*
" beseeching ; in a Word, he acted the whole
" Fable so well, that *Demetrius* much pleas'd
" with the Spectacle, as the greatest Praise, that
" could be bestow'd upon him, cry'd out in a
" loud Voice, I *hear* my Friend, what you *act* ;
" nor do I only see them, but methinks you
" speak with your Hands.

This Instance not only shews the Difference
of these *Pantomimes* from our old dumb Shews,
but the Power of *Action*, which a *Player*
ought to study with his utmost Application. The
Orator at the Bar, and in the Pulpit, ought to
understand the Art of Speaking perfectly well ;
but *Action* can never be in its Perfection but on the
Stage, and in our Time the Pulpit and the Bar have
left off even that graceful Action, which was necessary to the Business of those Places, and gave
a just Weight and Grace to the Words they uttered.   And I wonder that our Ministers do not
a little more consider this Point, and reflect, that
they speak to the People as much as the Orators
of *Greece* and *Rome* ; and what Influence Action
had on them, will be evident from some Instances
we shall give in their proper Places.

Action indeed has a natural Excellence in
it, superiour to all other Qualities ; *Action* is
Motion, and Motion is the Support of Nature,
which without it would again sink into the slug-
gish Mass of Chaos.   Motion in the various and
regular Dances of the Planets surprizes and delights : Life is Motion, and when that ceases,
the

the Humane Body fo beautiful, nay, fo divine when enlivened by Motion, becomes a dead and putrid Coarfe, from which all turn their Eyes. The Eye is caught by any thing in Motion, but paffes over the fluggifh and motionlefs things as not the pleafing Objects of its View.

This Natural Power of *Motion* or *Action* is the Reafon, that the Attention of the Audience is fixt by any irregular or even fantaftic Action on the Stage of the moft indifferent Player; and fupine and drowfy, when the beft Actor fpeaks without the Addition of *Action.*

'Twas the Skill the ancient Players of *Athens* and *Rome* had in this, which made them not only fo much admir'd by the Great Men of thofe Times and Places, but rais'd them to the Reputation of being Mafters of two of the greateft Orators that *Athens* or *Rome* ever faw; and who had it not been for the Inftructions of the Actors *Satyrus*, *Rofcius*, and *Æfopus*, had never been able to convey their admirable Parts to the World.

Demofthenes being, after many unfuccefsful Attempts, one Time exploded the Affembly, went home with his Head muffled up in his Cloak, very much affected with the Difgrace; in this Condition *Satyrus* the Actor follow'd him, being his intimate Acquaintance, and fell into Difcourfe with him. *Demofthenes* having bemoan'd himfelf to him, and his Misfortune, that having been the moft induftrious of the Pleaders, and having fpent almoft the whole

Strength

Strength and Vigour of his Body in that Employment, yet could he not render himſelf acceptable to the People ; That Drunkards, Tarpaulins, Sots, and illiterate Fellows found ſo favourable a Hearing, as to poſſeſs the Pulpit, while he himſelf was deſpis'd. What you ſay (replied *Satyrus*) is very true, but I will ſoon remove the Cauſe of all this, if you will repeat ſome Verſes to me out of *Sophocles*, or *Euripides*. When *Demoſthenes* had pronounc'd after his way, *Satyrus* preſently repeating the ſame Verſes with their proper Tone, Mien, and Geſture, gave ſuch a Turn to them, that *Demoſthenes* himſelf perceiv'd they had quite another Appearance. By which being convinc'd how much Grace and Ornament accrues to Speech by a proper and due Action, he began to think it of litle Conſequence for a Man to exerciſe himſelf in declaiming, if he neglected the juſt Pronunciation or Decency of Speaking. Upon this he built himſelf a Place under ground (which remain'd in the Time of *Plutarch*) whither he retir'd every Day to form his Action, and exerciſe his Voice. To ſhew what Pains this great Man took as an Example to our young Actors, who think not themſelves oblig'd to take any at all, I ſhall proceed with *Plutarch*. In his Houſe he had a great Looking-Glaſs, before which he would ſtand and repeat his Orations, by that means obſerving how far his Action and Geſture were graceful or unbecoming.

The

The fame *Demosthenes,* when a Client came to him on an Affault and Battery ; he at large gave him an Account of what Blows he had receiv'd from his Adverfary, but in fo calm and unconcern'd a manner, that *Demosthenes* faid, Surely my good Friend thou haft not fuffer'd any one thing of what thou makeft thy Complaint : Upon which his Client warm'd, cry'd aloud—— *How* Demofthenes ? *Have I fuffer'd nothing ?* Ay marry, replies he, now I hear the Voice of a Man that has been injur'd and beaten. Of fo great Confequence did he think the Tone and Action of the Speaker towards the gaining Belief.

This was the Cafe of *Demosthenes,* as *Plutarch* affures us, (if I may credit the Tranflation, as without doubt I may;) and that of *Cicero* was not much different—— At firft (fays *Plutarch*) he was, as well as *Demosthenes,* very defective in Action, and therefore he diligently apply'd himfelf to *Rofcius* the Comedian fometimes, and fometimes to *Æfopus* the Tragedian. And fuch afterwards was the Action of *Cicero,* that it did not a little contribute to make his Eloquence perfuafive ; deriding the Rhetoricians of his Time, for delivering their Orations with fo much Noife and Bawling, faying, that it was their want of Ability to fpeak, which made them have Recourfe to bellowing, as lame People who cannot walk, get on Horfe-back and ride.

The

The fame might be faid to many of our bawling Actors, of which number *Æfopus* was not, yet fo poffeffed with his Part, that he took his acting to be fo real, and not a Reprefentation, that whilft he was on the Stage reprefenting *Atreus* deliberating on the Revenge of *Thyeftes*, he was fo tranfported beyond himfelf, that he fmote one of the Servants haftily croffing the Stage, and laid him dead on the Place.

But my Lord *Bacon*, in his *Advancement of Learning*, gives us a Hiftory from the *Annals* of *Tacitus*, of one *Vibulenus*, formerly an Actor on the Stage, but at that time a common Soldier in the *Pannonian* Garrifons ; which is a wonderful Inftance of the Power of Action, and what Force it adds to the Words. The Account is this.

This Fellow, on the Death of *Auguftus Cæfar*, had rais'd a Mutiny, fo that *Blæfus* the Lieutenant committed fome of the Mutineers to Prifon ; but the Soldiers violently broke open the Prifon-Gates, and fet their Comrades at Liberty ; and this *Vibulenus*, in a Tribunitial Speech to the Soldiers, begins in this manner—— " You " have given Life and Light to thefe poor in- " nocent Wretches—— but who reftores my " Brother to me, or Life to my Brother ? Who " was fent hither with a Meffage from the Le- " gions of *Germany* to treat of the common " Caufe ; and this very laft Night has he mur- " der'd him by fome of his Gladiators, fome " of his Bravo's, whom he keeps about him

4 " to

" to be the Murderers of the Soldiers. Anfwer,
" *Blæfus,* where haft thou thrown his Body ;
" the moft mortal Enemies deny not Burial to
" the dead Enemy : When to his Corps I have
" perform'd my laft Duties in Kiffes, and flow-
" ing with Tears, command me to be flain at
" his Side, fo that thefe our Fellow-Soldiers
" may have leave to bury us.—— He put the
Army into fuch a Ferment and Fury by this
Speech, that if it had not immediately been
made appear, that there was no fuch Matter, that
he never had any Brother, the Soldiers would
hardly have fpar'd the Lieutenant's Life ; for he
acted it as if it had been fome Interlude on the
Stage.

There is not fo great a Pathos in the Words
uttered by the Soldier, as to ftir the Army into
fo very great a Ferment, they muft therefore receive almoft their whole Force from a moft moving and pathetic Action, in which his Eyes,
Hands, and Voice join'd in a moft lively Expreffion of his Mifery and of his Lofs. 'Tis
true that, when an Army is tumultuous in it
felf, it is no difficult matter to run them into
Madnefs ; but then it muft be done by fome,
who either by their former Intereft there, had
purchas'd an Opinion among them, or fome one
who by the Artfulnefs of his Addrefs fhould
touch their Souls, and fo engage them to what
he pleafes. The later I take to be our Cafe in
Vibulenus, who by the Advantage of his Skill
in Action recommended himfelf and his fuppofi-

titious

titious Caufe fo effectually to them, as to make
the General run a great hazard of his Life for an
imaginary Murder.

This has made fome of the old Orators give
the fole Power and fovereign Command in Speech
to Action, as I have read in fome of thofe learned Men who have treated of this Subject in *Englifh* and *French*.   And I am perfuaded, that our
Parfons would move their Hearers far more, if
they added but graceful Action to loud Speaking.
This often fets off indifferent Matter, and makes
a Man of little Skill in any other Part of Oratory, pafs for the moft eloquent ; this, I have
read, was the Cafe of *Trachallus*, who tho none
of the beft Orators of his Time for the Compofition and Writing part, yet excell'd all the
Pleaders of that Age, his Appearance and Delivery was fo plaufible and pleafing.   The State-
linefs of his Perfon and Port, the Sparkling of
his Eyes, the Majefty of his Looks, and the
Beauty of his Mien ;   and his *Voice* added to
thefe Qualities, which not only for Gravity and
Compofednefs came up to that of a *Tragedian*,
but even excell'd any Actors, that ever yet trod
the Stage, as my Author affures us from *Quintilian*.   *Philiftus*, on the other hand, for want
ot thefe Advantages of Utterance, loft all the
Beauty and Force of his Pleadings, tho for Language and the Art of Compofition excell'd all
the *Greeks* of his Time.

The fame Advantage of *Pericles* and *Hortenfius*, with this difference, *Hortenfius* afcrib'd all

I   the

the Succefs of his Pleadings to the Merit of the Writing, and convinc'd the World of his Error by publifhing his Orations; *Pericles*, tho 'tis faid he had the Goddefs Perfuafion on his Lips, and that he thundred and lightned in an Affembly, and made all *Greece* tremble when he fpoke, yet would never publifh any of his Orations, becaufe their Excellency lay in the ACTION.

What I have faid here of *Action* in general, and the particular Examples I have given of it, is I believe fufficient to fatisfy any one, that is ftudious of Excellence on the Stage, that it ought to be his chief Aim and Application. But next to this is the Art of Speaking, in which alfo a Player ought to be perfectly skill'd; for as a learned Country-man of ours obferves——
" The Operation of Speech is ftrong, not only
" for the Reafon or Wit therein contained, but
" by its Sound. For in all good Speech there
" is a fort of Mufic, with Refpect to its Mea-
" fure, Time and Tune. Every well-meafur'd
" Sentence is proportional three ways, in all its
" Parts to the Sentences, and to what it is in-
" tended to exprefs, and all Words that have
" Time allow'd to their Syllables, as is fuitable
" to the Letters whereof they confift, and to
" the Order, in which they ftand in a Sentence.
" Nor are Words without their Tune or Notes
" even in common Talk, which together com-
" pofe that Tune, which is proper to every Sen-
" tence, and may be prick'd down as well as
" any mufical Tune: only in the Tunes of
" Speech

" Speech the Notes have much lefs Variety,
" and have all a fhort Time. With Refpect al-
" fo to Time and Meafure, the Poetic is lefs
" various and therefore lefs powerful, than that
" of Oratory ; the former being like that of a
" fhort Country Song repeated to the End of the
" Poem, but that of *Oratory* is vary'd all along,
" like the Divifions, which a skilful Mufician
" runs upon a Lute.

He proceeds to our former Confideration, faying —— " The Behaviour and Gefture is alfo of
" Force ; as in Oratory fo in Converfe, confift-
" ing of almoft as many Motions, as there are
" moveable Parts of the Body, all made with
" a certain agreeable Meafure between one an-
" other, and at the fame time anfwerable to
" that of Speech, which when eafy and unaf-
" fected is becoming.

A Maftery in thefe two Parts is what com-
pleats an Actor : And I hope the Rules I fhall
give for both will be of Ufe to fuch as have
truly a Genius for this *Art* ; the Rules of which,
like thofe of Poetry, are only for thofe, who have
a Genius, and are not perfectly to be underftood
by thofe, who have not.

To begin therefore with *Action*, the Player is
to confider, that it is not every rude and unde-
figning *Action*, that is his Bufinefs, for that is
what the Ignorant as well as skilful may have,
nor can indeed want : But the Action of a Player
is that, which is agreeable to Perfonation, or the
Subject he reprefents. Now what he reprefents

D   is

is Man in his various Characters, Manners, and Passions, and to these Heads he must adjust every Action ; he must perfectly express the Quality and Manners of the Man, whose Person he assumes, that is, he must know how his Manners are compounded, and from thence know the several Features, as I may call 'em, of his Passions. A Patriot, a Prince, a Beggar, a Clown, *&c.* must each have their Propriety, and Distinction in Action as well as Words and Language. An *Actor* therefore must vary with his Argument, that is, carry the Person in all his Manners and Qualities with him in every Action and Passion ; he must transform himself into every Person he represents, since he is to act all sorts of Actions and Passions. Sometimes he is to be a Lover, and know not only all the soft and tender Addresses of one, but what are proper to the Character, that is in Love, whether he be a Prince or a Peasant, a hot and fiery Man or of more moderate and flegmatick Constitution, and even the Degrees of the Passion he is possessed with. Sometimes he is to represent a choleric, hot and jealous Man, and then he must be throughly acquainted with all the Motions and Sentiments productive of those Motions of the Feet, Hands, and Looks of such a Person in such Circumstances. Sometimes he is a Person all dejected and bending under the Extremities of Grief and Sorrow ; which changes the whole Form and Appearance of him in the Representation, as it does really in Nature. Sometimes
times

times he is diftracted, and here Nature will
teach him, that his Action has always fomething wild and irregular, tho even that regularly; that his Eyes, his Looks or Countenance,
Motions of Body, Hands and Feet, be all of a
Piece, and that he never falls into the indifferent
State of Calmnefs and Unconcern. As he now
reprefents *Achilles*, then *Æneas*, another Time
Hamlet, then *Alexander* the Great and *Oedipus*,
he ought to know perfectly well the Characters
of all thefe Heroes, the very fame Paffions dif-
fering in the different Heroes as their Characters
differ : The Courage of *Æneas*, for Example, of it
felf was fedate and temperate, and always attended with good Nature ; that of *Turnus* join'd
with Fury, yet accompany'd with Generofity
and Greatnefs of Mind. The Valour of *Mezentius* was favage and cruel ; he has no Fury
but Fiercenefs, which is not a Paffion but Habit,
and nothing but the Effect of Fury cool'd into a
very keen Hatred, and an inveterate Malice.
Turnus feems to fight to appeafe his Anger, *Mezentius* to fatisfy his Revenge, his Malice and
barbarous Thirft of Blood. *Turnus* goes to the
Field with Grief, which always attended Anger,
whereas *Mezentius* deftroys with a barbarous
Joy; he's fo far from Fury, that he is hard to
be provoked to common Anger ; who calmly killing *Ondes*, grows but half angry at his
Threats ;

At whom Mezentius *fmiling with a mingl'd Ire.*

Thus, 'tis plain, he has not the Fury of *Turnus*, but a Barbarity peculiar to himself, and a savage Fiercenefs, according to his Character in the tenth Book of *Virgil*.

To know thefe different Characters of eftablifhed Heroes, the Actor need only be acquainted with the Poets, who write of them; if the Poet who introduces them in his Play have not fufficiently diftinguifh'd them. But to know the different Compofitions of the Manners, and the Paffions fpringing from thofe Manners, he ought to have an Infight into Moral Philofophy, for they produce various Appearances in the Looks and Actions, according to their various Mixtures. For that the very fame Paffion has various Appearances, is plain from the Hiftory Painters, who have followed Nature. Thus *Jordan* of *Antwerp*, in a Piece of our Saviour's being taken from the Crofs, which is now in his Grace the Duke of *Marlborough*'s Hands, the Paffion of Grief is exprefs'd with a wonderful Variety; the Grief of the Virgin Mother is in all the Extremity of Agony, that is confiftent with Life, nay indeed that leaves fcarce any Signs of remaining Life in her; that of St. *Mary Magdalen* is an extreme Grief, but mingled with Love and Tendernefs, which fhe always exprefsed after her Converfion for our bleffed Lord; then the Grief of St. *John* the Evangelift is ftrong but manly, and mixt with the Tendernefs of perfect Friendfhip; and that of *Jofeph* of *Arimathea* fuitable to his Years and Love for

Chrift,

Chrift, more folemn, more contracted in himfelf, and yet forcing an Appearance in his Looks. *Coypel*'s Sacrifice of *Jeptha*'s Daughter has not unluckily exprefs'd a great Variety of this fame Paffion. The Hiftory Painters indeed have ob-ferv'd a Decorum in their Pieces, which wants to be introduc'd on our Stage; for there is never any Perfon on the Cloth, who has not a Con-cern in the Action. All the very Slaves in *Le Brun*'s Tent of *Darius* participate of the grand Concern of *Sifigambis Statira*, &c. This would render the Reprefentation extremely folemn and beautiful; but on the Stage, not only the Su-pernumeraries, as they call them, or Attendants, mind nothing of the great Concern of the Scene, but even the Actors themfelves, who are on the Stage, and not in the very principal Parts, fhall be whifpering to one another, or bowing to their Friends in the Pit, or gazing about. But if they made Playing their Study, (or had in-deed a Genius to their Art) as it is their Bufi-nefs, they would not only not be guilty of thefe Abfurdities, but would, like *Le Brun,* obferve Nature where-ever they found it offer any thing that could contribute to their Perfection. For he was often feen to mind a Quarrel in the Street betwixt various People, and there not only ob-ferve the feveral Degrees of the Paffion of Anger rifing in the Quarrel, and their different Recefs, but the diftinct Expreffions of it in every Face that was concern'd.

Our

Our Stage at the beſt indeed is but a very cold Repreſentation, ſupported by loud prompting, to the eternal Diſguſt of the Audience, and ſpoiling the Decorum of the Repreſentation ; for an imperfect Actor affronts the Audience, and betrays his own Demerits. I muſt ſay this in the Praiſe of Mr. *Wilks,* he always takes Care to give the Promptor little Trouble, and never wrongs the Poet by putting in any thing of his own ; a Fault, which ſome applaud themſelves for, tho they deſerve a ſevere Puniſhment for their equal Folly and Impudence. They forget *Hamlet's* Advice to the Players—— *And let thoſe who play your Clowns ſpeak no more, than is ſet down for them ; for there be of them that will of themſelves laugh to ſet on ſome Quantity of barren Spectators to laugh too ; tho in the mean time ſome neceſſary Queſtion of the Play be then to be conſider'd. That's* VILLANOUS, *and ſhews a moſt* PITIFUL *Ambition in the* FOOL *that uſes it.* This is too frequently done by ſome of our popular but half Comedians. But it is, I think, a greater Fault in a *Tragedian,* who through his Imperfectneſs in his Part ſhall ſpeak on any Stuff, that comes in his Head, which muſt infallibly prejudice the true Expreſſion of the Buſineſs of the Play, let it be Paſſion, Deſcription, or Narration. But notwithſtanding this Supinity in general of too many of our modern Players, we have ſometimes ſome of them who are in earneſt ; for I remember I once ſaw Mr. *Benjamin Johnſon* (our preſent *Roſcius*) act

Numphs

Numphs with such an Engagement in the Part, that I could not persuade my self, that it was acting but the Reality ; tho this often depends on the Poet in his furnishing his Characters with Matter enough to engage the Player to enter entirely into it, but a good Player will help out an indifferent Poet.

But this Address in the Performance can never be obtain'd without the last Degree of Perfectness, for without that the Player can never be free from the Apprehension of being out. Among those Players, who seem always to be in earnest, I must not omit the Principal, the incomparable Mrs. *Barry*; her Action is always just, and produc'd naturally by the Sentiments of the Part, which she acts, and she every where observes those Rules prescrib'd to the Poets by *Horace*, and which equally reach the Actors.

We weep and laugh as we see others do,
He only makes me sad, who shews the way,
And first is sad himself; Then Telephus
I feel the Weight of your Calamities,
And fancy all your Miseries my own ;
But if you ACT *them ill I sleep or laugh.*
Your Look must needs alter as your Subject does,
From kind to fierce, from wanton to serene.
For Nature forms and softens us within,
And writes our Fortune's Changes in our Face.
Pleasure enchants, impetuous Rage transports,
And Grief dejects, and wrings the tortur'd Soul;
And these are all interpreted by Speech.

But

But he, whose Words and Fortunes disagree,
Absurd, unpity'd grows a public Jest.
Lord *Roscommon*'s Translation.

She indeed always enters into her Part, and is
the Person she represents. Thus I have heard
her say, that she never said, *Ah ! poor* Castalio !
in the *Orphan*, without weeping. And I have
frequently obferv'd her change her Countenance
feveral Times as the Difcourfe of others on the
Stage have affected her in the Part she acted.
This is being throughly concern'd, this is to
know her Part, this is to exprefs the Paffions in
the Countenance and Gefture.

The Stage ought to be the Seat of Paffion in
its various kinds, and therefore the Actor ought
to be throughly acquainted with the whole Nature of the Affections, and Habits of the Mind,
or elfe he will never be able to exprefs them
juftly in his Looks and Geftures, as well as in
the Tone of his Voice, and manner of Utterance.
They muft know them in their various Mixtures,
and as they are differently blended together in
the different Characters they reprefent; and then
that Rule of the prefent Duke of *Buckingham*
will be of ufe to the Player as well as Poet.

————*For they muft look within to find*
Thofe fecret Turns of Nature in the Mind ;
Without this Part in vain wou'd be the whole,
And but a Body all without a Soul.

Then

Then that Conduct of the other Hopes of the *English* Stage, Mrs. *Bradshaw*, (of whom we might say in Acting, as one said of *Taſſo* in Poetry, that if he was not the beſt Poet, he had hindred *Virgil* from being the only Poet ; ſo that if ſhe be not the beſt Actreſs the Stage has known, ſhe has hindred Mrs. *Barry* from being the only Actreſs) would certainly be very juſt ; for a Friend of mine diſcourſing with her of the Action of the Stage, ſhe told him, *that ſhe endeavour'd firſt to make her ſelf Miſtreſs of her Part, and left the Figure and Action to Nature.*

Tho a great Genius may do this, yet Art muſt be conſulted in the Study of the larger Share of the Profeſſors of this Art ; and we find ſo great a Man as *Demoſthenes* perfected himſelf by conſulting the Gracefulneſs of the Figure in his Glaſs : And to expreſs Nature juſtly, one muſt be Maſter of Nature in all its Appearances, which can only be drawn from Obſervation, which will tell us, that the Paſſions and Habits of the Mind diſcover themſelves in our Looks, Actions and Geſtures.

Thus we find a rolling Eye that is quick and inconſtant in its Motion, argues a quick but light Wit ; a hot and choleric Complexion, with an inconſtant and impatient Mind ; and in a Woman it gives a ſtrong Proof of Wantonneſs and Immodeſty. Heavy dull Eyes a dull Mind, and a Difficulty of Conception. For this Reaſon we obſerve, that all or moſt People in
Years,

Years, fick Men, and Perfons of a flegmatic Conftitution are flow in the turning of their Eyes.

That extreme Propenfion to Winking in fome Eyes, proceed from a Soul very fubject to Fear, arguing a Weaknefs of Spirit, and a feeble Difpofition of the Eye-lids.

A bold ftaring Eye, that fixes on a Man, proceeds either from a blockifh Stupidity, as in Rufticks; Impudence, as in Malicious Perfons; Prudence, as in thofe in Authority, or Incontinence as in lewd Women.

Eyes enflam'd and fiery are the genuine Effect of Choler and Anger; Eyes quiet, and calm with a fecret kind of Grace and Pleafantnefs are the Offspring of Love and Friendfhip.

Thus the Voice, when loud, difcovers Wrath and Indignation of Mind, and a fmall trembling Voice proceeds from Fear.

In like manner, to ufe no Actions or Geftures in Difcourfe, is a Sign of a heavy and flow Difpofition, as too much Gefticulation proceeds from Lightnefs; and a Mean betwixt both is the Effect of Wifdom and Gravity; and if it be not too quick, it denotes Magnanimity. Some are perpetually fidling about their Cloaths, fo that they fcarce are drefs'd till they go to Bed, which is an Argument of a childifh and empty Mind.

Some caft their Heads from one fide to the other wantonly and lightly, the true Effect of Folly and Inconftancy. Others think it effential

to

to Prayer, to writh and wreft their Necks a-
bout, which is a Proof of Hypocrify, Superfti-
tion, or Foolifhnefs. Some are wholly taken
up in viewing themfelves, the Proportion of their
Limbs, Features of their Faces, and Graceful-
nefs of Mien ; which proceeds from Pride, and
a vain Complaifance in themfelves; of this number are Coquets.

In this manner I might run through all the
Natural Actions, that are to be found in Men of
different Tempers. Yet not to difmifs the Point
without a fuller Reflection, I fhall fubjoin here
the Signification of the various Natural Geftures
from a Manufcript of a Friend of mine, which
he affur'd me was taken from a learned Jefuit
who wrote on this Subject.

Every Paffion or Emotion of the Mind has
from Nature its proper and peculiar Countenance,
Sound and Gefture ; and the whole Body of
Man, all his Looks, and every Sound of his
Voice, like Strings on an Inftrument, receive
their Sounds from the various Impulfe of the
Paffions.

The Demiffion or hanging down of the Head
is the Confequence of Grief and Sorrow. And
this therefore is a Pofture and Manner obferv'd
in the Deprecations of the Divine Anger, and
on fuch occafions ought to be obferv'd in the I-
mitations of thofe things.

A lifting or toffing up of the Head is the Gefture of Pride and Arrogance. Carrying the Head
aloft is the fign of Joy, Victory and Triumph.

A

A hard and bold Front, or Fore-head is look'd on as a Mark of Obftinacy, Contumacy, Perfidioufnefs and Impudence.

The Soul is moft vifible in the Eyes, as being, according to one, the perfect Images of the Mind; and, as *Pliny* fays, they burn, yet diffolve in Floods; they dart their Beams on Objects, and feem not to fee them; and when we kifs the Eyes, we feem to touch the very Soul.

Eyes lifted on high fhew Arrogance and Pride, but caft down exprefs Humblenefs of Mind : Yet we lift up our Eyes when we addrefs our felves in Prayer to God, and afk any thing of him.

Lifting in vain his burning Eyes to Heav'n.
Virgil.

Denial, Averfion, Naufeating, Diffimulation, and Neglect, are exprefs'd by a turning away of the Eyes.

A frequent Winking, or tremulous Motion of the Eyes, argues malicious Manners, and perverfe and noxious Thought and Inclinations.

Eyes drown'd in Tears difcover the moft vehement and cruel Grief, which is not capable of Eafe ev'n from Tears themfelves.

To raife our Eyes to any thing or Perfon, is an Argument of our Attention to them with Defire.

The Hand put on the Mouth is a Token of Silence by Conviction, and is a Ceremony of the Heathen Adoration. The

The Contraction of the Lips and the scant Look of the Eyes expresses the Gesture of a diriding and malicious Person. Shewing the Teeth, and streightening the Lips on them, shews Indignation and Anger.

To turn the whole Face to any thing is the Gesture of one, who attends and has a peculiar Regard to that one thing. To bend the Countenance downward argues Conscioufness and Guilt; and, on the contrary, to lift up the Face is a Sign of a good Conscience or Innocence, Hope and Confidence.

The Countenance, indeed, is chang'd into many Forms, and is commonly the most certain Index of the Passions of the Mind. When it is pale it betrays Grief, Sorrow, and Fear, and Envy, when it is very strong. A louring and dark Visage is the Index of Misery, Labour and vehement Agitations of the Soul.

In short, as *Quintilian* observes, the Countenance is of very great Power and Force in all that we do. In this we difcover when we are suppliant, when minacious, when kind, when sorrowful, when merry; in this we are lifted up and cast down; on this Men depend; this they behold, and this they first take a View of before we speak; by this we love some, and hate others; and by this we understand a Multitude of things.

The Arm extended and lifted up signifies the Power of doing and accomplifhing something; and is the Gesture of Authority, Vigour, and

Victory.

Victory. On the contrary, the holding your Arms clofe is a Sign of Bafhfulnefs, Modefty, and Diffidence.

As the Hands are the moft habil Members of the Body, and the moft eafily turn'd to all fides, fo are they the Indexes of many Habits.

But we have two Hands, the Right and the Left, we fometimes make ufe of one, fometimes of the other, and fometimes of both, to exprefs the Paffion and Habit. The chief Forms of which I fhall mention,

The lifting of one Hand upright, or extending it, expreffes Force, Vigour and Power. The Right Hand is alfo extended upwards as a Token of Swearing, or taking a folemn Oath; and this Extenfion of the Hand fometimes fignifies Pacification, and Defire of Silence.

The putting of the Hand to the Mouth is the Habit of one, that is filent and acting Modefty; of Admiration and Confideration. The giving the Hand is the Gefture of ftriking a Bargain, confirming an Alliance, or of delivering ones felf into the Power of another. To take hold of the Hand of another expreffes Admonition, Exhortation, and Encouragement. The reaching out an Hand to another implies Help and Affiftance. The lifting up both Hands on high is the Habit of one who implores, and expreffes his Mifery. And the lifting up of both Hands fometimes fignifies Congratulation to Heaven for a Deliverance, as in *Virgil*;

His

His Hands now free from Bands he lifts on high,
In grateful Action to th' indulgent Gods.

The holding the Hands in the Bofom is the
Habit of the Idle and Negligent. Clapping the
Hands, among the *Hebrews* fignify'd deriding,
infulting, and exploding; but among the *Greeks*
and the *Romans,* it was, on the contrary, the
Expreffion of Applaufe. The Impofition of
Hands fignifies the imparting a Power, in con-
fecrating of Victims.

In fhort, *Quintilian* fays of the Hands ———
" It is a difficult matter to fay what a number
" of Motions the Hands have, without which all
" Action wou'd be maim'd and lame, fince thefe
" Motions are almoft as various as the Words we
" fpeak. For the other Parts may be faid to
" help a Man when he fpeaks, but the Hands
" (as I may fay) fpeak themfelves. Do we
" not by the Hands defire a thing? Do we not
" by thefe promife? call? difmifs? threaten?
" act the Suppliant? exprefs our Abomination
" or Abhorrence? our Fear? By thefe do we
" not afk Queftions? deny? fhew our Joy,
" Grief, Doubt, Confeffion, Penitence, Mode-
" ration, Plenty, Number, and Time? Do not
" the fame Hands provoke, forbid, make Sup-
" plication, approve, admire, and exprefs Shame?
" Do they not in fhewing of Places and Perfons,
" fupply the Place of the Adverbs and Pronouns?
" Infomuch that in fo great a Variety or Diver-
" fity

" fity of the Tongues of all Nations, this feems
" to remain the univerfal Language common
" to all.

It were to be wifh'd that this Art were a little reviv'd in our Age, when fuch ufeful Members, which of old contributed fo much to the
Expreffion of Words, fhould now puzzle our
Players what to do with them, when they feldom or never add any Grace to the Action of
the Body, and never almoft any thing to the
Explanation or fuller Expreffion of the Words
and Paffions. But to go on with my Text a very
little farther.——

The ftamping of the Feet among the *Hebrews*
fignify'd Derifion and Scoffing. Among the
Greeks, &c. Imperioufnefs. A conftant and direct Foot is the Index of a fteady, certain, conftant, and right Study and Aim of our Defigns.

On the contrary, Feet full of Motion are the
Habit of the inconftant and fluctuating in their
Counfels and Refolves. And the *Greeks*
thought this in Women a fign of a flagitious
Temper.

Thus I have gone through my Jefuit's Obfervations of the feveral Geftures and Pofitions of
the feveral Parts and Members of the Body.
And tho fome of them may to a hafty View
feem trifling, and others of no great Importance,
yet I am perfuaded, that a Man of true Judgment may find fome fecret Excellencies in them,
which may afford him great Helps in the ren-
dering his Geftures beautiful and expreffive.

There

There is no greater Proof of this, than the Example I have already urg'd of the *Pantomime* and *Demetrius* the *Cynic* Philofopher, who cry'd out to him, *I hear my Friend what you act ; nor do I only fee them, but methinks you fpeak with your* Hands. But this Speaking with the Hands, (as 'tis here call'd) I find contain a great deal of the Reprefentation of the dancing dumb Shows of the *Mimes* and *Pantomimes.* It may be perhaps objected, that thefe Motions of the Hands were fo well known to the Frequenters of the Theatres, that, like our talking on our Fingers with thofe, who underftand it, there would be no Difficulty in the Reprefentation ; but that if any Stranger or Foreigner fhould have been there, it would have been nothing but an unintelligible Gefticulation, and what *Shakefpear* calls it *unexplicable dumb Shews* ; whereas if thefe Actions and Geftures were drawn from their Natural Significancy, according to thofe Marks I have already given, or others referr'd to by my Quotation of *Quintilian*, they muft be intelligible to all Nations, on firft Sight to *Barbarians,* who never faw them before, as well as to *Greeks* and *Romans,* who convers'd with them every Day.

I allow the Objection, but fhall remove it by a farther Account of the very fame *Pantomime,* who liv'd in the Time of *Nero :* The Story is this——— " A *Barbarian* Prince, who came " from *Pontus* to *Rome,* about fome Bufinefs " with *Nero,* among other Entertainments faw

E " this

" this Dancer perfonate fo lively, that tho he
'· knew nothing of what was fung, being half
" a *Grecian*, yet he underftood all.   Being
" therefore to return to his Country after this
" Entertainment of *Nero*'s, and bid ask what
" he would and it fhould be granted, reply'd,
" give me the Dancer, and you will infinitely
" pleafe me.   *Nero* asking him of what ufe he
" would be to him? My Neighbour *Barbarians*
" (faid he) are of different Languages, nor is
" it eafy for me to find Interpreters for them;
" this Fellow, therefore, as often as I have need,
" fhall expound to me by his Geftures. So clear
and intelligible were his Actions and Geftures,
and fo derived from the Nature of the thing
reprefented; which is a Proof, that there are
certain Natural Significations of the Motions of
the Hands, and other Members of the Body,
which are obvious to the Underftanding of all
fenfible Men of all Nations.   If thofe which
I have given you from my *Jefuit* be not, yet I
am very fure, that many of them are explain'd
by him, which will be plain to a ferious Con·
fiderer.

Gefture has therefore this Advantage above
mere Speaking, that by this we're only underftood by thofe of our own Language, but by
Action and Gefture (I mean juft and regular
Action) we make our Thoughts and Paffions intelligible to all Nations and Tongues. 'Tis, as
I have obferv'd from *Quintilian*, the common
Speech of all Mankind, which ftrikes our Un·-
der-

derftanding by our Eyes, as effectually, as Speaking does by the Ears ; nay, perhaps, makes the more effectual Impreffion, that Senfe being the moft vivacious and touching, according to *Horace*, as I find him in my Lord *Rofcommon's* Verfion ;

> *But what we hear moves lefs, than what we fee,*
> *Spectators only have their Eyes to truft,* &c.

I think I have already affign'd a tolerable Rea-fon why *Movement* and *Action* fhould teach us fo fenfibly ; nay, the very Reprefentation of them in *Painting* often ftrikes our Paffions, and makes Impreffions on our Minds more ftrong and vi-vid, than all the Force of Words. The chief Work is certainly done by Speech in moft other ways of public Difcourfe, either at the *Bar*, or in the *Pulpit*; where the Weight of the Reafon and the Proof are firft and moft to be confider'd: But on the Stage, where the Paffions are chiefly in View, the beft *Speaking*, deftitute of *Action* and *Gefture* (the Life of all Speaking) proves but a heavy, dull, and dead Difcourfe.

This, in fome meafure, will likewife reach all things deliver'd in Public, fince I find *Pliny the younger* talking of People in his Days reci-ting of their Speeches, or Poems, by either rea-ding them themfelves, or by having them read by others, tells us, that this reading them was a very great Difadvantage to the Excellence of their Performance either way, leffening both

their

their *Eloquence* and *Character*, since the principal Helps of *Pronunciation*, the *Eyes* and the
Hands, could not perform their Office, being
otherwise employ'd to read, and not adorn the
Utterance with their proper Motions; insomuch
that it was no manner of wonder, that the Attention of the Audience grew languid, on so
unactive an Entertainment. On the contrary,
when any Discourse receives Force and Life, not
only from the Propriety and Graces of Speaking
agreeable to the Subject, but from a proper *Action* and *Gesture* for it, it is truly touching, penetrating, transporting; it has a Soul, it has Life,
it has Vigour and Energy not to be resisted. For
then the *Player*, the *Preacher*, or *Pleader*, holds
his Audience by the Eyes, as well as Ears, and
engrosses their Attention by a double Force.
This seems to be well represented in some Words
of *Cicero* to *Cæcilius*, a young Orator, on
his first Cause, who would needs undertake the
Action against *Verres*, in Opposition to *Hortensius*.
After he has shown his Incapacity in many
Points to accuse *Verres*, both in Ability, and in
not being free from a Suspicion of a share in the
Guilt, he comes at last to the Power and Art of
his Adversary *Hortensius* —— *Reflect*, (says he)
*consider again and again what you are going to
do! for there seems to me to be some Danger not
only of his oppressing thee with his Words; but
even of his confounding and dazling the Eyes of thy
Understanding with his* GESTURE, *and the* MO-
TION *of his Body, and so entirely drive thee from*
thy

thy Defign, and all thy Thoughts. The fame *Cicero*, in his Books of *Oratory*, tells us, that *Craffus* pleading againft *Brutus*, deliver'd his Words with fuch an Accent and fuch a Gefture, that he perfectly confounded the later, and put him out of Countenance, fixing his Eyes ftedfaftly on him, and addreffing all his Action up to him, as if he would devour him with a *Look* and a *Word.*

But to make thefe Motions of the Face and Hands eafily underftood, that is, ufeful in the moving the Paffions of the Auditors, or rather Spectators, they muft be properly adapted to the thing you fpeak of, your Thoughts and Defign; and always refembling the *Paffion* you would exprefs or excite. Thus you muft never fpeak of mournful things with a gay and brifk Look, nor *affirm* any thing with the Action of *Denial*; for that would make what you fay of no manner of Authority or Credit; you would gain neither Belief nor Admiration. You muft alfo have a peculiar Care of avoiding all manner of *Affectation* in your *Action* and *Gefture,* for that's moft commonly ridiculous and odious, unlefs where the Actor is to exprefs fome Affectation in the Character he reprefents, as in *Melantha* in *Marriage Ala-mode,* and *Millamant* in *the Way of the World.* But even then that very Affectation muft be unaffected, as thofe two Parts were admirably acted by Mrs. *Montfort* and Mrs. *Bracegirdle.* But your *Action* muft appear purely Natural, as the genuine Offspring

E 3 of

of the things you exprefs, and the *Paffion*, that moves you to fpeak in that manner.

In fine, our *Player, Pleader,* or *Preacher,* muft have that nice Addrefs in the Management of his Geftures, that there may be nothing in all the various Motions and Difpofitions of his Body, which may be offenfive to the Eye of the Spectator ; as well as nothing grating and difobliging to the Ears of his Auditors, in his Pronunciation ; elfe will his Perfon be lefs agreeable, and his Speech lefs efficacious to both, by wanting all that *Grace*, Virtue, and Power, it would otherwife obtain.

'Tis true, it muft be confefs'd, that the Art of Gefture feems more difficult to be obtain'd, than the Art of Speaking ; becaufe a Man's own Ear may be judge of the Voice, and its feveral Variations, but cannot fee his Face at all, and the Motion of the other Parts of the Body, but very imperfectly. *Demofthenes,* as I have faid, to make a true Judgment how far his Face and Limbs mov'd and kept to the Rules of good Action and Gefture, fet before him a large *Looking-Glafs* fufficient to reprefent the whole Body at one View, to direct him in diftinguifhing betwixt *Right* and *Wrong,* decent and indecent Actions ; but yet, tho this might not be unufeful, it lies under this Difadvantage, that it reprefents on the Right what is on the Left, and on the contrary, on the Left what is on the Right Hand ; fo that when you make a Motion with your *Right-Hand,* the Reflection makes it
seem

feem as done by the *Left*, which confounds the Gefture, and gives it an aukward Appearance : And to rectify this Appearance to you from the Glafs, by giving the Motions by the contrary Hands, might contract fuch an ill Habit, as ought with the utmoft Caution to be avoided.

As to all the other Parts of Action indeed a Glafs may prove very advantageous, fince in it you have a faithful Reprefentation not only of the *Face* in all its Variations of the Countenance, but of the whole Body likewife in all its Poftures and Motions, and the Agreeablenefs and Harmony of one to the other, and the Parts with the Whole, and the Whole with the Parts. So that you may thus eafily difcover any *Habit* or *Gefture* that wants Grace, and Agreeablenefs, and any Action, which may add them to your Perfon, and in them that Force and Influence to you utter.

For want of fuch a Glafs there is but a more difficult thing to be apply'd to, and that is fome Friend, who is a perfect Mafter in all the Beauties of *Gefture* and *Motion*, and can correct your Errors, as you perform before him, and point out thofe *Graces*, which wou'd render your Action compleatly charming. 'Tis true, that fome have advis'd the Learner to have fome excellent Pattern always before his Eyes, and urge, that *Hortenfius* was fo to *Rofcius* and *Æfopus*, who always made it their Bufinefs to be prefent at his *Pleadings* with that Attention as to improve themfelves fo far by what they faw, as to carry

E 4 away

away his fine Actions and *Gesture,* and practice
afterwards on the Stage, what they had seen at
the *Bar:* Yet can I not allow of this Imitation
in Acting ; for when a very young Player con-
ceives a strong Opinion of any one of received
Authority on the Stage, he at best becomes a
good Copy, which must always fall short of an
Original. Besides, this Instance of the two *Roman* Players will not reach our Case, since they
were established Players, had fixt their Characters, and manner of Playing ; and only did by
Hortensius what a Player now might do by the
fine Pieces of History-Painting, carry off the
beautiful Passions and Positions of the Figures,
or the particular Appearance of any one Passion.
But after all it puzles me, who am not acquainted so well with the Ancients, how to reconcile
this of *Roscius* and *Æsopus* learning Gesture of
Hortensius, and instructing *Cicero* in the same :
'Tis true I have been inform'd, that *Hortensius*
was Senior to *Cicero,* and therefore they might
be thought to have paid that to the Bar in *Cicero,* which they had borrow'd from the Bar in
Hortensius. But let this be as it will, the Con-
troversy is not of that Moment as to detain us
any longer.

But it may be objected, that what I have
deliver'd all this Time seems rather to dwell
upon *Generals,* than to come to any Particulars.
I confess in this Art it is much an easier Matter
to discourse in a general Manner, than to deliver particular Rules for the Direction of our
Actions.

Actions. Yet I believe I may venture to say, that as general as my Difcourfe may feem to fome, thofe, who have any true Genius to *Playing*, will find fuch particular Inftructions, as may be of very great ufe to them ; and this Art, as well as moft others, but efpecially *Poetry*, delivers fuch Rules, that are not eafily underftood without a *Genius*.

However, to gratify thofe, who require greater Particularities, I fhall add fome particular Rules of Action ; which juftly weigh'd, will be of ufe to the *Bar* and the *Pulpit*, as well as the *Stage*, provided, that the Student allow a more ftrong, vivid and violent Gefture to the *Plays*, than to either of the other.

I fhall therefore begin with the *Government, Order,* and *Balance,* as I may fay, of the whole Body ; and thence I fhall proceed to the Regiment and proper Motions of the *Head,* the *Eyes,* the *Eye-brows,* and indeed the whole *Face* ; and I fhall conclude with the *Actions* of the *Hands,* more *copious* and *various,* than all the other Parts of the Body.

The Place and Pofture of the Body ought not to be chang'd every Moment, fince fo fickle an Agitation is trifling and light : Nor, on the other Hand, fhould it always keep the fame Pofition, fixt like a Pillar or Marble Statue. For this, in the firft place, is unnatural, and muft therefore be difagreeable, fince God has fo form'd the Body with Members difpofing it to Motion, that it muft move either as the Impulfe of the

Mind

Mind directs, or as the neceffary Occafions of the Body require. This heavy Stability, or thoughtlefs Fixtnefs, by lofing that *Variety,* which is fo becoming of and agreeable in the Change and Diverfity of Speech and Difcourfe, and gives Admiration to every thing it adorns, lofes likewife that Genteelnefs, and Grace, which engages the Attention by pleafing the Eye. Being taught to dance will very much contribute in general to the graceful Motion of the whole Body, efpecially in Motions, that are not immediately embarrafs'd with the Paffions.

That the Head has various *Geftures* and *Signs, Intimations* and *Hints,* by which it is capable of expreffing *Confent, Refufal, Confirmation, Admiration,* and *Anger,* &c. is what every one knows, who has ever thought at all. It might therefore be thought fuperfluous to treat particularly of them. But this Rule I muft lay down on this Head in general, firft that it ought not to be lifted up too high, and ftretched out extravagantly, which is the Mark of *Arrogance* and *Haughtinefs*; but an Exception to this Rule will come in for the *Player,* who is to act a Perfon of that Character. Nor on the other fide fhould it be *hung down* upon the Breaft, which is both difagreeable to the Eye, in rendring the *Mien* clumfy and dull; and would prove extremely prejudicial to the *Voice,* depriving it of its *Clearnefs, Diftinction,* and that *Intelligibility,* which it ought to have : Nor fhould
the

the Head always lean towards the Shoulders, which is equally ruftic and affected, or a great Mark of *Indifference, Languidnefs*, and a *faint Inclination.* But the Head, in all the calmer Speeches at leaft, ought to be kept in its juft *Natural State* and *upright Pofition.* In the Agitation indeed of a *Paffion*, the Pofition will naturally follow the feveral Acceffes and Receffes of the Paffion whether *Grief, Anger*, &c.

We muft farther obferve, that the Head muft not be kept always like that of a Statue without Motion; nor muft it on the contrary be moving perpetually, and always throwing it felf about on every different Expreffion. It muft therefore, to fteer between this *Scylla* and *Carybdis*, and fhun thefe ridiculous Extremes, turn gently on the Neck, as often, as Occafion requires a Motion, according to the Nature of the thing, turning now to one fide, and then to another, and then return to fuch a decent Pofition, as your Voice may beft be heard by all or the Generality of the Audience. To this I may add, that the Head ought always to be turn'd on the fame fide, to which the *Actions* of the reft of the Body are directed, except when they are employ'd to exprefs our Averfion to Things, we refufe; or on Things we deteft and abhor: For thefe Things we reject with the *Right Hand*, at the fame time turning the Head away to the *Left.*

But the greateft Life and Grace of *Action* derive themfelves from the *Face.* For this Reafon:

son: *Craſſus* in *Cicero* remarks, that *Roſcius*, tho
ſo excellent a Player, loſt his Admiration among
the *Romans* on the Stage, becauſe the Maſque
on his Face deny'd the Audience the ſight of thoſe
Motions, Charms, and *Attractions*, which were
to be diſcover'd in the Countenance. I confeſs
I am extremely ſurpriz'd at the Ancients Uſe
of thoſe Masks on the Stage, which they call'd
the *Perſonæ* ; nor could I imagine how they
were made, not to deſtroy that Grace and Beauty of Acting, in the Management of the Lineaments of the Face, which by all that we have
of that kind muſt be entirely hid; and yet what
Plutarch tells us of *Demoſthenes* and *Cicero*, is a
Proof, that the Players of *Athens* and *Rome* were
abſolute Maſters of Speaking and Action. 'Tis
true, there is much in the *Voice* to expreſs the
Paſſion artfully, yet certainly the ſeveral Figu-
rations of the Countenance, as of the *Eyes, Brows,
Mouth*, and the like, add the moſt touching and
moſt moving Beauties. But this Obſervation
before-mention'd ſatisfies me, that thoſe were
entirely loſt by the *Perſonæ* ; which is a Proof,
that in whatever they excell'd our Actors, we
have the Advantage in the making the Repreſentation perfect, by enjoying the Benefit of expoſing all the Motions of the Face.

The Character which *Lucian* gives (as I find
it in Dr. *Jaſper Maine*'s Tranſlation) of thoſe
Perſonæ, makes them extremely ridiculous, and
by his Deſcription of the reſt of the Tragic Equipage would make us very much doubt their
Ex-

Excellence in the other Parts of Acting.———
" What a deform'd and frightful Sight (fays
" he) is it to fee a Man rais'd to a prodigious
" Length, ftalking on exalted Bufkins, his Face
" difguis'd with a grim Vizard, widely gaping,
" as if he meant to devour the Spectators ; I
" forbear to fpeak of his ftuff'd Breafts and
" Fore-bellies, which make an adventitious
" and artificial Corpulency, left his unnatural
" Length fhould carry a Difproportion to his
" Slendernefs.

Surely fuch a Figure as *Lucian* gives our *Tra-*
gedian, muft not only render him incapable of
giving the Body all its juft Motions and graceful Geftures, of which we are talking, and
which the great Writers, as I am told, celebrate
fo much ; but muft be ridiculous to a Farce.
But tho what *Lucian* reprefents, may be look'd
upon as in the Time of the Corruption of the
Roman Stage, yet the *Cothurni* and the *Perfonæ*
were in ufe among the *Greeks,* and muft have been
extremely prejudicial to the Beauty of the Reprefentation. The Reafon I have heard given for the
firft was the common Opinion, that the Heroes of
former Times were larger and taller, than the Men
our Cotemporaries ; and I believe the firft Ufe
of the Vizard, which fucceeded the befmeering
the Face with Lees of Wine in the Time of
Thefpis, was chiefly to exprefs the Looks and
Countenance of the feveral Heroes reprefented,
according to their Statues and Portraictures,
which made the Player always new to the Audience ;

dience; whereas we coming always on the Stage with the fame Face, put a Force on the Imagination of the Audience to fancy us other than the fame Perfons.

But I think I have found out a way, which, if maturely ftudy'd, would obtain this Variety of Countenance more artfully, and at the fame time infpire the Actor better with the Nature and Genius of his Part. I remember that fome Years ago I read a *French* Book written by one *Gafferel* a Monk; who tells us, that when he was at *Rome* he went to fee *Campanella* in the Inquifition, and found him making abundance of Faces; that he at firft imagin'd, that thofe proceeded from the Torments he had undergone in that *Ecclefiaftical Slaughter-Houfe*; but he foon undeceiv'd him, by enquiring what fort of Countenance fuch a Cardinal had, to whom he had juft before fent; for he was forming his Countenance, as much as he could, to what he knew of his, that he might know what his Anfwer wou'd be.

If therefore a Player was acquainted with the Character of his Hero, fo far as to have an Account of his Features and Looks; or of any one living of the fame Character, he would not only vary his Face fo much by that means, as to appear quite another Face; by raifing, or falling, contracting, or extending the Brows; giving a brifk or fullen, fprightly or heavy turn to his Eyes; fharpening or fwelling his Noftrils, and the various Pofitions of his Mouth, which
by

by Practice would grow familiar, and wonderfully improve the Art of Acting, and raise the noble Diversion to greater Esteem. The studying History-Painting would be very useful on this Occasion, because the Knowledge of the Figure and Lineaments of the Represented (and in History-Pieces almost all, who are represented are to be found) will teach the Actor to vary and change his Figure, which would make him not always the same, as I have said, in all Parts, but his very Countenance so chang'd, that they would not only have other Thoughts themselves, but raise others in the Audience. Some carry their Heads aloft and stately, others pucker their Brows, look with a piercing Eye, and the like, as I have just said ; and these things throughly consider'd by the Player, would in every part make him a new Man; and with more Beauty supply the *Persona* of the Ancients, and raise our Stage to a greater Merit, than theirs could pretend to, which depriv'd the Audience of the noblest and most vivacious Part of the Representation, in the Loss of the Motions of the Face ; of which we ought to take a peculiar Care, since it is on that, which the Audience or Spectators generally fix their Eyes the whole Time of the Action.

Exercise and frequent Practice ought to reform the least Error in this particular, because in the Performance every one presently discovers it, tho you see it not your self. The surest way of correcting your self in this is either a Looking-Glafs, or a judicious Friend, who can and will let you know what Countenance is agreeable, and what the contrary. But this is a general Rule, without any Exception, that you adjuft all the Lines and Motions of the Face to the Subject of your Difcourfe, the Paffion you feel within you, or fhould according to your Part feel, or would raife in thofe, who hear and fee you. You muft likewife confider the Quality you reprefent, as well as the Quality of thofe to whom you fpeak ; for even in great Degrees of the Paffions the Difference and Diftance of that has a greater or lefs Awe upon the very Appearance of the Paffion. The *Countenance* muft be brightened with a pleafant Gayety on things, that are agreeable, and that according to the Degrees of their being fo ; and likewife in *Joy*, which muft ftill be heighten'd in the Paffion of *Love* ; tho indeed the *Countenance* in the Expreffion of this Paffion is extremely various, participating fometimes of the Tranfports of Joy, fometimes of the Agonies of Grief ; it is fometimes mingled with the Heats of Anger, and fometimes fmiles with all the pleafing Tranquillity of an equal Joy. Sadnefs or Gravity muft prevail in the *Countenance*, when the Subject is grave, melancholy or forrowful ; and Grief is to be expreffed according to its various Degrees of Violence. *Hate* has its peculiar Expreffion compofed of *Grief*, *Envy*, and *Anger*, a Mixture of all which ought to appear in the Eye. When you bring

I

or

or offer Comfort, Mildnefs and Affability ought
to fpread o'er your Countenance, as *Severity*
fhould when you cenfure or reprehend. When
you fpeak to Inferiors, or to little People, and
your own Quality is great, Authority and Gravity ought to be in your Face ; as Submiffion,
Humility, and Refpect or Veneration, when you
addrefs to thofe above you.

The Management of the Eyes in an *Orator*
at the *Bar*, or in the *Pulpit*, feems fomething
different from what they muft be in a *Player*,
tho, if we make the reft of the Actors on the
Stage with him at the fame time his Auditors,
the Rules for one will reach the other ; for fo
indeed they are, for all the Regard that is to be
had to the Audience is that they fee and hear
diftinctly, what we act and what we fpeak ;
that they may judge juftly of our Pofitions,
Geftures and Utterance, in regard to each o-
ther.

The Orator therefore muft always be cafting
his Eyes on fome or other of his Auditors, and
turning them gently from fide to fide with an
Air of Regard, fometimes on one Perfon, and
fometimes on another, and not fix them immove-
ably on one Part of your Auditors, which is
extremely unaffecting and dull, much lefs moving, than when we look them decently in the
Face, as in common Difcourfe. This will hold
good in Playing, if apply'd according to my
former Rule ; for indeed I have obferv'd frequently fome Players, who pafs for great ones,

F   have

have their Eyes lifted up to the Galleries, or Top of the Houſe, when they are engag'd in a Diſcouſe of ſome Heat, as if indeed they were conning a Leſſon, not acting a Part ; and *Theophraſtus* himſelf (as I find him quoted) condemn'd *Tamariſcus*, a Player of his Time, who when ever he ſpoke on the Stage, turn'd his Eyes from thoſe, who were to hear him, and kept them fixt all the while on one ſingle and inſenſible Object. But Nature acts directly in a contrary manner, and yet ſhe ought to be the Player's as well as Poet's Miſtreſs. No Man is engag'd in Diſpute, or any Argument of Moment, but his Eyes and all his Regard are fixt on the Perſon, he talks with ; not but that there are times according to the Turn or Criſis of a Paſſion, where the Eyes may with great Beauty be turn'd from the Object we addreſs to ſeveral Ways, as in Appeals to Heaven, imploring Aſſiſtance, to join in your Addreſſes to any one, and the like.

When you are free from Paſſion, and in any Diſcourſe,which requires no great Motion, as our modern Tragedies too frequently ſuffer their chief Parts to be, your Aſpect ſhould be pleaſant, your Looks direct, neither ſevere nor aſide, unleſs you fall into a Paſſion, which requires the contrary. For then Nature, if you obey its Summons, will alter your Looks and Geſtures. Thus when a Man ſpeaks in *Anger* his Imagination is inflam'd, and kindles a ſort of Fire in his Eyes, which ſparkles from them in

ſuch

such a manner, that a Stranger, who understood not a Word of the Language, or a deaf Man, that could not hear the loudest Tone of his Voice, would not fail of perceiving his Fury and Indignation. And this Fire of their Eyes will easily strike those of their Audience, which are continually fixt on yours; and by a strange sympathetic Infection, it will set them on Fire too with the very same Passion.

I would not be misunderstood, when I say you must wholly place your Eyes on the Person or Persons you are engag'd with on the Stage; I mean, that at the same time both Parties keep such a Position in Regard of the Audience, that even these Beauties escape not their Observation, tho never so justly directed. As in a Piece of History-Painting, tho the Figures direct their Eyes never so directly to each other, yet the Beholder, by the Advantage of their Position, has a full View of the Expression of the Soul in the Eyes of the Figures. Thus in the *Psyche* and *Cupid* of *Coypel*; Her Eyes are directed to him as he descends on the Wing, and his to her glowing with Love and Desire, and yet all this is seen in him by those, who view the Picture. *Titian* has drawn the same Story, I mean the Loves of *Cupid* and *Psyche*; but as She lies on the Bed naked, we see nothing but her Back-parts, tho *Cupid* advances his Knee to the Bed, with his Eyes fixt on her Face, which are turn'd from the Spectator. I know not what the *Italian*'s Fancy was, to imagine that the

F 2   Back-

Back-parts of the Miſtreſs of Love ſhould be more agreeable, than her Face. But this *en paſ-ſant* —— To return to the Subject.

The Looks, and juſt Expreſſion of all the other Paſſions, has the ſame Effect, as this I have mention'd of Anger. For if the *Grief* of another touches you with a real Compaſſion, Tears will flow from your Eyes, whether you will or not. And this Art of Weeping, as I have read, was ſtudy'd with great Application by the ancient Players; and they made ſo extraordinary a Progreſs in it, and work'd the Counterfeit ſo near a Reality, that their Faces uſed to be all over blurr'd with Tears when they came off the Stage.

They us'd ſeveral means of bringing this paſſionate Tenderneſs to a Perfection; yet this they found the moſt effectual. They kept their own private Afflictions in their Mind, and bent it perpetually on real Objects, and not on the Fable, or fictitious Paſſion of the *Play*, which they acted. The ſame Author gives us two notable Examples of this: The firſt is of one *Polus*, a famous Actor; he had refrain'd the Stage for ſome time, after the Death of a beloved Son, for the Grief for that Loſs had ſo ſenſibly affected him, and thrown him into ſuch a Melancholy, that he had no Thoughts of ever returning to his Theatrical Employment; but being at laſt once more on the Stage, and oblig'd to act *Electra* carrying the ſuppos'd Urn of her Brother *Oreſtes*, he went to the Grave

of

of his own beloved Child, and brings his Urn on, inftead of the fuppos'd Urn of *Oreſtes*; which fo mov'd him, and melted his Heart into fuch Compaſſion and Tendernefs, at the Sight of that real Object of Sorrow, that he broke out into fuch loud Exclamations, and fuch unfeigned Tears, as fill'd the whole Houfe with Grief, Weeping, and Lamentations.

The other Example is of the famous and wealthy Player *Æſopus*, who by his rare Art in this particular did a great Piece of Service to the Common-wealth of *Rome*, in applying his Art to the recalling of *Cicero* from Baniſhment. For he underſtanding, that fuch a thing was in Agitation with the People, acted a Play of *Accius*, in which were fome admirable Verfes on the Exile of *Telamon*, and the horrible Calamities of *Priam* and his Family. In the fpeaking of thefe Verfes, the real Sufferings of his Friend fo affected him, that he made the imaginary Sufferings of the Poetical Perfon fo moving, that he drew Floods of Tears from thofe, who were indifferent, and made his very Enemies bluſh with Tears in their Eyes at his Affliction. And this fo mollify'd the People towards *Cicero*, and gave them fuch a Difpofition towards his Recalling and Re-eſtabliſhment in his former Dignities, that he was foon after brought home in Triumph; and, as my Author affures me, *Cicero* himfelf tells us, with the utmoſt Gratitude, what his cordial Friend, this great Actor, had done for him on this Occafion.

The

The Player therefore, nay, and the Orator too, ought to form in his Mind a very ftrong Idea of the Subject of his Paffion, and then the Paffion it felf will not fail to follow, rife into the Eyes, and affect both the Senfe and Under-ftanding of the Spectators with the fame *Tender-nefs.* The Performance of this is exprefs'd in *Shakefpear's Hamlet* admirably well, and fhould be often confider'd by our young Players. ——

Ham. *Is it not monftruous that the Player here,*
　But in a Fiction, in a Dream of Paffion,
　Could force his Soul fo to his whole Conceit,
　That from her working all his Vifage warm'd,
　Tears in his Eyes, Diftraction in his Afpect ;
　A broken Voice, and his whole Function fuiting
　With Forms to his Conceit ? And all for nothing !
　For HECUBA !
　What's HECUBA *to him, or he to* HECUBA,
　That he fhould weep for her ? What wou'd
　　he do
　Had he the Motive, and the Cue for Paffion
　That I have ? He would drown the Stage with
　　Tears ;
　And cleave the general Ear with horrid Speech ;
　Make mad the Guilty, and appal the Free ;
　Confound the Ignorant, and amaze indeed
　The very Faculty of Eyes and Ears.

This fhews, that our *Shakefpear* had a juft Notion of Acting, whatever his Performance was ; for in thefe few Lines is contain'd almoft
　　　　　　　　　　　　　　　all

all that can be faid of Action, Looks and Gefture. Here we find the *Soul* forc'd fo to his
whole Conceit, *&c.* The firft place is the fixing this in the *Soul*, to engage that throughly in
the Paffion, and then from her Working will
his Vifage warm, his Eyes flow with Tears,
and Diftractions fpread over all his Face ; nay,
then will his Voice be broken, and every Faculty of his Body be agreeable to this ftrong E-
motion of the Soul. Tho in the firft feven
Lines he feems to have expreffed all the Duties
of a Player in a great Paffion ; yet in the following feven he derives a yet ftronger Action
when the Object of Grief is real ; which jufti-
fies what the Ancients practis'd in heightning
their Theatrical Sorrow, by fixing the Mind on
real Objects ; or by working your felf up by a
ftrong Imagination, that you are the very Perfon and in the very fame Circumftances, which
will make the Cafe fo very much your own,
that you will not want Fire in Anger, nor
Tears in Grief : And then you need not fear
affecting the Audience, for Paffions are wonderfully convey'd from one Perfon's Eyes to another's ; the Tears of *one* melting the Heart of
the *other*, by a very vifible Sympathy between
their Imaginations and Afpects.

You muft lift up or caft down your Eyes, according as the Nature of the Things you fpeak
of : Thus if of Heaven, your Eyes naturally
are lifted up ; if of Earth, or Hell, or any
thing terreftrial, they are as naturally caft down.

Your

Your Eyes muſt alſo be directed according to the
Paſſions, as to deject them on things of Diſgrace, and which you are aſham'd of ; and
raiſe them on things of Honour, which you can
glory in with Confidence and Reputation. In
Swearing, or taking a ſolemn Oath, or Atteſta-
tion of any thing, to the Verity of what you
ſay, you turn your Eyes, and in the ſame Action lift up your Hand to the thing you ſwear by,
or atteſt.

　Your Eye-brows muſt neither be immoveable,
nor always in Motion ; nor muſt they both be
rais'd on every thing that is ſpoken with Eager-
neſs and Conſent, and much leſs muſt one be
rais'd, and the other caſt down ; but generally
they muſt remain in the ſame Poſture and Equality, which they have by Nature, allowing them
their due Motion, when the Paſſions require it ;
that is, to contract themſelves, and frown in
Sorrow ; to ſmooth and dilate themſelves in
Joy ; to hang down in *Humility,* &c.

　The *Mouth* muſt never be writh'd, nor the
Lips bit or lick'd, which are all ungenteel and
unmannerly Actions, and yet what ſome are frequently guilty of ; yet in ſome Efforts or Starts
of Paſſion, the Lips have their ſhare of Action,
but this more on the Stage, than in any other
public Speaking, either in the Pulpit, or at the
Bar ; becauſe the Stage is or ought to be an
Imitation of Nature in thoſe Actions and Diſcourſes, which are produc'd betwixt Man and
Man by any Paſſion, or on any Buſineſs, which
can

can afford Action ; for all other has in reality
nothing to do with the *Scene*.

Tho to shrug up the Shoulders be no Gesture
allow'd in Oratory, yet on the Stage the Character of the Person, and the Subject of his Difcourfe, may render it proper enough ; tho I confefs, it feems more adapted to Comedy, than
Tragedy, where all fhould be great and folemn,
and with which the graveft of the Orators Actions will agree. I have read of a pleafant Method, that *Demofthenes* took to cure himfelf of
this Vice of Action, for he at firft was mightily
given to it ; he us'd to exercife himfelf in declaiming in a narrow and ftreight Place, with
a Dagger hung juft over his Shoulders, fo that
as often as he fhrugg'd them up, the Point, by
pricking his Shoulders, put him in mind of his
Error : which in time remov'd the Defect.

Others thruft out the Belly, and throw back
the Head, both Geftures unbecoming and indecent.

We come now to the Hands, which as they
are the chief Inftruments of Action, varying
themfelves as many ways, as they are capable of
exprefling things, fo is it a difficult matter to
give fuch Rules as are without Exception.
Thofe Natural Significations of particular Geftures, and what I fhall here add, will, I hope,
be fome Light to the young Actor in this particular. Firft, I would have him look back to
what I have faid of the *Action* of the Hands, as
to their Expreffion of *Accufation, Deprecation,*
                                              Threats,

Threats, Desire, &c. and to weigh well what those Actions are, and in what manner expressed ; and then considering how large a share those Actions have in all manner of Discourse, he will find that his Hands need never be idle, or employed in an insignificant or unbeautiful Gesture.

In the Beginning of a solemn Speech, or Oration, as in that of *Anthony* on the Death of *Cæsar,* or of *Brutus,* on the same Occasion, there is no Gesture at least of any Consideration, unless it begin abruptly, as O ! JUPITER, *Oh! Heav'ns ! is this to be born ? the very Ships then in our Eyes, which I preserv'd,* &c. extending here his Hands first to Heav'n; and then to the Ships. In all regular Gestures of the Hands, they ought perfectly to correspond with one another, as in starting in a Maze, on a sudden Fright, as *Hamlet* in the Scene betwixt him and his Mother, on the Appearance of his Father's Ghost ————

Save me, and hover o'er me with your Wings, You Heavenly Guards !

This is spoke with Arms and Hands extended, and expressing his Concern, as well as his Eyes, and whole Face. If an Action comes to be used by only one Hand, that must be by the *Right,* it being indecent to make a Gesture with the *Left* alone ; except you should say any such thing as,

Rather

Rather than be guilty of so foul a Deed,
I'd cut this Right Hand off, &c.

For here the Action must be expressed by the *Left* Hand, because the *Right* is the Member to suffer. When you speak of your self, the *Right* not the *Left* Hand must be apply'd to the Bosom, declaring your own Faculties, and Passions; your Heart, your Soul, or your Conscience, but this Action generally speaking, should be only apply'd or expres'd by laying the Hand gently on the Breast, and not by thumping it as some People do. The Gesture must pass from the *Left* to the *Right*, and there end with Gentleness and Moderation, at least not stretch to the Extremity of Violence. You must be sure as you begin your Action with what you say, so you must end it when you have done speaking; for Action either before or after Utterance is highly ridiculous. The Movement or Gestures of your Hands must always be agreeable to the Nature of the Words, that you speak; for when you say, *Come in* or *approach*, you must not stretch out your Hand with a repulsive Gesture; nor, on the contrary, when you say, *Stand back*, must your Gesture be inviting; nor must you join your Hands, when you command Separation; nor open them, when your order is *closing*; nor hang them down, when you bid *raise such a thing*, or *Person*; nor lift them up, when you say, *throw them down*. For all these Gestures
would

would be fo vifibly againft Nature, that you would be laugh'd at by all that faw or heard you. By thefe Inftances of faulty Action, you may eafily fee the right, and gather this Rule, that as much as poffible every Gefture you ufe fhould exprefs the Nature of the Words you utter, which would fufficiently and beautifully employ your Hands.

It is impoffible to have any great Emotion or Gefture of the Body, without the Action of the Hands, to anfwer the Figures of Difcourfe, which are made ufe of in all Poetical, as well as Rhetorical Diction ; for Poetry derives its Beauty in that from Rhetoric, as it does its Order and Juftnefs from Grammar ; which furprizes me, that fome of our modern taking Poets value themfelves on that, which is not properly Poetry, but only made ufe of as an Ornament, and drawn from other Arts and Sciences.

Thus when *Medea* fays,

Thefe Images of Jason,
With my own Hands I'll ftrangle, &c.

'tis certain the Action ought to be exprefs'd by the Hands to give it all its Force.

In the lifting up the Hands to preferve the Grace, you ought not to raife them above the Eyes ; to ftretch them farther might diforder and diftort the Body ; nor muft it be very little lower, becaufe that Pofition gives a Beauty

to

to the Figure : Besides, this Posture being general on some Surprize, Admiration, Abhorrence, &c. which proceeds from the Object, that affects the Eye, Nature by a sort of Mechanic Motion throws the Hands out as Guards to the Eyes on such an Occasion.

You must never let either of your Hands hang down, as if lame or dead ; for that is very disagreeable to the Eye, and argues no Passion in the Imagination. In short, your Hands must always be in View of your Eyes, and so corresponding with the Motions of the Head, Eyes and Body, that the Spectator may see their Concurrence, every one in its own way to signify the same thing, which will make a more agreeable, and by Consequence a deeper Impression on their Senses, and their Understanding.

Your Arms you should not stretch out sideways, above half a Foot from the Trunk of your Body, you will otherwise throw your *Gesture* quite out of your Sight, unless you turn your Head also aside to pursue it, which would be very ridiculous.

In Swearing, Attestation, or taking any solemn Vow or Oath, you must raise your Hand ; an Exclamation requires the same Action : But so that the *Gesture* may not only answer the *Pronunciation*, or *Utterance*, but both the Nature of the thing, and the Meaning of the Words. In public Speeches, Orations, and Sermons, it is true your Hands ought not to be always in Motion, a Vice which was once call'd the *Babling*

ling of the Hands ; and perhaps, it may reach some Characters, and Speeches in Plays; but I am of Opinion, that the Hands in Acting ought very seldom to be wholly quiescent, and that if we had the Art of the *Pantomimes*, of expressing things so clearly with their Hands, as to make the Gestures supply Words, the joining these significant Actions to the Words and Passions justly drawn by the Poet, would be no contemptible Grace in the Player, and render the Diversion infinitely more entertaining, than it is at present. For indeed *Action* is the Business of the Stage, and an Error is more pardonable on the right, than the wrong side.

There are some *Actions* or *Gestures*, which you must never make use of in Tragedy, any more than in Pleadings, or Sermons, they being low and fitter for Comedy or Burlesque Entertainments. Thus you must not put your self into the Posture of one *bending a Bow, presenting a Musquet*, or playing on any Musical Instrument, as if you had it in your Hands.

You must never imitate any lewd, obscene or indecent Postures, let your Discourse be on the Debaucheries of the Age, or any thing of that Nature, which the Description of an *Anthony* and *Verres* might require our Discourse of.

When you speak in a *Prosopopæia*, a Figure by which you introduce any (thing or) Person speaking, you must be sure to use such Actions only, as are proper for the Character, that you speak for. I can't remember at present one in

3   Tra●

Tragedy, but in Comedy *Melantha*, when she speaks for a Man, and anfwers him in her own Perfon, may give you fome Image of it. But thefe feldom happen in Plays, and in Orations not very frequently.

Thus I have gone through the Art of Action or Gefture, which tho I have directed chiefly for the Stage, and there principally for Tragedy, yet the *Bar* and the *Pulpit* may learn fome Leffons from what I have faid, that would be of mighty ufe to make their Pleadings and Sermons of more Force and Grace. But, I think, the *Pulpit* chiefly has need of this Doctrine, becaufe that converfes more with the Paffions, than the *Bar* ; and treats of more fublime Subjects, meritorious of all the Beauty and Solemnity of Action. I am perfuaded, that if our Clergy would apply themfelves more to this Art, what they preach would be more efficacious, and themfelves more refpected ; nay, have a greater Awe on their Auditors. But then it muft be confefs'd it is next to impoffible for them to attain this Perfection, while that Cuftom prevails of reading of Sermons, which no Clergy in the World do but thofe of the Church of *England*. For while they read they are not perfect enough in what they deliver, to give it its proper Action and Emphafis, either in Pronunciation or Gefture. But the *Tatler* has handled this particular very well ; and if what he has faid will have no Influence upon them, it will be much in vain for me to attempt it.

The

The *Comedians*, I fear, may take it amifs, that I have had little or no Regard to them in this Difcourfe. But I muft confefs, tho I have attempted two or three Comical Parts, which the Indulgence of the Town to an old Fellow has given me fome Applaufe for ; yet Tragedy is, and has always been, my Delight. Befides, as fome have obferv'd, that Comedy is lefs difficult in the Writing ; fo I am apt to believe, it is much eafier in the Acting ; not that a good *Comedian* is to be made by every one that attempts it, but we have had, almoft ever fince I knew the Stage, more and better *Comedians*, than *Tragedians* ; as we have had better *Comedies*, than *Tragedies* writ in our Language, as the Critics and knowing Judges tell us. But being willing to raife Tragedies from their prefent Neglect, to the Efteem they had in the moft polite Nation, that ever *Europe* knew, I have endeavour'd to contribute my Part towards the improving of the Reprefentation, which has a mighty Influence on the Succefs and Efteem of any thing of this Nature.

I might here add fome Obfervations on the Errors in the Action of our prefent Players ; but as that would be an invidious Tafk, fo they may eafily be difcover'd by thofe Rules I have laid down of a juft Performance. I fhall therefore now proceed to the other Duty of a Player, which is the Art of *Speaking* ; which, tho much the leaft confiderable, yet according to our modern *Tragedies*, I mean thofe, which have

been

been beft receiv'd, is of moft Ufe.　For thofe
Poets have very erroneoufly apply'd themfelves
to write more what requires juft *Speaking,* than
juft Acting.　And our Players, generally fpeaking, fall very much fhort of that Excellence ev'n
in this, which they ought to aim or arrive at;
but too plainly prove what *Rofeneraus* defcribes—
An Airy of Children, little Tafes, they cry out on the
Top of the Queftion, and are moft tyrannically
clapt for't; thefe are now the Fafhion, and fo be-
rattle the common Stages (fo they call'em) that many
wearing Rapiers are afraid of Goofe-Quills, and
dare fcarce come thither.　And tho in what I have
before quoted from *Hamlet* (in his Account of the
Actor's Action and Behaviour) do happily exprefs
the Soul and Art of Acting, which *Shakefpear* has
drawn the compleat Art of Gefture in miniature, in
the quoted Speech, yet all the Directions, which he
gives, relate (except one Line) wholly to *Speaking.*

HAMLET.　" Speak the Speech, I pray you,
" as I pronounc'd it, trippingly on the Tongue.
" But if you mouth it, as many of our Players
" do, I had as lieve the Town-Cryer had fpoke
" my Lines.　Nor do not faw the Air too much
" with your Hand thus, but ufe all gently; *For*
" *in the very Torrent, Tempeft, and I may fay*
" *the Whirlwind of Paffion, you muft acquire and*
" *beget a Temperance, that may give it Smooth-*
" *nefs.*　Oh! it offends me to the Soul to fee a
" robuftous, *perriwig-pated* Fellow tear a Paf-
" fion to Tatters, to very Rags, to fplit the Ears
" of the Groundlings, who for the moft part
　　　　　　　　　　　　　　　　" are

" are capable of nothing but inexplicable *dumb*
" *Shows* and *Noife.*   I could have fuch a Fel-
" low whipt for o'erdoing Termagant : It out-
" *Herod's Herod.*   Pray you avoid it ———— Be
" not too tame neither, but let your own Dif-
" cretion be your Tutor.   Suit the *Action* to the
" *Word,* the *Word* to the *Action,* with this fpe-
" cial Obfervance, that you o'ertop not the Mo-
" defty of *Nature.*   For any thing fo overdone
" is from the Purpofe of Playing, whofe End
" both at the firft and now was and is to hold
" as 'twere the Mirror up to *Nature* ; to fhow
" Virtue her own Feature ; fcorn her own I-
" mage,   and the very Age and Body of the
" Time, his Form, and Preffure.   Now this
" over-done, or come tardy of, tho it make the
" Unskilful laugh, cannot but make the Judici-
" ous grieve : *The Cenfure of which* ONE, *muft*
" *in your Allowance o'erfway a* WHOLE THEA-
" TRE *of others.*   Oh ! there be Players, that
" I have feen play, and heard others praife,
" and that highly, (not to fpeak it prophanely)
" that neither having the Accent of *Chriftians,*
" nor the Gate of *Chriftian,* Pagan, or *Norman,*
" have fo *ftrutted* and *bellow'd, that I have*
" *thought fome of Nature's Journey-Men had*
" *made Men, and not made them well, they imi-*
" *tated Humanity fo abominably.*
    Player. " I hope we have reformed that indif-
" ferently with us, Sir.
    Ham. " Oh ! reform it altogether.   And let
" thofe, who play the Clowns, fpeak no more,
                                  " than

" than is fet down for 'em; for there be of them,
" who will themfelves laugh, to fet on fome
" Quantity of barren Spectators to laugh too;
" tho in the mean time, fome neceffary Que-
" ftion of the Play be then to be confider'd :
" that's villanous, and fhews a moft *pitiful Am-*
" *bition* in the Fool, that ufes it.

If we fhould confider and weigh thefe Directions well, I am perfuaded they are fufficient
to inftruct a young Player in all the Beauties of
Utterance, and to correct all the Errors he might,
for want of the Art of Speaking, have incurr'd.
By pronouncing it *trippingly on the Tongue,* he
means a clear and difembarrafs'd Pronunciation,
fuch as is agreeable to Nature and the Subject
on which he fpeaks.   His telling the Actor, that
he had as lieve the Town-Cryer fhould fpeak his
Lines, as one that mouth'd them, is very juft;
for if Noife were an Excellence, I know not who
would bear away the Palm, the *Cryer,* or the
Player; I'm fure the Town-Cryer would be lefs
faulty, his Bufinefs requiring Noife. *Nor do not
faw the Air with your Hand thus,* but *ufe all* GENT-
LY : This is the only Precept of Action, which is
extremely juft; and agreeable to the Notions of
all, that I have met with on my full Enquiry a-
mong my learned Friends, who have read all that
has been wrote upon Action, and who reckon *rude*
and *boiftrous* Geftures among the faulty; Art always directing a moderate and gentle Motion,
which *Shakefpear* expreffes by *ufe all gently.* Befides,
this *fawing of the Air,* expreffes one, who is very
much

much at a Lofs how to difpofe of his Hands, but knowing that they fhould have fome Motion, gives them an aukward Violence. The next Obfervation is extremely mafterly——*For in the very* TORRENT, TEMPEST, *and I may fay the Whirlwind of Paffion, you muft acquire and get a Temperance, that may give it* SMOOTHNESS. I remember among many, an Inftance in the Madnefs of *Alexander* the *Great*, in *Lee*'s Play, Mr. *Goodman* always went through it with all the Force the Part requir'd, and yet made not half the Noife, as fome who fucceeded him ; who were fure to bellow it out in fuch a manner, that their Voice would fail them before the End, and led them to fuch a languid and enervate Hoarfenefs, as entirely wanted that agreeable *Smoothnefs*, which *Shakefpear* requires, and which is the Perfection of beautiful Speaking ; for to have a juft Heat, and Loudnefs, and yet a *Smoothnefs* is all that can be defir'd. *Oh! it offends me to the Soul*, he goes on—— Methinks fome of our young Gentlemen, who value themfelves for great Players, nay, and Judges too of the Drama, fet up for Critics, and who cenfure and receive or reject Plays, fhould be afham'd of themfelves, when they read this in *Shakefpear*, whofe Authority they feem fo fond of on other Occafions ; but it is with them here, as with fome Enemies of Reafon on other Occafions, who are againft Reafon, when Reafon is againft them, tho none fo clamorous for it at other Times, that is, they are fonder of Error,

than

than Truth, when they can be more remarkable, and clapt by the *Million*, by continuing in their Error, than by quitting it— But that is a *pitiful Ambition* indeed, and unworthy a Mafter of any Art. *Tully* likens thefe Bellowers to Criples, that fly to Noife to cover their Igno-rance, as the other to a Horfe to help their Lamenefs; and with this Noife they triumph with the Ignorant; but *Homer* never reckon'd *Stentor* among his fine Speakers. So that tho a ftrong and firm Voice be a very good Ingredi-ent in a Speaker, yet he ought to have a pecu-liar Care not to offend a nice Ear, by putting it upon the ftretch too much. For this Reafon when *Carneades* (not yet of fo great Autho-rity among the Philofophers) was declaiming in the Schools, the Mafter fent him word to moderate his Voice a little; but on his requi-ring a Pitch from him, the Mafter reply'd, let his Voice be your Tone, with whom you talk. So that the Loudnefs or Lownefs of the Voice is to be modell'd according to the Place of Speaking, and the Audience; that it be not too low, or too loud. An equal Care ought to be taken of the Action, that it be not rude and defultory, nor beyond Meafure active; *Quintus Haterius* had a Servant always behind him, when he fpoke in Public, who by touching his Garment, when the Ardour of Difcourfe had made him fly out, recall'd him to the juft Medi-um of Action. The Ancients indeed (if my Authors miflead me not) were extremely againft

G 3 that

that infolent toffing of the Body about, when there was no Occafion. *Sextus Titius* was a very fharp and loquacious Man, but was fo diffolute and enervate in his Action and Geftures, that a fort of Dance arofe out of his Gefticulation, which was call'd by his Name. Nor was *Manlius Sura,* whom when *Domitius Afer* had feen whilft he was Acting or Speaking, running up and down, dancing, toffing his Hands about, throwing down his Gown now, and then gathering it up again, he faid, this Man does not act or ufe Geftures, but miferably aims at fomething he does not underftand. Some of the Ancients, not content with this Agitation of the Body, that they like the Antifophift of *Virginius,* travell'd a many Miles in their Declamations ; which made *Caffius Severus* require fome Goal, or Bound to be fet them, as in Races, beyond which their Excurfions fhould not reach. Some ftrike their Chins, fome their Thighs, and fome their Foreheads in Trifles, and others perpetually buffet the Pulpit, or Place of Action ; fome proceed fo far, as to pull off their Hair. Thefe Vices of Action are not fit for any one, much lefs for grave People, and on grave Occafions. For tho the Paffions are very beautiful in their proper *Geftures,* yet they ought never to be fo extravagantly immoderate, as to tranfport the Speaker out of himfelf. Tho this has a peculiar Regard to the Bar and the Pulpit, yet has it an equal Authority over the Stage, allowing only for the greater Latitude, which

is

is proper to that Place, which would be ſhock-
ing in the other. But then *Shakeſpear* would
not have his *Player* too tame neither, for that
indeed is an Error in the other Extreme; it e-
nervates the Diſcourſe, and makes the whole
Paſſion languiſh, which ought to warm you
with a juſt and comfortable Heat, and enliven-
ing Fire. Altho Action be of great Uſe and
Force in *Speaking*, Sedateneſs being to be expreſs'd in ſome things, in others *Severity*, and
Vehemence, yet never Madneſs in any thing,
which happens to thoſe, who wanton in a ſort
of tragical and howling Voice upon every Trifle. Some, on the contrary, are viciouſly op-
poſite to theſe, who act ſo tamely and ſo coldly,
that when they ought to be angry, to thunder
and lighten, as one may ſay, they are no fuller
of Heat, than a wet Hen, as the Saying is; and
turn over a *Thyeſtean* Scene in the calm Tone of
a mere Reader; which made *Cicero* ſay to *Callidius*, when he ſedately told of his being like
to be poiſon'd, *If you did not feign all this Story,
could you deliver it in this manner ?* gathering
from his Action, that he ſpoke not feelingly e-
nough for a Reality. Such are fitter to comfort
the Sick, than to *ſpeak* in public. In this
much is left to the Nature of the Subject, and
for this Reaſon *Shakeſpear* leaves it to his Diſ-
cretion. Yet notwithſtanding he leaves his Diſ-
cretion to be his Guide, he ſoon directs that
Guide, by bidding him *ſuit the Action to the*
Words, *and the Words to the* Action; and

G   not

not *to overtop* the Modefty of, that is, to go beyond *Nature*, which is to be the Rule of juft
Acting. But then the fame Difficulty will arife
here as in Writing, where all fides agree, that
Nature is the fovereign Guide and Scope; but
then they are not fo agreed in what *Nature* is:
The Skilful lay down thofe Signs, Marks, and
Lineaments of *Nature*, that you may know
when fhe is truly drawn, when not; the Un-
fkilful, which is the greater and more noify
part, leave it fo at large, that it amounts to no
more, than every one's Fancy, which would
make Contradictions Nature; for what pleafes
one, he calls Nature; what pleafes another,
that he calls Nature; and I heard once a Man
of the Stage, in great Vogue for I know not what
off the Stage, fay *Nonfenfe* was natural, when
Nature has been urg'd as the Rule of good Writing; whether he meant it a *Witticifm* or not, I
never thought it worth while to examine, being fenfible, that NONSENSE is very natural to
fome, ev'n tho they fet up for, and are ev'n admir'd by a Set of People for their Wit.

I inftance this, to fhow that there feems a
Neceffity of fome Marks, or Rules to fix the
Standard of what is *Natural*, and what not,
elfe it is a loofe vague Word of no manner of
Ufe or Authority. But this is what *Shakefpear*
fuppofes our Actor to know, and therefore he
proceeds to tell him what the End of a Player
was and is, *viz. to hold as it were the Mirrour
up to Nature, to fhew Virtue her own Feature*;
fcorn

fcorn her own Image, and the very Age and Body of the Time, his Form and Preffure. To attain a juft Praife in which, befides the Knowledge of them, the Player muft neither over or under-act his Part. As I have already laid down fuch Obfervations, as may be of great Ufe to the *Actor* in his Acting and Gefture, fo I fhall now fet down fome, which will give an Infight into the Art of *Speaking,* or regulating and modelling the Voice in fuch a manner, as may render the Utterance pleafing to the Ear.

Before I come to the Directions for the Beauties of Speaking, I think it will not be amifs to infert here a Paper given me by a Friend, of the feveral natural Defects and Vices of a Voice, taken from the 26th Chapter of the Second Book of *Julius Pollux's Onomaftics,* which he makes about twenty in number.

The firft he calls *Black,* drawing the Metaphor from the Eyes to the Ears. For as Black ftrikes the Eyes more dully, fo does this fort of Voice penetrate the Ears with greater Difficulty, and carries with it lefs of the Pleafant, but fomething on the contrary of the *difmal* and *horrid.*

Next the *dufky* or *brown,* differs from the Black only, by being fomething lefs obfcure, but is yet very far from that Brightnefs of a pure Tone of Voice.

Rough or *unpleafant,* fuch as your very ftrong Voices generally are, with which the pleafing Sweetnefs is feldom mingled ; and *Seneca* puts

it

it down for a wonder, that *Caffius Severus* retain'd a Sweetnefs in his Voice, tho it was extremely ftrong and robuft; for it feldom happens, that the fame Voice is both fweet and folid.

The oppofite to this he calls *fmall* or *weak*, fuch is their Voice, who feem rather to pip like a young Chicken, than to fpeak like humane kind.

Strait or *flender*, which is flenderly melted thro' the narrow Channel of the Throat, and fills not the Ears of the Hearers.

Dufucous, that which is not heard without Difficulty, or that which is very importunately troublefome to the Ears.

That which by *Fabius* is call'd *fubfurd* or *deafifh*, which wanting vocal Emiffion, detains the Sound within; like the Harper *Afpendius*, who could touch the Harp fo, that no body but himfelf could hear the Sound.

The *confus'd*, which is not diftinguifh'd with full articulate Sounds.

The *jarring*, untuneable, abfonous, and unharmonious.

Unmelodious, neglected, without Beauty or Grace.

Rude, uncouth, untractable, unmanageable, like unbroken Colts.

Unperfuafive, that is not adapted to Perfuafion, fuch as theirs, who have a perpetual Identity of Tone in Difcourfe; a *Monotony*.

Rigid,

Rigid, that which with Difficulty admits any Variation.

Hard or *harſh*, which offends the Ears with a ſort of bouncing and cracking Noiſe.

Deſultory or *broken*, which is when the Diſcourſe leaps or bounds, as it were with unequal Diſtances and Sounds, confuſedly mixing ſhort and long, flat and ſharp, high and low, ſo that the Diſcourſe goes lamely on with the Inequality of all theſe together ; the ſame is call'd the *fickle* or *inconſtant*.

The *auſtere*, *ſour* or *diſmal*, which ſtrikes the Ears with an unpleaſant Sound, ſomething like that of creaking Wheels.

The *infirm* or *feeble*, by which the weak and broken Breath is ſpread and diſpers'd into a hoarſe Smallneſs.

Brazen, which like the vehement Clinking of Braſs is perpetually aſſaulting our Ears.

The *ſharp* or *acute*, which ſtrikes and penetrates the Ears with a ſhriller Sound, than it ought. For the moſt acute Sounds are not the moſt fit for Speaking in Public ; which is made too thin, too cutting, and of too great a Clearneſs.

The contrary Virtues enumerated by the ſame Author are theſe.

The *high*, which being ſent from good Lungs and Cheſt perfectly fills the Ears.

The *lofty*, that which is not only more fully heard, but by its own Firmneſs becomes durable.

The

The *clear*, that founds fprightly, and is not blurr'd with any Defects.

The *fmooth, fpreading, explicit.*

The *grave, bafs,* or *full,* fuch as generally is the Voice of the moft manly and robuft Singers, which if mingled with Sweetnefs is the moft valuable Voice, that is ; but when it wants this Sweetnefs, it fcatters and fpreads out into wild and defolate Enormity.

The *candid* and *pure,* which affects the Ears, as White does the Eyes, and is therefore contrary to the Vice of Voice call'd the *black.*

The *pure* and *fimple,* and as it were refin'd from all Vices and Defects.

The *fweet,* which delights with the Flower, as I may fay, of a good Grace.

The *alluring,* that abounds in delicate Modulating, and harmonious Warblings.

The *exquifite,* polifh'd and rich.

The *round* and *fimple,* and moft adapted to Perfuafion.

The *tractable* or *Voice at Command,* which eafily rifes from the loweft Note to the higheft, and with as much Eafe falls from the higheft to the loweft, and every where divides it felf into all the pleafing Variety of Notes.

The *flexible,* that is wholly without Roughnefs, Stiffnefs, that obeys the Modulation, as Wax does the Fingers.

The *voluble* or fwift, fuch as that of the beft Orators, in the clofeft and hotteft of the Argument.

The

The *delicious*, beautiful in a kind of graceful Softnefs.

The *founding* or *canorous*, fit to fing with Mufical Inftruments.

The *full*, *perfpicuous*, and eafy to be heard.

The *fplendid*, and *fhining* with an agreeable Softnefs.

Thefe are the feveral forts, or kinds of Voices, and their Virtues, which proceed merely from Nature, which yet receive from Art their Brightnefs, Improvement, and Perfection.

As thefe are the Virtues and Vices of the Voice, fo we fhall now proceed to the Beauties and Defects of *Pronunciation :* The chief Excellencies of which are agreed by the Mafters of the Art to be *Purity*, *Perfpicuity*, *Ornament*, and *Hability* or *Aptitude*.

PURITY is, as we may fay, a certain Healthfulnefs of Voice, which has in it nothing vicious ; which is obftructed by the Voice we have call'd *fubfurd* or deafifh, rude, noify, hard, rigid, inconftant or uncertain, thick or grofs ; or by one, that is fmall, ftrait, empty, infirm, foft, or effeminate. On the contrary, a Delivery, which is eafy, open, pleafant, genteel ; and in which nothing founds clownifh or foreign, is a great Help to *Pronunciation*, as *Quintilian* juftly obferves. *Cicero*, with equal Juftice, and for the fame Reafon, in his Book *de Oratore*, condemns a Voice, that is foft, womanifh, untuneable, abfurd, ungenteel and ruftical. And he directs his Speaker to a *Delivery*,

that

that is neither harſh, nor diſorderly, nor clown-
iſh, nor gaping, but cloſe, equal, or of the
ſame Tenor, and ſmooth. To theſe we muſt
add the Tone and Accent, by which Men are
known. This Virtue is obtain'd by Nature and
Uſe, which is of very great Conſequence in
theſe Affairs ; for which Reaſon Boys ſhould
inure themſelves to a right Pronunciation from
the Beginning ; ſince we find, that in learning
foreign Tongues, thoſe ſeldom reach the Purity
of them, who apply not themſelves to them till
in Years.

The PERSPICUITY, and Light of *Pronunciation* conſiſts of a certain articulate Expreſſion
of all the Syllables, and their proper Points and
Stops; of which theſe are the Precepts of *Quintilian.*

The *Pronunciation* will be *perſpicuous* and
clear, firſt if the whole Words are entirely
ſounded, part of which is ſometimes devoured,
part neglected by moſt, who by indulging and
dwelling too much on the Sound of the foregoing Syllables, expreſs not ſufficiently the laſt :
But as the making Words have a plain Pronunciation is neceſſary, ſo is it very troubleſome
and odious to run it to a Computation and Enumeration of every Letter, and we muſt obſerve
nicely in what Place the Diſcourſe is to be ſuſtain'd, and as it were ſuſpended. And this, as
is plain, is to be attain'd by Art.

The ORNAMENT is the cultivating and Clearneſs of the Voice ; and to this a great Help is

I　　　　　　　　　　　　na-

naturally deriv'd from a Voice, that is eafy, great, happy, flexible, firm, fweet, durable, clear, pure, penetrating, high, and adorn'd indeed with all thofe Virtues, we have already enumerated out of *Julius Pollux*. To this we muft add, the beautiful Compofition of the whole Inftrument or Body, as the Firmnefs of the Cheft and Lungs, Goodnefs of Breath, and that not eafily giving way to, or failing under Labour and Fatigue.

HABILITY or APTITUDE is a pleafing Variety of *Pronunciation*, according to the Diverfity of the Subject, and in a conftant Equality. For as the beft Style is perpetually equal or confiftent with it felf, and yet is according to the Subject now grave, now florid, and now gently abated ; fo is a valuable Utterance always the fame, and never deviating from its Excellence, yet derives all its Beauty and Glory from thofe agreeable Varieties, which according to the Nature of the Things it delivers, it admits. It is impoffible to exprefs how great and charming the Grace of the Art of varying the Voice, how much it enlivens the Hearers, and refrefhes the Speaker himfelf by an agreeable Change of his Labour. On the contrary, a *Monotony*, or perpetually Speaking in the fame unvary'd Tone, quite deftroys the Speaker, and difpirits the Auditors, making them languifh under a tirefome Ofcitation. As we cannot always ftand, or fit, or walk, but relieve our felves by an alternate Ufe of them, fo in *Pronunciation*, we love a

grate-

grateful Variation of the Voice directed by a juſt Equality.

The Voice therefore, according to *Quintilian*, in *Joy* ſhould be full, ſimple, pleaſant, and flowing; in *Diſpute*, extended with all its juſt Force and Nerves; in *Anger*, vehement and ſharp, or acute, cloſe, compact, mixt with frequent Reſpirations; but more ſlow in raiſing *Envy*, ſince few but Inferiours have Recourſe to this.

In Inſinuations, Confeſſions, Atonements and the like, the Voice muſt be gentle and temperate; when you perſuade, admoniſh, promiſe, or Comfort it ought to be grave; and contracted in Fear, and Baſhfulneſs and Modeſty; ſtrong in Exhortations, in Diſputations round, fine and ſmooth; in Pity and Compaſſion, turning dolefully, and as it were on purpoſe more obſcure. In Expoſitions and Diſcourſes, direct; and in a Tone, that is a Medium betwixt an acute and grave. It is rais'd with our Paſſions, and falls again with them, being higher or lower according to either. Whoever can do all this has attain'd the higheſt Perfection of *Pronunciation*.

Cicero, in his 3d Book *de Oratore*, divides Pronunciation into many kinds; into *gentle* and *fierce*; contracted and diffus'd; with a continu'd Breath, and with an Intermiſſion of the ſame; *broken* or *cut*; with a varying or direct Sound; ſlender and *great*. Theſe, ſays he, are expos'd for Colours to the Actor, as to the Painter to draw his Variations.

Anger

Anger loves an acute Sound, vehement, and full of Refpirations.

Commiferation or *Pity*, one that is flexible, full, interrupted, and doleful.

Fear, one low, not without Hefitation, and abject.

Force and *Power*, one vehement, earneft, imminent, but carry'd on with a certain Gravity.

Pleafure, one effufive, gentle, tender, joyful, and remifs.

Grief and *Trouble*, one grave, and opprefs'd with every ftraining.

Thus far my Paper, in which, I think, is contain'd the Art of Speaking beautifully on all Occafions; for there is nothing, that an Actor can talk of on the Stage, whether in Paffion, or out of Paffion, a Pleader at the Bar, or the Divine in the Pulpit, but what muft fall under fome of thefe Heads. I therefore recommend to the Study of my *Speaker* a perfect Application to what is here deliver'd. Yet, as this may not appear fo obvious to many, who may defire to underftand this Art, and may be capable of arriving at fome Perfection in it ; I fhall proceed to give my Learner fome more plain Lights, and which may ferve, as a thorough Paraphrafe and Explanation of what I have here deliver'd.

The firft Confideration in the Art of Speaking, is to fatisfy the Ear, which conveys all Arts and Sciences to us, and is the natural Judge of the Voice. The Speaker therefore ought to be heard and underftood with Eafe and Pleafure,

to

to which a Voice clear, fweet and ftrong, is neceffary to be heard all over the Audience. Such a Voice as *Quintilian* gives *Trachallus*, would be very ufeful, who pleading a Caufe in one of the four Courts in the *Julian Forum*, was not only heard in that but in all the reft, fo well as to be underftood, and merit Applaufe; but tho every Man cannot obtain a Voice like this, yet if he cannot fill the Place, where he fpeaks, he's not fit to fpeak.

Some Men have fuch a Voice naturally, others attain it by the Improvement of Art and Exercife. As has been faid of *Demofthenes*, who was as defective in Speaking as in Action and Gefture: He had naturally a weak Voice, and Impediment in his Speech, and a fhort Breath; and venturing withal thefe Difqualifications to fpeak in public twice, he was hifs'd both Times. But by his Induftry and Application, he remov'd all thefe Obftructions. He daily in his under-ground Apartment exercis'd himfelf, by fpeaking what he had read aloud, fo that his Organs gradually open'd, and his Voice fenfibly clearing, grew every Day ftronger, than the former. His Tongue was fo grofs and clumfy, that he mumbled his Words, nor could utter them clear and plain; nay, he could not pronounce an (R) at all; he was fo fhort winded, that he could not fpeak many Words together without taking his Breath, which was but a fort of broken-winded Pronunciation; and thefe Difficulties produc'd a wonderful Difficulty, which was the furmounting

ing

ing the great Noife of a Publick Affembly.

Firft, he cur'd the Groffnefs of his Tongue, by putting Peble-ftones in his Mouth, whilft he fpoke for fome time ; he cur'd himfelf of his fhort Breath, by running up Hills, and repeating upright as he went fome Verfes, or Sentences of Speeches, which he had by Heart ; which ftrengthen'd his Lungs, and made him long-winded : The Noife of Public Affemblies he conquer'd by Speaking with his utmoft Contention of Voice in his Orations to the Roaring of the Sea, when loudeft, and fo became the moft compleat Speaker of his Age.

'Tis true *Demofthenes* overcame thefe Difficulties, or at leaft Hiftorians make us believe fo ; but this fhould be no Reafon for admitting any one into a Play-houfe, who lies under fuch Defects, as this great Orator, by unfpeakable Diligence, remov'd. For if a Man's Voice be good for nothing, by Reafon of any Indifpofition of the Organs, as the Tongue, Throat, Breaft, or Lungs ; if he have any confiderable Lifping, Hefitation, or Stammering, he is not proper for the Stage, the Pulpit, or the Bar.

But I have given this Inftance of *Demofthenes*, for the Sake of fome, who may be on the Stage, and furnifh'd with an admirable Genius, yet for want of Breath, or by the Feeblenefs of their Voice, cannot exert their other beautiful Qualities. Let them always fpeak out in their private Study, and in *Rehearfals* ; it is an exer-

cife;

cife, which has been judg'd beneficial to the
Health, provided, that you do not overftrain
your Voice. Thus we find in *Plutarch,* (for I
read all the Ancients I can meet with in
French or *Englifh*) whilft he advifes other
bodily Exercifes for the Health of others, to
thofe, who fpeak in *Public,* be it on the Stage,
or elfewhere, he prefcribes Difcourfing, or making Speeches often, or Reading with as exalted a Voice, as Nature will well bear ; and he
fays, it is his Opinion, that this Exercife is more
healthy, and ufeful for this End, than all others;
fince while the other Motions fet only the Limbs
at work, and ftir the external Members, the
Voice employs a nobler part of the Body, and
ftrengthens the Lungs, from which it receives
its Breath ; it augments the natural Heat, thins
the Blood, cleanfes the Veins, opens all the Ar-
teries, prevents every Obftruction, and hinders
the grofs Humours from thickening into Di-
ftempers.

Let every Syllable have its diftinct and full
Sound and Proportion, when you ufe this Exercife, and then you need not fear muffling your
Words, or Stammering. But befides this Vice
of Utterance, you muft avoid a broad way of
fpeaking with your Mouth wide open, and of
bellowing out a great Sound, but fo confus'd
and inarticulate, that tho you may be heard a
great way off, yet the Sound will convey no
more to the Underftanding, than the Roaring
of a Bull, or any other Beaft. This proceeds

from

from an Affectation, and a falfe Opinion, that this enormous Loudnefs gives a Majefty and Force to what they fay; whereas it robs it of its Articulation, which is the very Being of Speech, and hinders its being underftood, which is the very End of Speaking.

There are, in fhort, two things to make the Speaker heard and underftood without Difficulty; firft, a very diftinct and articulate Voice, and next a very ftrong and vigorous Pronunciation. The firft is the moft important; for an indifferent Voice, with a diftinct Pronunciation, fhall be far more eafily underftood, than one, that is ftronger and more audible, but which does not articulate the Words fo well.

But it is not fufficient to be heard without Difficulty, but it ought to be the Object of your Endeavours to be heard with Pleafure and Satisfaction. To this End you muft confider, whether your Voice have any of the fore-mention'd Vices or Defects, whether it be harfh, hoarfe, or obfequious, and enquire into the Caufe, whether it be from Nature, or an ill Habit; for 'tis your Bufinefs to render your Voice as fweet, foft, and agreeable to the Ear, as you poffibly can. If the Defect proceeds from only an *ill Habit*, you ought to practice a contrary manner, if you would make your felf fit for this Affair. But if it proceed from Nature, in the Defect of any, or all of the Organs of the Body employed in it, tho we have the Examples of *Cicero* and *Demofthenes* of Succefs, yet

H 3   at

at this time, and in this Employ, I think, it is scarce worth the while to aim, by a great deal of uncertain Labour, at the correcting Nature, when there are other Employments fitter for you.

Next to the Finenefs of the Tone, the Variation of it is what will make the Auditors pleas'd and delighted with what they hear; you ought therefore to employ much Care and Time in learning the Art of varying the Voice, according to the Diverfity of the Subjects, of the Paffions you would exprefs or excite, ftronger or weaker, higher or lower, as will be moft agreeable to what you fay.

Tho I have already touch'd on this Point both in my Remarks on what I quoted from *Shakefpear* about Speaking, and in the Paper inferted on the Virtues of *Pronunciation*, yet I cannot difmifs this Subject without fome farther Reflections, becaufe we have had fome Actors of Figure, who have an admirable Tone of Voice, the Beauty of which they have perverted into a Deformity, by keeping always in the very fame Identity of Sound, in the very fame Key, nay, the individual Note; for as in Mufic, fo in Speaking, 'tis the Variety, which makes the Harmony; and as for a Fidler or Lutinift, or any other Performer in Mufic, to ftrike always the fame String and Note, would be fo far from tolerable Mufic, that it would be ridiculoufly infufferable and dull, fo can nothing grate the Ear fo much, or give the Auditors a greater

Dif-

Difguft, as a Voice ftill in the fame Tone, without Divifion or Variety.

'Tis true, this Vice is too general among moft Speakers, but not in the laft Degree. Few arrive to the true Art of varying the Voice with that Beauty and Harmony, which is in Nature, becaufe they do not ftudy what the Words, Subject, and Paffion to be exprefs'd properly require. A good Voice, indeed, tho ill manag'd, may fill the Ear agreeably, but it would be infinitely more pleafing, if they knew how to give it the juft Turns, Rifings, Fallings, and all other Variations fuitable to the Subjects and Paffions. But thofe very fine Voices, which in fpight of their being ill govern'd pleafe, are very uncommon. But this Vice renders fuch Voices, as are ordinarily met with, to the laft Degree difagreeable.

But this *ftiff Uniformity of Voice* is not only difpleafing to the Ear, but difappoints the Effect of the Difcourfe on the Hearers ; firft, by an equal way of Speaking, when the Pronuncia-tion has every where, in every Word and eve-ry Syllable the fame Sound, it muft inevitably render all Parts of the Speech equal, and fo put them on a very unjuft Level. So that the Power of the Reafoning Part, the Luftre and Ornament in the Figures, the Heart, Warmth, and Vigor of the paffionate part being exprefs'd all in the fame Tone, is flat and infipid, and loft in a fupine, or at leaft immufical Pronunciation. So that, in fhort, that which ought to ftrike and ftir up the Affections, becaufe 'tis fpoken all

alike,

alike, without any Diſtinction or Variety, moves them not at all. Next there is no greater Opiate in Speaking, nothing ſo dull and heavy, and fit to lull us aſleep, as a whole Diſcourſe turning ſtill on the ſame *Note* and *Tone*; and indeed it ſavours of the Cant, which was formerly in ſome of the Diſſenter's Pulpits, which they have of late very much reform'd in their young Men.

I believe a great deal of this is owing to our erroneous way of Education, where the School-Miſtreſſes firſt, and afterwards the Maſters, teach or ſuffer the Boys to cant out their Leſſons in one unvary'd Tone for ſo many Years, which grows up with us, and is not overcome at laſt without Application; tho Nature and Reaſon, if we would conſult them, would guide us into a more pleaſing and excellent Road.

Nature tells us, that in Mourning, in Melancholly, in Grief, we muſt and do expreſs our ſelves in another ſort of Tone and Voice, than in Mirth, in Joy, in Gladneſs: Otherwiſe in Reproof of Crimes, *&c.* than in Comforting the Afflicted: Otherwiſe when we upbraid a Man with his Faults, than when we aſk Pardon for our own; otherwiſe when we threaten, than when we promiſe, pray, or beg a Favour; otherwiſe when we are in a good Humour, the Paſſions all calm, and the Mind in perfect Tranquillity, than when we are rais'd with Anger, or provok'd by ill Nature.

This

This *Variation* is fo founded in Nature, that fhould you hear two People, in a Language you do not underftand, talking together with Heat, the one in *Anger*, the other in *Fear*; one in *Joy*, the other in *Sorrow*, you might eafily diftinguifh the Paffions from each other by the different Tone, and Cadence of their Voice, as well as by their Countenance and Gefture; nay, a blind Man, who could not obferve thofe, by the Voice would eafily know the Diftinction.

From this it is plain, that as this Variation of the Voice is founded in Nature, fo the nearer you approach to Nature, the nearer you come to Perfection; and the farther you are from her, the more vicious is your *Pronunciation*. The lefs affected the better, for a natural Variation is much the beft; the eafieft way of arriving at which, is a juft Obfervation of common Dif-courfe, and to mind how you fpeak your felf in Converfation; how a Woman expreffes her Paffion for an Injury receiv'd, her Grief for the Lofs of a Hufband, or any thing dear to her, and from thefe Obfervations endeavour to form your Pronunciation in public, with this only dif-ference, that you confider how much louder your Voice ought to be to be heard in all thofe Particulars, at fuch a Diftance as the Stage, the Bar, or the Pulpit. The beft Actors change their Voice according to the Qualities of the Perfons they reprefent, and the Condition they are in, or the Subject of their Difcourfe; al-ways fpeaking in the fame Tone on the Stage,

as

as they would do in a Room, allowing for the Diftance.

We muft, therefore, vary the Voice, as often as we can ; but the only Difficulty is to know how to do it artfully, and with Harmony ; to the accomplifhing which, I fhall give the following Directions.

There are three chief Differences of *Highnefs* or *Lownefs*, of *Vehemence* and *Softnefs*, and *Swiftnefs* and *Slownefs*. The Speaker therefore is to obferve a juft Meafure in all thefe Diftinctions thro' all that he has to fay. He muft be fure to keep a true Medium of the Voice, both the Extremes being vicious and difagreeable. Firft, as to its *Height*, you muft have a Care of either raifing it always to the higheft Note it can reach, or letting it down to the *loweft*. To ftrain it always to the Height, would be a *Bawling* or a *Monotony*, a Cant, or Identity of Sound. For befides the Ungenteelnefs and Indecency of the Clamour and Noife to the Hearer, it wears the Throat of the Speaker into a Hoarfenefs, and the Ears of the Hearer into an Averfion. To fink the Voice likewife into the loweft and moft bafe Note, and to keep it always in the fame Tone, would be to mutter, not to fpeak, and few of the Audience would be able to hear a Word, that was faid.

Nor muft a Man force his Voice perpetually to the laft Extremity ; for not being able to fuftain it long in that Key, it would fail him all of a fudden ; like the String of a Mufical Inftrument, that breaks when fcrew'd up too high.

With-

Without obferving thefe Directions, he would either like *Adrian* the *Phœnician*, mention'd by *Philoſtratus*, lofe his Voice in the midſt of his Difcourfe, and murmur out the later part in fo low a Tone as not to be heard ; or like *Zoſimus* the Freedman of *Pliny* the younger, over-ſtraining himfelf, vomit Blood, and endanger his Life. A Man of a weak Conſtitution, and in Years, ought to have a Care of fuch an intemperate way of Speaking, left he incur the Fate of King *Attalus.* He (as I have read) made once a Speech at *Thebes*, in a public Affembly, in which being tranfported into an Action too violent for the Debility of his old Age, he was of a fudden ſtruck fpeechlefs, and without the leaft Motion or Appearance of Life ; fo that he was forc'd to be carry'd home to his Lodgings, whence foon after being convey'd to his Palace at *Pergamus*, he dy'd.

On the other fide, you ought not to be too fupine or remifs either in your *Action* or *Speaking*, becaufe fo effeminate and foft a Diffolution of the *Voice* betrays a Feeblenefs, and deftroys the Energy of what you fay, nor raifes the Paffions of any one, that hears above a common and difpaffionate Difcourfe.

Next, as to the Swiftnefs and Volubility, it ought not to be precipitate. This was the Fault of one *Serapion*, of whom *Lucillius* gives *Seneca* an Account, and fays, That his Fancy flow'd fo quick, that hudling Word on Word, one Tongue feem'd not fufficient for the Precipitation

tion of his *Pronunciation*. But this, on feveral Accounts, is a very vicious way of Speaking. This Vice is not only unfeemly on all grave Subjects, but an Obftacle to the End propos'd by them, which is Perfuafion. For without allowing Time to confider what you fay, how can you convince? But on the Stage indeed the Cafe is fomething different, becaufe there are Parts, and fome particular Speeches, where fuch an extravagant Volubility is beautiful ; as in feveral Places of the Part of *True Wit* in the *Silent Woman*, and fome other Parts : But that we fhall fee anon, when we come clofer to Particulars. This running on Poft without any Paufe, is alfo prejudicial to the Speaker himfelf; for there is nothing hurts the Lungs more, than fuch a Violence and Precipitation of Speech, as allows no Intermiffion for the regular drawing the Breath, which has caft fome into Confumptions, and coft them their Lives.

But when I give Caution againft this Vice, I would not have you throw your felf into the contrary Extreme ; for when I would not have you run fo very faft with your Tongue, I would not have you fuppofe, that I prefcribe fuch a Slownefs of Utterance, that is like a fick Man's Walking, who can hardly draw one Leg after the other ; whereas what I aim at is, that the Tongue of the Speaker fhould keep Pace with the Ear of the Auditors, being neither too fwift for them to follow, nor too flow for their Attention. I find in an Author on this Subject,

Vicians

Vicians noted for this, that his Slowneſs of Delivery was ſo great, that he ſpoke ſcarce three
Words together without a Pauſe, or Intermiſſion. But there can be no manner of Pleaſure to
hear a Man drawl out his Words at this Rate ;
his Speech, to be of Value, muſt be more florid,
but then it ought to glide like a gentle Stream,
and not pour down like a rapid Torrent.

There is a certain Latitude for the Variation
of the Voice, extending to five or ſix Tones ;
ſo that the Speaker has room enough for varying
his Voice, without ſtriking on the two Extremes,
by forming out of theſe five or ſix Notes a juſt
and delightful Harmony.

Next, the Speaker muſt govern his Voice, in
Regard of its Violence and Softneſs, with ſuch
a Moderation, that tho he force it not to that
laſt Extremity, which hurts Nature in himſelf,
as well as jars upon the Ear of the Hearer ;
nor languiſh, on the other hand, ſo far, as to fall
into the loweſt Degree of Softneſs and Effeminacy, he may yet give his *Pronunciation* more or
leſs Vehemence, or Mildneſs, according to the
different State of his Subject, and the Quality
of his Speech. But in this, as well as in the
Swiftneſs and *Slowneſs*, he muſt let the Subject
and Paſſions of his Diſcourſe be the Guide of
his Judgment. Nor muſt he, when he would
vary his Voice, ſtart out of one Tone into another with too remarkable a Diſtinction of the
latter from the former ; but ſlide from one to
the other with all the Moderation, Softneſs

2   and

and Addrefs in the World ; elfe to thofe, who fee you not, it will feem the Speech of fome other Perfon.

Were I fure of fuch Readers, as could reduce thefe general Rules to particular Cafes, I need not give my felf the Trouble of defcending to Particulars : But that there may be no Help wanting, that I am able to procure, I fhall come to Rules for all the feveral Variations of the Voice, tho they might in fome Meafure be gather'd from what has been urg'd on this Head, both in what regards the Quality of the Subjects, the Nature of the Paffions, the feveral Parts of the Difcourfe, the Figures made ufe of, and the Varieties of Words and Phrafes.

I fhall begin with the Subjects, of which there are feveral forts ; as, *Things Natural, the good or evil Actions of Men, the happy or unfortunate Events of Life,* &c. All which ought, as they are of a very different kind, to be fpoken with as different an Air and Accent. In fpeaking of Things Natural, when you defign only to make your Hearers underftand you, there is no need of Heat or Motion, a clear and diftinct Voice and Utterance is fufficient ; becaufe the informing the Underftanding being here all the Bufinefs, the moving the Will and Paffions has nothing to do. But if from this you rife to ftrike your Auditors with Admiration of the Wonders of Providence, in its *Beauty, Wifdom* and *Power,* you muft do it in a grave Voice, and a Tone full of Admiration.

If

If your Difcourfe be on the Actions of Men, either as *juft*, and *honourable*, which you would by Praife recommend to the Efteem or Imitation of thofe, who hear you ; or *unjuft* or *infamous*, which you would deter them from by Invective; the Voice muft be adapted to the Quality of either; expreffing the Juft and Honeft with a full, lofty, and noble Accent, with a Tone of Satisfaction, Honour, and Efteem ; but the *unjuft*, *infamous*, or *difhonourable*, with a ftrong, violent and paffionate Voice, and a Tone of Anger, Difdain and Deteftation.

If your Difcourfe be on the Events of human Life, thofe are fome fortunate or happy, others unfortunate and miferable ; you muft likewife vary your Voice according to the Difference. When you congratulate the Fortunate, your Tone and Accent is brifk and chearful ; when you condole the Unfortunate, the Accent muft be fad and mournful.

As all the Subjects of Natural Things are not alike for their Grandeur, Beauty and Luftre, as the Heavens and Earth, the Planets and Herbs and Infects, and therefore not to be deliver'd with the fame Voice, and State of Magnificence of *Pronunciation* ; fo are not the Actions and Events of human Life happy or unhappy, good or bad, of the fame Import ; a great and profligate Crime, or a barbarous and extraordinary Cruelty, are of greater Confequence, than a little and common Peccadillo. The Intereft and Honour of Life is of greater Importance, than
the

the Intereft of many; the brave Actions of an illuftrious Conqueror, of a MORDANT or an EUGENE, than thofe of a *Wat Tyler* or *Jack Straw*; the Deftruction or Safety of a *whole Kingdom*, than the Lofs or Gain of a *private Perfon*. So they require a different, and fome a more vehement Accent and Pronunciation, than others; for a great Tone and Accent to trivial and common Occurrences, would be as ridiculous and abfurd, as to fpeak in a plain, low, unconcern d familiar Tone on the moft noble and illuftrious Affairs.

Tho thefe things perhaps, at firft View, may feem more clofely to relate to fet Speeches, Orations, or Sermons, yet if the Actor will throughly confider them, they are of no lefs Concern to him, fince whatever he fpeaks of on the Stage, will fall under fome of thefe Heads, or, at leaft, thefe Subjects will often fall in his way to difcourfe of in Tragedy. But what follows will, beyond Contradiction, be of immediate Ufe to him, fince it is directive of the Accents and Tones according to the Paffions; and the Paffions are or ought always to be in every Part of the *Tragic Scene*; and which, if more introduc'd by our Poets, would get them much more Reputation, as well as Money.

If the *Speaker* will but weigh thefe Subjects, I have juft mention'd, well, and ftrongly imprint them in his Imagination, they will infallibly give fuch lively Ideas, as muft raife in himfelf the Paffions of *Joy* or *Sorrow*, of Fear or
Boldnefs,

Boldnefs, of Anger or Compaffion, of Efteem or of Contempt ; and if thefe are fully and emphatically reprefented, and utter'd with that *Variety* of Tone and Cadence, which they ought to be, they cannot fail of moving the very fame Affections in his Auditors.

When you are therefore to fpeak, you ought firft with Care to confider the Nature of the Thing of which you are to fpeak, and fix a very deep Impreffion of it in your own Mind, before you can be throughly touch'd with it your felf, or able by an agreeable Sympathy to convey the fame Paffion to another. The String of a mufical Inftrument founds according to the Force and Impulfe of the Mafter ; if the Touch be gentle and foft, the Sound is fo too ; if ftrong, the Sound is vivid and ftrong. It is the fame in Speaking as in Mufic, if violent Paffion produce your *Speech*, that will produce a violent Pronunciation ; but if it arife only from a tranquill and gentle Thought, the Force and Accent of the Delivery will be gentle and calm ; fo that the Speaker ought firft to fix the Tone and Accent of his Voice to every Paffion, that affects him, be it of Joy or Sorrow, that he may by a fympathetical Force convey it to others.

Thus will he beft exprefs *Love* by a gay, foft and charming Voice ; his *Hate*, by a fharp, fullen, and fevere one ; his *Joy*, by a full flowing and brifk Voice ; his *Grief*, by a fad, dull and languifhing Tone ; not without fometimes interrupting the Continuity of the Sound with a
Sigh

Sigh or Groan, drawn from the very inmoft of the Bofom. A tremulous and ftammering Voice will beft exprefs his *Fear*, inclining to Uncertainty and Apprehenfion. A loud and ftrong Voice, on the contrary, will moft naturally fhow his *Confidence*, always fupported with a decent Boldnefs, and daring Conftancy. Nor can his Auditors be more juftly ftruck with a Senfe of his *Anger*, than by a Voice or Tone, that is fharp, violent and impetuous, interrupted with a frequent taking of the Breath, and fhort Speaking. Thus *Hotfpur* in *Henry* IV. of *Shakefpear*.

Hotf. *He faid he would not ranfom* MORTIMER,
　Forbad my Tongue to fpeak of MORTIMER,
　But I will find him when he lies afleep,
　And in his Ear I'll hollow MORTIMER.
　Nay, I'll have a Starling fhall be taught to
　　　fpeak
　Nothing but MORTIMER, *and give it him,*
　To keep his Anger ftill in Motion.
　Why look ye, I am whipt and fcourg'd with
　　　Rods,
　Nettl'd and ftung with Pifmires, when I hear
　Of his vile Politician Bullingbrook, *&c.*

And King *Lear* in the fame Poet.

LEAR. *Detefted Kite, thou lyeft !*
　My Train are Men of choice and rareft Parts,
　That all Particulars of Duty know,
　　　　　　　　　　　　　　　　　And

And in the moſt exaƈt Regard ſupport
The Worſhips of their Names ! O moſt ſmall
    Fault !
How ugly didſt thou in CORDELIA *ſhow ?*
Which like an Engine wrench'd my Frame of
    Nature (*Love,*
From the fixt Place ; drew from my Heart all
And added to the Gall. O LEAR ! LEAR !
    LEAR !
Beat at this Gate that let thy Folly in,
And thy dear Judgment out.——

And again immediately.

Hear ! Nature hear ! dear Goddeſs hear !
Suſpend thy Purpoſe if thou doſt intend
To make this Creature fruitful,
Into her Womb convey Sterility ;
Dry up in her the Organs of Increaſe,
And from her Dewgate Body never ſpring
A Babe to honour her. If ſhe muſt teem,
Create her Child of Spleen, that it may give,
And be a thwart, diſnatur'd Torment, like her.
Let it ſtamp Wrinkles in her Brow of Youth ;
With cadent Tears fret Channels in her Cheeks,
Turn all her Mother's Pains and Benefits
To Laughter and Contempt ; that ſhe may feel
How ſharper than a Serpent's Tooth it is
To have a thankleſs Child.

Both theſe Speeches, with that of *Hotſpur,*
muſt be ſpoke with an elevated Tone and enra-
         I 2   ged

ged Voice, and the Accents of a Man all on Fire, and in a Fury next to Madnefs. The fame may be faid of *Othello* in the following Speech.

OTH. *Villain ! Be fure thou prove my Love a*
 Whore ;
 Be fure of it ; *give me the Ocular Proof,*
 Or by the Worth of my eternal Soul,
 Thou hadft better have been born a Dog,
 Than anfwer my wak'd Wrath ——
 If thou doft flander her, or torture me,
 Never pray more ; *abandon all Remorfe*
 On Horrors Head, Horrors accumulate ;
 Do Deeds to make Heav'n weep, all Earth
  amaz'd,
 For nothing canft thou to Damnation add
 Greater than that.

Old Capulet in Romeo and Juliet.

How now !
How now! chop Logic ? What's this ?
Proud ! and I thank you ! and I thank you not !
Thank me no Thankings ; *nor proud me no*
 prouds ;
But fettle your fine Joints 'gainft Thurfday
 next,
To go with Paris *to* St. Peter's *Church,*
Or I will drag thee in a Hurdle thither.
Out you Green-ficknefs Carrion ; *out you Bag-*
 gage ;
Out you Tallow-Face.

And

And before in the fame Play.

Old Cap. *He fhall be endur'd.*
What good Man Boy—I fay he fhall. Go to----
Am I the Mafter here or you ? Go to ——
You'll not endure him ! God fhall mend my Soul,
You'll make a Mutiny among the Guefts !
You'll fet cock-a-hoop ! you'll be the Man !

'Tis plain from the Expreffions between fhort
Sentences in both thefe Speeches, that the Actor
fhould fpeak puffing and blowing, and take his
Breath at every Point, as if his Paffion had
choak'd up his Delivery, and he could not for
Anger and Choler utter more Words together.
The fame may be faid of the firft Speech of
Hotfpur's.

I cannot but here give a Defcription of a vali-
ant Anger, or the Heat of a noble Warrior in
Fight, out of *Shakefpear's Harry* V. becaufe it
gives a lively Image of all the Looks and Actions
belonging to it.

Hen. *But when the Blaft of War blows in our*
    Ears,
Then imitate the Action of the Tyger.
Stiffen the Sinews, fummon up the Blood ;
Difguife fair Nature with hard-favour'd Rage ;
Then lend the Eye a terrible Afpect ;
Let it pry through the Portage of the Head,
Like the Brafs Cannon let the Brow o'erwhelm it,

As fearfully as does a galled Rock
O'erhang and jutty his confounded Base,
Swell'd with the wild and wasteful Ocean.
Now set the Teeth, and stretch the Nostrils wide,
Hold hard the Breath, and bend up ev'ry Spirit
To its full Height.———

If a Player would study this Speech, he would find such Looks and Motions would inspire him with more Life on the Reprefentation of such a Character, than he would otherwife feel.

To move Compaffion, the Speaker muft exprefs himfelf with a foft, fubmiffive and pitiful Voice, as *Arthur* in King *John*, when *Hubert* fhows him the King's Order for burning out his Eyes with a hot Iron.

Arth. *Have you the Heart ? When your Head*
    did but ake,
I knit my Handkerchief about your Brows,
(The best I had, a Princess wrought it me)
And I did never ask it you again ;
And with my Hand at Midnight held your Head,
And like the watchful Minutes to the Hour,
Still and anon chear'd up the heavy Time,
Saying, What lack you ? and where lies your
    Grief ?
Oh! what good Love may I perform for you ?
Many a poor Man's Son would have lain still,
And not have spoke a loving Word to you,
But you at your sick Service had a Prince, &c.
                                                And

And *Anthony* in *Julius Cæsar,* in the Beginning of his Speech on *Cæsar's* Death.

ANT. *Friends,* Romans, *Country-men, lend me*
      your Ears,
  I come to bury CÆSAR, *not to praise him.*
  The Evil, that Men do, lives after them,
  The Good is oft interred with their Bones.
  So let it be with CÆSAR. *The noble* BRUTUS
  Has told you, CÆSAR *was ambitious.*
  If it were so, it was a grievous Fault,
  And grievously has CÆSAR *answer'd it.*
  Here under Leave of BRUTUS *and the rest,*
  (For BRUTUS *is an honourable Man,*
  So they are all, all honourable Men)
  Come I to speak in CÆSAR's *Funeral.*
  He was my Friend, faithful and just to me ;
  But BRUTUS *says he was ambitious,*
  And BRUTUS *is an honourable Man,* &c.

'Tis plain, that *Arthur* spoke (if it were well acted) with a low Tone, and slender and humble Accents, pleading for his Life ; turning his Voice on such Tones, as were fittest to incline the Affections. The same may almost be said of *Anthony's* Speech, where he pleaded to the People to move their Pity first, and then to raise a stronger Passion, nay, even their Rage ; endeavouring first to melt them with a low and submissive Voice, and yet not without Passion, but that Passion is mingled with a great deal of

I 4   Ten-

Tendernefs, that fhew'd a Mind fenfibly touch'd and afflicted with the Oppreffion and Murther of his Friend.

I have read in a *French* Author, that *Cicero* in his *Tufculan Queftions*, tells us, that the whole Theatre was fill'd with Melancholly and Grief, when the Actor pronounc'd thefe Words, of the Ghoft of an unbury'd Corps.

Awake, O Mother ! break off your carelefs
    Slumbers,
Think on your wretched Son, yet uninterr'd ;
Cover, oh ! cover foon his poor defencelefs Body,
From wild devouring Beafts of Prey,
That foon my fcatter'd Limbs and mangled Corps
May bear away, &c.

Tho this was fpoke with a deplorable Voice, yet to do this well, there are feveral Manners of foftening the Voice neceffary to exprefs the different Qualities of the Words uttered, and the Characters of the Things mention'd in the Difcourfe ; which are much better convey'd to the Learner *vivâ voce*, than by Precept.

But to proceed to other *Paffions,* and the Variations and Inflections of the Voice proper to them : If you were to give the Character of a great and brave *Hero,* with a vifible Efteem of him, he muft do it with a lofty and magnificent Tone, and a Voice noble as the Theme— As if you were fpeaking of the Earl of *Peterborough.*

His

His Merits are too Public *to need a Recital, his Friends with Joy, and his Enemies with Regret confess, and all* Europe *is Witness to them with Amazement ; nothing can be said of his Courage or Conduct, of which there are not attested Proofs in the Hands of all Men : The Taking and Relief of* Barcelona, *the Stony Cliffs of* Albocaçar, *the Surrender of* Nules *and* Molviedro, *the Relief of* Valentia, *and the Reduction of that Kingdom, and the Promise of all* Spain, *by the particular Force of his own Genius, and various other Wonders, testified by that Royal Hand, into which his Valour and Conduct only put a* Scep-tre. *What should I say of his Generosity, a heavenly Quality, and which must be visible in all the Actions of a Hero truly great ! What, I say, can I speak, equal to those noble Proofs, which remain on Record to all Posterity ? He was always liberal of his* Own Treasure, *but justly frugal of* That *of the* Public ; *when he took whole Countries almost without Men, and maintain'd Armies without Money. But what can all the Art of the best Orator say, equal to that unparallel'd Act of Beneficence to the* Public, *when his Lordship refus'd a Compensation for the Loss of his Baggage at* Huete ; *where, with a Generosity peculiar to his Lordship, he transferred the Amends due to himself to the Advantage of the Public, by obliging the Inhabitants to furnish the Confederate Army with Magazines of Corn (sufficiently then wanted by them) large enough to suffice a Body of* 20000 *Men for two Months. This*

This is an Action, as unfashionable, as noble, and
too likely to raise Envy, as well as Admiration,
when the Public *is the Bubble of private Interest,*
and Heroes have the Art of uniting their own Gain
with the public Good.

Should this be spoke in a low and languishing
Voice, it would be flat, cold and insipid, and
altogether beneath the Honour of the Hero ;
but let them be spoke with that noble Accent,
and be animated with a lofty Tone of Voice, a-
greeable to the Hero's Spirit and Magnificence,
then they will not appear wholly unworthy of
the Subject.

If a Man is to speak in Contempt of any one,
he ought to exprefs that Contempt in the fcorn-
ful *Tone*, but without any Eagernefs, Paffion, or
Violence of *Voice*, for thofe fhow *Anger* ; and
where there is Anger, juftly fpeaking, there is
not Contempt, the Object of which is fuppos'd
to be below our Anger, and unable to give us
Pain. Any thing therefore of this Nature muft
be fpoke calmly, and without any great Emotion ; for if you fpeak on this Occafion with a
paffionate Voice, difcovering a great Concern or
Indignation, you plainly contradict your own
Defign, your Contempt being exprefs'd in only
Words, and not in Deeds ; you muft therefore
always avoid this Error, when you treat any
Man with Scorn and Derifion, or expofe the
Folly of any ridiculous Argument or Thing :
for to be vehement on a Trifle, would be like
using

ufing a Club againſt a Worm, which you might
cruſh to pieces with your Foot.

But if you have had any Inhumanity, **or**
barbarous Injuſtice offer'd you, of which you
would complain, you muſt then ſpeak after quite
another manner ; you muſt expreſs your Grie-
vance and your Affliction in a Tone more elevated and ſtrong, proportioning your Paſſion and
Vehemence of Voice to the Greatneſs of the Injuſtice done you ; for to ſpeak without Emotion
in ſuch a Caſe, is to perſuade the Hearer, that
you do not feel the Injury, for if you did, it
would produce an Utterance much more outra-
gious. A Client coming to *Demoſthenes*, on a Caſe
of Affault and Battery, related his Story with
ſo little Concern, that he plainly told him, he
could not believe, that there was the leaſt Reality in what he ſaid ; on which the Client reply-
ing with a loud Voice and agitated Spirit, *How!
do you not believe me ?* Ay now (ſays he) I believe you, this is the Voice of a Man, that has
felt the Baſtinado. And this Art of Speaking
was ſo well known to the Ancients, that I find
Cicero quoted on this Occaſion, urging the Calm-
neſs and Indifference of *Callidius's* Pleading,
where Heat and Concern were requr'd, as an
Argument againſt the Reality of what he pleaded for his Client.

I cannot paſs from this Head of varying the
Voice according to the Paſſion you are to ex-
preſs, without this Rule, (which indeed will be
of more uſe to the Bar and Pulpit, by Reaſon of
the

the Length of their Difcourfe, than to the Stage, tho it be not unufeful even to that) when you come to cool on a violent Paffion, and recover your felf from a Tranfport, you ought to lower the Tone of your Voice in fuch a manner, as may exprefs that Languidnefs of your Faculties and Speech, which the Stretch and Extent of your Paffion has produc'd. And I would advife all thofe, who would fpeak with Beauty and Harmony in thefe various Infledtions of the Voice, often to read with Caution and Attention aloud the beft and moft paffionate Tragedies, and thofe Comedies, which may afford the greateft Variety, and fuch Dialogues as approach neareft to the Stile of the Dramatic Poets. For as a certain Author obferves, nothing can be more ferviceable to the Improvement of Adtion and Eloquence.

I muft, by the way, add a Word or two, which the Stage has not much to do with, unlefs in fuch Speeches, as imitate Orations, or folemn and public Addreffes, which have not a Right to have much place in the Drama ; and that is, the Art of varying the Voice according to the feveral parts of the Oration, Pleading, Sermon, or Difcourfe, which you deliver.

You muft therefore begin with a low and modeft Voice, both in Regard of that Deference, which you fhould pay to the Auditors, and for the better Management of your Voice, taking with you the calm State of the Hearers, when you begin to fpeak, and to raife it by degrees up

to

to fuch a Height of Paffion and Warmth, as may be neceffary for your Purpofe, and the Energy of the Subject ; elfe firft you would put your felf out of Breath, for want of a prudent Conduct at your firft ftart, fo that you would be unable to return to that Moderation, which allows ways to heighten the reft and more important parts of your Speech to a degree above the Beginning.

On the other hand, I do not propofe, that you fhould begin in fo very low a Voice, as not to be heard by more, than a few, who ftand or fit neareft to you ; but tho you muft fpeak even at firft with a Voice fo clear and diftinct, that every individual Perfon of your Audience, that attends, may hear you without Difficulty or Trouble ; yet it muft contain nothing of that Force and Energy, which is proper to Paffion. I am therefore only for having the Beginning infinuating, foft and eafy, delivered in a Tone more low, and an Addrefs more humble, than the other Parts of the Difcourfe.

This Rule, 'tis true, does admit of an Exception ; for there are fome Beginnings, which do not fall under it, which are thofe, which we call *abrupt*, as that of *Ajax* in *Ovid*.

Before the Ships, ye Gods, then muft I plead ?
And is ULISSES *then compar'd to me ?*

Nor

Nor has the Speaker any Occafion of raifing his Voice to any great ftretch of Paffion in the *Propofition* or Narration of his Difcourfe, this being the Place of informing his Hearers in the Matters in Queftion; fo that the Voice here has only need of being a degree higher, than in the Beginning : But he muft take Care to be ve ry diftinct and articulate, it being the Ground-work of the Whole, and the For and Vigour of the following Reafons and Arguments taking all their Life from hence; it ought therefore to be perfectly heard and underftood, or the Foundation being defective, the Fabric muft fall to the Ground. The Difference of Actions and Events in the *Narration* muft vary the manner of the Delivery ; yet this is not the proper part of the Speech, for the Contention of Voice, which muft be chiefly refin'd for the other parts : For the greateft Strefs of the Difcourfe lies in confirming our own Arguments, and refuting thofe of the Adverfary. When the Speaker comes to the fumming up the whole, after the Confutation, he ought to make a little Paufe, and begin it again with a lower Tone, and a different Accent from the laft Cadence of his Voice ; then raifing himfelf, he fhould break out into a louder Voice, and carry it on to the End with more Gaiety, Magnificence, and Tri- umph of Pronunciation, which would feem born of his Affurance in the Juftice of his Caufe, now fufficiently made good, and the Conviction and Satisfaction of his Hearers in that and his

In-

Integrity. And then he should conclude with Joy and Satisfaction.

But to omit none of those Helps to this Art, which I have been able to meet with in my little Reading, I must add a few Words, which will assist in this varying the Voice, a Quality so necessary for a Speaker of any kind in *Public*, and that is, by running through those Modes of Speech, or Manners of expressing the Mind, which I find call'd Figures of Speech, or *Rhetoric* ; which some call the Lights of Speech, deriving to it both Grace and Variety, there being so peculiar an Air, Ornament and Novelty proper to each, that they are spoken with a different Tone from the rest of the Discourse. I begin therefore with that, which is call'd an EXCLAMATION.—— As it would be ridiculously flat and insipid to pronounce this with no louder a Voice and more passionate Accent, than the rest of the Discourse ; so the very Nature of the thing gives you the Reason of it ; as, *Oh Horror ! O unheard of Cruelty ! unequall'd Impiety ! to stand in fear neither of Man nor God! What a Feast was that of* THYESTES ! *Oh! monstrous Barbarity ! to feed the Father with the Flesh of his own Son ! to make the Parents Bowels the Grave of his own Child! Well might the fiery Chariot of the Sun turn back, and not give Light to so hellish a Deed,* &c. To speak these Words without an Elevation of Voice, would be to make them flat and insipid, and to rob them of their Force and Energy.

2　　　　　　　　　　　　　　The

The fame exclamatory way of Speech muſt be uſed in Swearing, or a ſolemn Denunciation, Oath or Vow ; as, that which I find quoted of *Demoſthenes,* in his Oration for *Cteſiphon,* which was, it ſeems, much admir'd by the Ancients. In that Point you have not fail'd, no—— *I ſwear by our great Anceſtors, who won the Battle of* MARATHON *with ſo much Hazard and Bravery ! by thoſe, who maintain'd the Fight at* PLATEA *with ſo much Generoſity and Glory ! by thoſe, who contended with ſo much Courage in the Sea-Fight of* SALAMIS ! *by thoſe, who ſo bravely fell at* ARTEMISIUM ! *and by all thoſe gallant Warriors, whoſe Deeds merited public Monuments with all the Enſigns of Honour, Fortune and Fame !*

It cannot be doubted but *Demoſthenes,* who had ſtudy'd Action and Utterance with ſo much Application, ſpoke this with that Elevation of Tone, and Contention of Voice, as was neceſſary to touch his Hearers with Warmth, and not chill them with a calm Indifference of *Pronunciation.*

There is a Figure, which comes, or may come often, into the Speeches of the Pulpit, which is the Introduction of ſome other Perſon ſpeaking, which they call a *Proſopopæia,* and this has been often us'd on the Stage, in Comedies eſpecially, as in the former Inſtance I have given of *Melantha,* if that ought not rather to be referr'd to a *Diologiſm.* That the Perſon ought to change his Voice, who introduces this,

is

is evident, and that by the Character of him he introduces, that he may fhew, that it is not he but the Perfon introduc'd, that fpeaks. For In-ftance: If a grave, venerable old Man be thus brought in, the *Force* of the Voice, and the manner of Utterance muft be grave and fevere, and fo anfwerable to the Perfon ; and thus if a young Rake or *Debauchee* be introduc'd, it muft be loofe and effeminate.

When you addrefs your Speech to any Man or thing by way of *Apoftrophe*, you ought to con-fider your own Defign, and the Circumftances of him that you addrefs to. If you direct your Difcourfe to any thing inaminate, you muft raife your Voice above the ordinary and com-mon Tone, as to one deaf, or who want their perfect Hearing ; as, *Oh ! facred Thirft of Gold, how you conftrain our mortal Breafts,*&c. *Ye Walls ! ye Beds ! ye confcious Pillows tell,* &c. Thus if you addrefs your felf to Heaven, you muft do it in a higher Strain and loftier Tone of Voice, than if you were fpeaking to Men, who are here on a Level with you ; *To thee, O* Jove ! *I make my laft Appeal. Ye Stars, ye wandring Planets of the Night, and thou bright Sun the Source and Prince of Light, I call you all to witnefs my true Fire,* &c.

When you bring in two Perfons in a *Dialogue* talking together, by way of Queftion and An-fwer, you muft certainly change your Voice by turns, as if two Men, or a Man and Woman, were talking together ; of which, that which

K   I

I have now twice already mention'd will be a juft Example.

Upon all thefe Conferences and Dialogifms, we muft always obferve to pronounce the Anfwer with a different Tone from the laft Cadence of the foregoing Queftion or Objection.

When the Speaker prefles his Adverfary clofe, and infifts upon the fame Arguments ftill, prefling it home upon him feveral ways, over and over again, 'till he feems afham'd of it, and confounded at the Repetition, his Voice muft be *brifk*, prefling and infulting, where he lays the main Strefs of what he aims at—— My Author furnifhing me with fo good an Example of this from *Cicero*, when he defends *Ligarius* againft *Tubero*, who accus'd him to *Cæfar*, as having been in *Pompey*'s Army at *Pharfalia*; and I choofe it rather than any Inftance from the *Drama*, becaufe that Speech is famous for having made *Cæfar* drop his Papers, and declare himfelf vanquifh'd by Eloquence, when he had decreed, that he would not forgive *Ligarius* before he came to hear him—— *What*, Tubero, *did you in the Battle of* Pharsalia *with your Sword drawn ? At whofe Breaft did you aim the Point ? What was the Senfe of your Weapon ? the Defign of your Arms ? and the Intention of your Appearance there ? Where were your Thoughts, your Defires, your Wifhes, your Expectations ? What meant thofe Eyes, that Zeal, that Paffion, that Hand, that Weapon ? But I urge this Matter too hard upon him. The Youth is afham'd, and*

in

in Confusion at the Conviction. I'll say no more.

When you avow your Liberty of Speaking without Fear, let the Danger be what it will, which the Rhetoricians call *Parrhasia*, the Voice must be full and loud, exalted with Confidence of Succefs or Boldness, not to be daunted with any Apprehension. Nor can I omit an Example of this likewise from the same Orator, becaufe it is excellent and pathetic. *Oh ! Clemency moſt admirable ! and worthy of eternal Praiſe, Honour, and Memory !* CICERO *has the Boldneſs to confeſs himſelf guilty before* CÆSAR *of a Crime, for which he cannot ſuffer another to be wrongfully accus'd ; nor is he under any Apprehenſions from the Reſentment of his Judge on this Account. Behold how undaunted I am, Sir, in the Confidence of your Goodneſs , behold the great Lights of Generoſity and Wiſdom, which from your Aſpect favour me in what I ſay, I will raiſe my Voice to a Loudneſs, if I can, ſufficient to make all the People of* Rome *hear what I ſay ! The War now being not only began, but almoſt ended, I went over to your Enemy's Camp freely, voluntarily, on my own Choice, before this finiſhing Blow put an end to it at* PHARSALIA.

In a *Gradation* or *Climax*, the Voice muſt with the Sentence climb up by several Degrees of the Sentence to the Period ; as, *Luxury is born in the City, out of Luxury there is a Neceſſity that Avarice ſhould ariſe, from Avarice muſt*

ſpring

spring audacious Boldness, which must beget all manner of Wickedness and Mischief.

> MARS *saw the Nymph, and seeing did desire,*
> *And having wish'd, he quench'd his amorous Fire.*
> *The Eye the dangerous Poison soon let in,*
> *And by the Eye the Heart began to sin,*
> *Till the whole Body did the Crime complete,* &c.

The *Suppression* or *Aposiopesis,* is a suppressing of what might be farther urg'd; and in this the Speaker must lower his Voice a Tone or two, and pronounce the foregoing Words, that introduce it with the highest Accent; as, *Æolus* in *Virgil.*

> *Which I——*
> *But first the raging Floods, 'tis fit that I compose.*

In a *Subjection,* where several Questions are put, and an Answer subjoin'd to ev'ry one of them : He that speaks must vary his Voice, by giving the Question one Tone, and the Answer another; either by asking the Question higher, and giving the Answer lower, or the contrary, according to the Place where he would have the Force lie.

In the *Opposition* or *Antithesis,* the Contraries must be distinguish'd by giving one a louder Tone, than the other; as, *Truth breeds us Enemies, Flattery Friends.* The Romans *hate*

PRI-

PRIVATE *Luxury,* but love PUBLIC *Magnifi-cence.*

Repetition or *Anadiplofis,* which is a Repetition of the fame Word, and the Speaker muft give the Word in the fecond place a louder and ftronger Sound, than in the firft place.

> *Y*° *Harmonious Nine, to* GALLUS *tune my Song,*
> *To* GALLUS, *whofe Love,* &c.
> *And yet he lives, not only lives, but comes*
> *Into the very Senate-Houfe.*

There is another Repetition, where the fame Word is more, than once repeated, either in the Beginning of feveral Sentences, or in the feveral Claufes of the fame Sentence, where the Word muft be founded always in the fame Tone, but differently from the other Parts of the Difcourfe. *Does not the Nightly Guards of the Palace touch you at all? Not at all the Watches of the City? Not at all the Peoples Fear? Not at all the Agreement of all honoura-ble Men? Not at all this fortify'd Place of the Senate-Meeting,* &c. *You lament the Lofs of three* Roman *Armies,* MARK ANTONY *deftroyed them: You refent the Death of fo many noble Ci-tizens,* MARK ANTONY *was their Death; the Authority of the Senate is invaded,* MARK AN-TONY *invades it.*

As for Sentences, fome are very fhort, and thofe not fpoken in a Breath, would be maim'd; there are others, which are fomething longer,

yet

yet withal do not exceed the Power of an eafy Pronunciation, in one Breath if you can ; for a Period fo pronounc'd, founds rounder and handfomer, and appears with more Beauty and Force, than it would do with feveral Breathings. To this End you muft endeavour by Practice to attain a long Wind, as *Demofthenes* did by the Inftructions of *Neoptolemus* the Actor. But when the Period is long, you ought to fetch your Breath at the feveral Members of the Periods, that is to fay, after two Points, or a *Semi-colon*, or at leaft after a *Comma*, for to do it otherwife or oftner, would be extremely difagreeable. For nothing is more intolerable and clownifh, than to break off in the middle of a Word or Expref-fion. 'Tis proper to make a Paufe at the End of every Period ; but it muft be fhort on thofe, that are fhort, and longer on thofe, which are of greater Extent.

When you have a Period, that requires a great Contention and Elevation of Voice, you muft manage your Voice with the greater Moderation on thofe, which precede it ; but by employing your whole Force upon thofe, you are oblig'd to fpeak this more important one more languidly, which requires more Vigour and Vehemence. This was a Beauty, which was always obferv'd by the two famous Actors of the *Romans*, *Rofcius* and *Æfopus*. For in fpeaking thefe Verfes,

> *The noble Warriors generous Choice and Buckler,*
> *Is Honour, not the Plunder of the Field.*

he

he did not pronounce them with all that Vehemence of Action and Utterance, that some now would, but simply, and with Moderation, that he might exert himself in this following Exclamation, which naturally requir'd more Force and Emotion of Admiration and Astonishment.

What is't I see ! all arm'd, all arm'd he comes !
E'en to your Sacred Temples ! &c.

Nor did *Æsopus*, with the utmost Contention of Voice, say —— *Where shall I find Relief, and whither fly ?* but more softly and languidly, and without any immoderate Action ; the Force of which he reserv'd for the following Exclamation —— *O ! my Father ! O ! my Country ! O ! House of* PRIAM. —— which his Voice would not have supply'd without that Care. Thus the Painters represent some parts of a Picture in Shades and Distances, to heighten the rest with greater Light.

But tho I have said something of Sentences in their several Kinds, yet I must add a Hint or two of Words likewise.— In them you must regard the common Pronunciation of Custom, and the Conversation of those, who speak well ; avoiding the ill Accent, and Pronunciation of the several Dialects of the different Countries, either in the Quantities of Syllables, or the Sound of the Vowels, either longer or shorter, or broader or narrower ; and you must avoid

K 4   these

thefe Faults, not only in the Country People, but of thofe of the City and Court it felf, where Affectation often deftroys the genuine and juft Pronunciation. Next remember to pronounce emphatical Words with an Emphafis, Force and Diftinction ; as, *certainly, affuredly, infallibly, undoubtedly, neceffarily, abfolutely, exprefly, manifeftly,* which are Words of a very ftrong and pofitive Pronunciation. Words of Praife and Extolling ; as, *admirable, incredible, incomparable, ineffable, ineftimable, glorious, glittering, pompous, triumphant, illuftrious, heroic, auguft, majeftic, adorable,* which are Terms of Honour, and muft be pronounc'd in a magnificent Tone. Or Words, that exprefs our Difpraife or Deteftation ; as, *cruel, hainous, wicked, deteftable, abominable, execrable, monftrous,* and fuch like, are all to be pronounc'd with a paffionate and loud Voice. Words that complain and lament ; as, *unfortunate, miferable, fatal, mournful, pitiful, deplorable, lamentable, forrowful,* require a melancholy Tone and Accent. There muft be a more, than common Strefs on Words of Quantity ; as, *grand, high, fublime, profound, long large, innumerable, eternal* ; as well as on Words of Univerfality ; as, *all the World, generally, every where, always, never.* Here the *Pronunciation* muft be grave, and of an high *Accent.* As for Terms of Leffening, or Contempt and Slight ; as, *pitiful, infignificant, little, low, mean, defpicable, feeble,* &c. they muft be pronounc'd with a very low, leffening, abject Voice,

and

and an Accent of the greateft Scorn and Difdain.
To fpeak otherwife in all thefe Cafes, than I
have laid down, would be ridiculous, and to
fpeak fo will effect that Variation of Voice,
which is fo neceffary to finifh a complete Speaker.
In fine, remember to pronounce all your Words
with an audible Voice, efpecially thofe, which
conclude a Period ; which is chiefly to be taken Care of, when the Period ends with Syllables of a weak and dull Sound in themfelves.

I have thus run through the whole Art of
Acting and *Speaking,* or rather, as *Shakefpear*
calls it, of ACTION and UTTERANCE, in which
I have had a juft Regard to the PULPIT and the
BAR, as well as to the STAGE ; in Complaifance to which, I have chofen to give Examples
rather oftentimes from *Oratory,* than from the
Drama, fince the *Actor* may learn his juft Leffons
from that former, as from the latter. I have,
in fhort, laid down fuch Rules, as if throughly
confider'd, and reduc'd judicioufly to Practice,
will form the *Gefture* with that Beauty, as to
ftrike the Eye with Wonder and Pleafure ; and
teach the Tongue to *utter* with that Grace and
Harmony, that the Ear will be equally ravifh'd,
and both convey fo fenfible a Delight to the
Mind, that the Succefs will be much more glorious in the *Pulpit* and on the Stage, than is at
prefent found from the Endeavours of either. I
confefs, I know not whether Oratory be at all
ufeful at the *Bar,* where *Evidence, Proofs,* and
Methods of Court, generally prevail, or where
Juftice

Juftice and Equity ought to carry the Point. Befides, the Subjects, which are furnifh'd at the Bar, are in themfelves *low* and mean, and afford nothing great and awful, as both the *Pulpit* and the *Stage* always do, or ought to do.

I have given you a Collection of the natural Significations of feveral *Geftures*, and fhown how Nature expreffes her felf in the feveral Emotions, which fhe feels ; I have fhewn you how Art improves thefe *Geftures*, and on what Occafions they are proper, and how to make them graceful ; I have likewife fhewn you how you are to model your Voice to make your Utterance harmonious, fhewn the Defects of *Voice* or *Tone*, and its Beauties and Varieties, and laid down Rules how you may avoid that intolerable Vice of *Monotony*, or always founding the fame Note on all Occafions, without any or with very little Variation. Thus I have run through the *Paffions*, the Figures of Diction, Sentences, nay, and even Words ; each of which afford infinite Variety to the Voice, if the Student will make it his Bufinefs to underftand and to practife them.

I fhall therefore now conclude with thofe Qualities and Qualifications of a *complete Actor*, which however difficult to attain they may feem, are yet fufficiently, from what I have faid, proved to be neceffary.

He ought, therefore, to underftand Hiftory, Moral Philofophy, Rhetoric, not only as far as it relates to Manners and the Paffions, but every

very other Part of it, at leaſt as far as it teaches the Rules of Elocution. He ought not to be a Stranger to Painting and Sculpture, imitating their Graces ſo maſterly, as not to fall ſhort of a *Raphael Urbin*, a *Michael Angelo*, &c. But that which is the moſt neceſſary Quality, that a Player ought to cultivate, which ſhould be open, and much at Command ; and the Praiſe *Thucidides* gave *Pericles*, he ſhould endeavour to obtain, that is, *to know what is fit, and to expreſs it.* He muſt know how to give the proper Graces to every Character he repreſents, thoſe of a *Prince* to a *Prince*, thoſe of a *Merchant* to a *Merchant*,, and ſo of all others ; for generally ſpeaking, let the Part be what it will, the Perſon, Mien, Action, Look, is the ſame, that is, that of the Player, not of the Perſon repreſented. He ſhould have farther a penetrating Wit and clear Underſtanding ; he muſt alſo be a good Critic in the Art of the Stage, I mean, in the Poetical Performances, that he may chooſe the Good, and reject the Ill.

Beſides theſe Qualifications of Mind, his Body ought to have ſeveral, that are not very common in our Days. He ſhould not be too tall, nor too low and dwarfiſh, but of a moderate Size ; neither over-fleſhy, which is prodigious, nor over-lean, like a Skeleton. . Tho this is a thing ſo little regarded by our Managers or Audience, yet I find, that it was of Conſequence in the nicer Nations of Antiquity, as thoſe Inſtances may ſhow, which *Lucian* tells you, were of a People,
ple,

ple, who were no dull Obfervers.—— " The
" Citizens of *Antioch* (fays he) are moſt inge-
" nious, and much addicted to the *Stage*, and
" ſo given to remark what is ſaid and done,
" that no Paſſage eſcapes them ; feeing, there-
" fore, on a Time a *little ſhort* Fellow enter,
" and act *Hector*, they cry'd out with one Voice,
" This is *Aſtyanax*, but where is *Hector?* An-
" other time, a great tall long Fellow acting
" *Capaneus*, attempting to ſcale the Walls of
" *Thebes*, they told him, he might mount the
" Walls without a Ladder ; at another Time a
" big and corpulent Dancer endeavouring to riſe
" high, we have need, cry'd they, to under-
prop the Stage, *&c.*

A Player, therefore, ſhould be of an active,
pliant and compacted Body, which may be improv'd by learning to dance, fence and vault.
With theſe Qualities and Qualifications, and a
thorough Knowledge of what I have written,
he may juſtly be allow'd a complete Player.
But before I put an End to this Diſcourſe, I ſhall
give an Inſtance or two of Affectation and Over-
acting from *Lucian*. " I once (fays he) faw a
" Dancer (or Actor, for in his Senſe they are
" the fame) who tho before of a good Reputa-
" tion for his Art, I know not by what miſ-
" chance, diſgrac'd himſelf by Over-Action.——
" For being to repreſent *Ajax* diſtracted after
" his being vanquiſh'd by *Ulyſſes*, he acted not a
" Madneſs, but was himſelf diſtemper'd. For
" he rent the Garment of one of thoſe, who
" ſtamp'd

" ftamp'd in Iron Shoes, and fnatching a Cor-
" net from one of the Fidlers, ftruck *Ulyffes*,
" who ftood by infulting on his Victory, fuch
" a Blow on his Head, that if his Helmet had
" not fav'd him, and born off the Violence of
" the Stroke, he had perifhed, and fal'n proftrate
" at his Feet.

" Tho the whole Theatre of Spectators, as
" mad as *Ajax*, ftampt, fhouted, and fhook their
" Cloaths ; for the Rout and Ideots, who knew
" not Decorum, nor were able to diftinguifh
" falfe Action from true, took this as a great
" Expreffion of Fury ; and the better bred and
" more underftanding, tho they blufh'd at what
" was done, yet fhew'd not their Diflike, as
" much as by their Silence, but colour'd the
" Actor's Folly by their Commendations, tho
" they faw not the Madnefs of *Ajax* acted, but
" that of the Reprefenter. So that not yet
" contented, the Gentleman play'd a Prank much
" more ridiculous ; for defcending into the Pit,
" he fat down betwixt two, who had been
" Confuls, who were much afraid of themfelves,
" left this frantic Actor fhould take one of them
" for a Sheep. Which Paffage fome extoll'd,
" others derided ; others fufpected, that his O-
" ver-Imitation had caft him into a real Mad-
" nefs. Others report, that after he came to
" himfelf, he was fo afham'd of what he had
" done, that upon the true Apprehenfion of his
" Diftemper, he fell fick for Grief, and plainly
" profefs'd it. For thofe of his Faction defiring

2   " him

" him to act *Ajax* over again to them, *When I*
" *come next on the Stage,* faid he; *in the mean*
" *time, 'tis enough for me once to have plaid the*
" *Madman.* But his chief Difcontent fprung
" from an *Antagonift* or *Anti-Actor,* who repre-
" fented *Ajax* raving fo gracefully and difcreet-
" ly, that he gain'd a great Applaufe.

Tho, I fear, I may have tir'd you with all
thefe Rules and Obfervations, which immediately relate to the Actors ; yet I cannot conclude
without faying fomething of our Theatrical
Dancing and Mufick, as being by *Ariftotle* himfelf allow'd part or an Appendix of the Stage.
Under the laft Head of Mufic, I fhall prefume
to fay fomething of *Opera's,* which have of late
been dangerous Rivals of the Drama, tho clogg'd
with many adventitious or accidental Abfurdities more, than the very *Opera* confider'd in it felf
contains, tho thofe are fo very many and very vifible, that they exclude it from the rational Diverfions.

I am fenfible, that what I am going to fay
may look like a Condemnation of my own Pra-
ctice, when I had the Management of the
Houfe, and that is in regard of good Dancing.
Yet confidering, that I was oblig'd, on Account
of Self-Defence, to enter into thofe Meafures,
I hope what I fay here cannot be look d on as a
Deviation from my own Principle ; or if it be,
I may be allow'd to alter my Opinion in things
of this Nature, when we find great Divines do
the fame every Day in Matters of far greater
Importance. I

I know very well, that in this I fhall run a-gainft the Stream of the Town, I mean of thofe, who generally make up the Audience ; but then I confider, that I am an old Man, and have con-tracted fuch a Value for the *Drama,* by fo long a Converfation with it, that I would willingly leave for a Legacy to my Succeffors, a Stage freed from thofe intolerable Burthens, under which it groans at prefent by the Depravity of the Tafte of the Audience, which as it has rifen in Dignity has (I am afraid) fal'n in Purity and Judgment.

About an hundred Years ago, there were a-bout five or fix Play-houfes at a Time in this Town, tho at that Time much lefs extended and populous, than at prefent, all frequented and full ; and the Players got Eftates, tho the Stage was yet in its Infancy, rude and uncultivated, without Art in the Poet, or in the Decorations, and fupported by the *Lower Sort of People,* and yet thefe LOWER SORT OF PEOPLE difcover'd a natural Simplicity and good Tafte, when they were pleas'd and diverted with a Drama fo na-ked, and unaffifted by any foreign Advantage.

But in our Times (forgive fo bold a Truth) the People of Figure, who in Reafon might have been expected to be the Guardians and Suppor-ters of the nobleft and moft rational DIVERSI-ON, that the Wit of Man can invent, which at once inftructs and tranfports the Soul, were the firft, nay, I may fay, the only People, who confpir'd its Ruin, by prodigal Subfcriptions for

3

Squeak-

Squeaking Italians, and cap'ring Monfieurs; and the more infamoufly to diftinguifh their poor and mean Diverfions from thofe more noble of the Public, they would have no Play at all mingled with them, left the World fhould think, that they pay'd any Deference to Poetry, Wit, and Senfe ; or that their Satisfaction and Delight reach'd farther, than their Eyes and Ears. But what was yet worfe, their Tafte was fo far funk, that they were pleas'd with what fhock'd a nice Ear, and what could not divert a curious Eye. For firft, the beft of *French Dancers* are without Variety ; their Steps, their Pofture, their Rifings are perpetually the *fame* UNMEAN-ING *Motion* ; a *French Dancer* being at beft but a *graceful Mover,* full of a brifk and fenfelefs Activity, unworthy the Eye of a Man of Senfe, who can take no Pleafure worth attending, in which the Mind has not a confiderable Share.

Were our modern Dancers like the *Mimes* and *Pantomimes* of the *Romans,* (tho even thofe grew into Efteem in the Wain and Corrup ion of that Empire) our Dotage on them might have been thought more excufable ; fince one of them, as I have fhewn from *Lucian,* by the Variety of his Motions and Gefticulations, would reprefent a whole Hiftory, with all the different Perfons concerned in it fo plainly and evidently, that every body, that faw him, perfectly underftood what he meant.

In

In this indeed it might be pretended, that there was fomething to ftrike the Mind, and rationally entertain it, every Action depending on the other, and all directed to one End. But to be fond of our modern Dancing is ftill to be Children, and fond of a Rattle, that makes perpetually the very fame Noife. All that could be faid of *Ballon*, (or any other Dancer of more Reputation) is, that his Motion was eafy and graceful, the Figures he threw his Body into, fine, and that he rofe high with Freedom and Strength ; or, in fhort, that he was an active Man. But is that, or would indeed the *Roman Pantomimes*, be a fufficient Ballance for the Lofs of the *Drama* to any Man of common Senfe ?

But before the Depravity of the *Roman State*, nay, ev'n in *Greece*, Dancing was efteem'd, and always perform'd in their Plays, either Traged es or Comedies, having thofe, which were proper and peculiar to each, and not to be ufed promif- cuoufly in both : nay, we find, that ev'n the *Pantomime* Art was in great Perfection, in which *Telefis* the Dancer was fo great a Mafter, that when he danc'd the feven Captains befieging of *Thebes*, he fet before the Eyes of the Spectators, by his Gefticulations and Motions all that they perform'd in that Siege.

Nay, Dancing was there in fo much Efteem, that *Socrates* being reflected on for frequenting too much the *Ægyptian* Performances of that kind, reply'd, that Dancing contain'd all Mufi-

L   cal

cal Exercifes ; and the ancient Poets *Thefpis,* *Cratinus, Phrynicus,* &c. were call'd Dancers, not only becaufe they added Dances to their Fables or Plays, but alfo becaufe they taught to dance. Nay, 'tis certain, that the Art of *Dancing* was fo much in Efteem in *Greece,* that *Pindar* calls *Apollo* himfelf the *Dancer.* But then we muft remember, that all thefe *Dances* contain'd not only an extraordinary Exercife for the Body, but an Inftruction to the Mind, both in the Subject reprefented by the Figures in the Art of War, which was taught by the *Pyrrhic* and other Dances.

For this Reafon I fuppofe, the Poets affign'd Dancing to Children, (except in the more robuft Performances of Warlike Dances) and the Figures of the Dances always exprefs'd the things, that were fung by the Voice, preferving always in them fomething manly and great, and they were call'd *Hyporchemata,* as it were, Dances fubfervient to the Voice ; and therefore they always condemn'd thofe, whofe Steps and Figures did not exprefs or correfpond to the Voice. 'Tis likewife plain from *Lucian,* that the *Mimes* and *Pantomimes* of his Time exprefs'd in Figures what they fung, whether the Rape of *Proferpina,* the Loves of *Mars* and *Venus,* or any other of the Poetical Fables : For in his Enumeration of the Faults of Dancers, he fays —— " There " are many, who out of Ignorance (for 'tis im- " poffible, that all fhould be knowing) com- " mit great Solecifms in Dancing, fuch, I mean, " whofe

" whofe Actions are irregular, and not to the
" Tune, as they fay, when the Foot fays one
" thing, and the Inftrument another : Others
" keep Proportion to the Mufic, but their Pre-
" fentments, as I have often feen, are difpropor-
" tion'd to the right Time. For you fhall have
" one, who endeavouring to act the Birth of
" *Jupiter*, and *Saturn's* eating his Children,
" dances the Sufferings of *Thyeftes*, by reafon
" of the Affinity of the Fables. Another being
" to act *Semele* burnt with Lightning, likens
" *Glauce* to her born long after, not enough re-
" garding the Song, that is fung.

But I fhall call into my Affiftance on this Subject a Manufcript lately left with me by a Friend,
better acquainted with thefe Matters, than I
can pretend with all my modern Helps to be.

Thefe Dances, fays a certain Author, were
in Imitation of thofe things, which the Words
of the Songs exprefs'd. One of them is thus
defcrib'd by *Xenophon*, in his *Expedition of Cyrus*,
as perform'd before them at a Feaft with *Seuthes*
the *Thracian*.

" After we had (fays he) peform'd our *Li-*
" *bations* to the Gods, and fung the *Pæana*, (that
" is, in plain *Englifh*, after we had faid Grace) firft,
" fome *Thracians* rofe up, and arm'd danc'd to the
" Flute, rifing lightly and high, waving and
" brandifhing their Swords, till two of them to
" the Tune dealing Blows to each other, that when
" one of them fell artificially down, they all
" imagining that he was wounded, fhriek'd out

L. 2   " aloud.

" aloud. Immediately he, who feem'd to have
" wounded him, as he lies there fpoils him of
" his Arms, and finging the Praifes of *Sitalcas*,
" makes his Exit. The Reft of the *Thracians*
" then take up the fuppos'd dead, (who indeed
" had felt no harm) and bear him off. After
" this enter'd the *Magnefians* and the *Œnianes*,
" and perform'd the Dance call'd *Semlutes* with
" their Arms, which is thus.

" A Plough-man with his Arms by his Sides
" drives in the Oxen and Plough, and fows his
" Corn, turning every Minute from one fide to
" the other, as if he were afraid, or apprehen-
" five of fome Danger. Prefently a Robber ap-
" proaches, and the Plough-man handling his
" Arms, fights the Robber, (putting himfelf be-
" twixt him and his Plough) adapting all the
" Motions of his Body to the Notes of the
" Flutes ; but in the End the Robber vanquifh-
" ing the Plough-man, binds him, and bears
" him off ; and fometimes, on the contrary, the
" Plough-man the Robber.

There were indeed many Kinds of Dancing
among the Ancients, which fome, according to
Homer, reduce to three ; the firft was call'd *Cu-
biftic*, which *Xenophon* and *Suidas* fay was an
Art of Dancing on the Head, whilft they acted
various Motions and Gefticulations with their
Hands and Legs. The fecond fort was call'd
Sphæriftic, or the *Play at Ball*, becaufe they
danc'd playing with a *Ball*, all the while they
kept Time to the Mufic. The third kind was

4   plainly

plainly call'd *Orchesis* or *Dancing*. *Plato*, in his Book of Laws, divides Dancing into *Military*, Peaceable or proper for Peace, and the Medium betwixt both. That he call'd Military, which imitated by rising on high, or falling back, or inclining to any side, the Assaults of Enemies, their Attacks, Evasions, and Defences, and resembled by various Figures the *Darters*, or those, who fight with close Weapons ; and *Plato* was so fond of this sort of Dance, that he ordains in his Republic, that some should be paid by the *Public* to teach it to both Men and Women ; believing, that by this alone there would be a very great Help obtain'd towards the Perfection of military Discipline. In Confirmation of which we find, that the *Lacedemonians* receiv'd Dancing among their Exercises as useful to War.

It would swell this Discourse too much, to pick all, that the Authors yet extant could furnish on the several Heads of these two Divisions of Dancing, that is, of *Homer* and *Plato* ; I shall therefore keep wholly to the last of the former, that is, the *Orchesis* or *Simple Dancing*, deferring to speak of the *Cubistic* and *Spæristic* till some other time.

Aristotle, in the Beginning of his Poetics, having said, that all the Parts and Kinds of Poetry agree in this, that they are all Imitations; he divides Imitations into divers Kinds, or ways of Imitation, as by *Harmony*, or *Verse*, &c. or into Degrees, as *better*, or *like*, or *worse* ; or

into

into divers Modes or Forms and Manners, as A-
ction, or Introduction, or Narration, or affu-
ming the Person of others, or not ; and proceeding, he says, this of Dancers, that they imitate
by Number alone without Harmony, for they
imitate the Manners, Paffions and Actions
by the numerous Variety of Gefticulation.
Hence it appears, that Dancing was nothing elfe
but a certain Faculty of imitating the Manners,
Paffions, and Actions of Men, by the Motions
and Geftures of the Body, made by a certain
Artifice, Number and Reafon. For when he
had told us in the feventh Book of his Politics,
that there was nothing in Nature, which more
fully exprefs'd the Similitude of things, than
Number and *Song*, he juftly adds, that Dancers
in the Imitations of Actions make ufe of *Number*. How this Imitation could be effected by
numerous Motions, *Plutarch* in his fifteenth Pro-
blem expreffes this moft clearly of all Men after
Ariftotle ; who tells us, that Dancing had three
Parts, the *Bearing, Figure,* and *Indication*; becaufe all Dancing confifts of Motions, Habitudes, or States of Body, and Paufes, as Harmony of Tones and Intervals, or Stops, he fays,
the *Bearing* or *Lation* was only the reprefenta-
tive moving of any Paffion or the Actions ; but
the *Figure* the Habitude or State of Body and
Difpofition, in which the Motion or *Bearing*
ended ; for the Dancers paufing near the Figure
or Image of *Apollo, Pan,* or *Bacchus,* their Bodies being form'd to their Likenefs, continu'd
ele-

elegantly a-while in that Posture. But that the
Indication was not properly an Imitation, but a
Declaration of some certain thing, either of the
Earth, or the Heavens, or something else relating
to either, exprefs'd by numerous and regular
Motions. As the Poets, when they imitate make
use of fictitious sometimes, or metaphorical
Words; but when they inform or inftruct,
employ only those, which are proper. In like
manner, the Dancers, when they imitate make
use of Figures, and Habitudes, or States of the
Body; but when they declare or inform, they
employ the things themselves with the forefaid
Indications. So that Art or Faculty of Dancing,
according to *Plato, Ariftotle,* and *Plutarch* confifts in Imitation, made only by Motion; and
the Dancers themselves do nothing else but imitate the Manners and Affections, by moving
themselves in Number, and ufing Gefticulations
in Order, by *Bearings* or *Lations,* or Figures; or
declare by Indications or Information; or else
at once declare to all the Manners, or reprefent
to all at once the Manners, Paffions and Actions of Men. Hence it was that *Simonides,*
with a great deal of Reafon, us'd to call *Dancing a filent Poefie, and Poefie a fpeaking Dancing.*

But *Plutarch,* even in his Time, complains,
that True Dancing was much degenerated from
Mufic, to which it was join'd, and faln from
that Celeftial Art, which it once was, into the
tumultuous and unlearned Theatres held a moft

ab-

abfolute and tyrannic Sway ; and there is no Man of Knowledge but is fenfible, from that Time to our Days, how much more it is corrupted.

It is not fufficiently known, who firft taught Men this fort of Dancing, unlefs you will allow what *Theophraftus* tells us in *Athenæus*, that *Andro,* a Flutinift of *Catana*, firft added to his Mufic apt and proper and elegant Motions ; whence the Ancients call'd Dancing *Sicilifing*, *Catana* being a City of *Sicily*. After whom *Cleophantes* of *Thebes* and *Æfchylus* invented many Figures of Dancing, which were call'd by a *Sicilian* Name *Balliomous,* as *Athenæus* infinuates from the Authority of *Epicharmus* ; and from this Name *Hieronymus Mercurialis* derives the *Italian* Name of *Balli,* as our *Balls* feems to be deriv'd from that.

Dances were perform'd to the Sound of Wind Mufic, or the Lute, or any other Inftrumental or Vocal Mufic. But *Homer, Plato, Xenophon, Ariftotle, Strabo, Plutarch, Gallia, Pollux,* and *Lucian,* give an Account of an infinite Number of various Kinds of Dancing. Thofe that were in moft Efteem deriv'd their Names either from the Countries where they were invented, or in great Requeft, or from the Inventor or Manner of Performance. Thofe which took their Names from Countries were, the *Laconic, Trœxenic, Empyrephyrian, Cretenfian, Ionic, Mantinean,* &c. From the Inventor and Manner of Performance, as the *Pyrrich* from one *Pyrrichus* a *Lacedæmonian,*

or,

or, as others would have it, from *Pyrrhus* the Son of *Achilles* ; in which Dances they danc'd arm'd either with a Song or without it, as we find by a piece of old *Baſſo Relievo.*

But theſe *Pyrrich* Dances were divided into ſeveral Kinds, or had ſeveral Names ; as, among the *Cretans,* the *Orſitan,* and *Epichidian* ; among the *Ænianenſetans,* and *Magnetes,* the *Carpeans,* which *Xenophon* mentions in the V. of his Expedition of *Cyrus.* There were beſides, thoſe call'd *Apochinos* or *Maɛtriſmos,* which were danc'd by Women, and for that Reaſon call'd *Martyriæ.* Others had greater Variety, and were more ſolemn; as, the *Daɛtil, Jambic, Emmelian, Moloſſic, Cordux, Sicinus, Perſian, Phrygian, Thracian,* and *Teleſias* ; the laſt ſo call'd from one *Tilenius,* who firſt danc'd it in Arms, in which Dance *Ptolemus* kill'd *Alexander* the Brother of *Philip.* Other Dances were call'd *Turning* or *Verſatile,* becauſe the Dancers turn'd round in a Ring.

There were other Dances call'd *Mad Dances* or *Cernophorus, Mongas, Thermauſtris,* or the popular or plebeian *Anthema,* in which the Dancers moving themſelves, ſung to the Tune they danc'd, *Where are my Roſes? Where are my Violets? Where are my Lillies? Where are my beauteous Swarms of Bees?* Some were ridiculous ; as, the *Sodis Mætriſmos, Apodimas, Sobas, Morphaſmus, Glaux,* and the *Lion.* There are beſides, the *Scenic Dances,* as the *Tragic, Comic, Satyric,* and the *Lyric,* as the *Porrichian,*

richian, Gymnopædican, and *Hyporchæmatican,*
the manner of Dancing all which is not the Bufinefs of our prefent Difcourfe; it is fufficient
to know, that in this third Divifion of Dancing
were not only all thefe Kinds, we have mention'd, but many more, to which *Lucian* appro-
priated a whole Book, and that they likewife
made ufe of a great Diverfity of Motions both
of the Hands and Feet. For fince all Motion is
compos'd of *impelling* and *drawing* according to
Ariftotle, fo the Dancers either thruft on their
Bodies, or drew them, either upwards or down-
wards, from the Right to the Left, and the contrary, backwards and forwards; from which
Motions afterwards were compos'd fimple Walking, Winding and Turning, Procurfion or Sal-
lies, Leaping or Rifing. Divarication or fpreading of the Legs to a Diftance, Claudication or
halting, Ingeniculation or a bowing the Knee, or
a Curtefying, Elation or bearing up haughtily,
the fhaking of the Feet, Permutation or *changing*
or altering the Motion, *&c.* out of all which the
whole Art of Dancing was perfected.

Tho this be but an imperfect Sketch of the
Excellence of the Dancing of the Ancients, and
gathered from fuch Fragments, as the Injury of
Time has left us; yet it is plain, that they were
all directed to exprefs or imitate fomething,
which was an Advantage, that few or none of
our modern (efpecially *French*) Dances have.

But fince there is no Man, who fhall accu-
rately confider the feveral Species of Dances in
ufe

ufe among the Ancients, but will find, that they did not want the Order of Time, Reafon, Proportion, and Mufical Harmony, and therefore may be apt to think them not unlike the Hobby-Horfe Dancing of our Days, which both Men and Women ufe for the promoting of Luft ; but there is no body but may perceive this Difference between theirs and ours, that theirs were employ'd as Exercifes often, and conducive to Health, ours after Supper, Feafts, and in the Night Time. Theirs were always directed to exprefs fome Paffion or Action, or Story of the Gods or Men, ours to nothing but frifking about to fhew a ufelefs Activity. And yet how much greater Deference has been paid to *L'Abbe, Ballon, Subligniy,* and the reft, than to *Otway, Shakefpear,* or *Johnfon ?* And while our own Poets were neglected, the *French* Dancers got Eftates ; and this by the Influence of thofe, who at the fame Expence might have made their own Names and their Country famous for the Encouragement of the politeft Arts and Sciences, now neglected to a Degree of Barbarity, greater, than moft Nations on this fide *Lapland.*

I muft own, that the Excufe of our Leaders feems greater and more reafonable in the Indulgence they fhew to Mufic, in their Subfcriptions for *Italian* Singers ; tho fo fenfible a Man as Monfieur St. *Evremont* evidently gives the Palm of Singing to his own Nation——" *Solus gallus* " *cantat,* fays he, *none but the* Frenchman *fings.* " I will not be injurious to all other Nations
" in

" in maintaining what an Author has publifh'd,
" the SPANIARD *weeps,* the ITALIAN *grieves,*
" the GERMAN *hollows,* the FLANDERKIN
" *howls,* and *only the* FRENCHMAN *fings* ; I
" leave him to all thefe pretty Diftinctions, and
" fhall only back my Opinion with the Autho-
" rity of *Loüigi,* who could not endure to hear
" an *Italian* fing Airs, after he had heard *Vyert,*
" *Hilaire,* and *La Petite Varenne* fing. Upon
" his Return to *Italy,* he made all the Muficians
" of that Nation his Enemies, faying openly
" at *Rome,* as he had at *Paris,* that to make
" pleafant Mufick, *Italian* Airs fhould be in a
" *French* Man's Mouth——It is very certain, he
" was much difgufted with the *Harſhneſs* and
" *Rudeneſs* of the *greateft* Mafters of *Italy,* when
" he had tafted the Sweetnefs of the *French,*
' the *Neatneſs* and *Manner* of the *French.*——
" The *Italians* with their Profoundnefs in Mufic,
" bring their Art to our Ears without any
" Sweetnefs, *&c.* Whether this Man of an
acknowledg'd fine Tafte be in the right or not,
I leave to the Judges of the Art; but I am fure,
if he has fhewed himfelf but an indifferent Critic in Mufic, he has fhewn himfelf a good *Patriot,* in preferring his own Country-men to a
Company of *Stroling Foreigners,* who in my
poor Opinion have little Advantage of either of
us, but that of coming a great way, and requi-
ring a great deal of Money, and the Witchery
of being a *Foreigner* ; when fcarce any Nation
has given us, for all our Money, better Singers,
than

than Mrs. *Tofts* and Mr. *Leveridge,* who yet being of our own Growth, maintain but a fecond or third Character among worfe Voices.

But were thefe Foreigners as excellent, as they themfelves would be thought, yet to be drawn wholly by Sound, tho the moft harmonious, that Art and Nature can fupply, is neither the greateft nor the jufteft Praife.

It muft, however, be allow'd, that Mufic difcovers a wonderful Power, a Power not to be refifted ; but I am afraid, that Power acts more on the Body, than the Mind, or by the Body on the Mind ; the Ear has a pleafing Senfation at melodious Sounds, and that gratifies the Mind, which cannot naturally be uneafy when the Body is delighted with agreeable Senfations : But this proves Mufic as tranfporting, as it is to be but a fenfual Pleafure, and deriving no part from Reafon, nor directing any part to the Gratification of the rational Soul. But then this Power and Force of *Mufic* is heighten'd by the Addition of Poetry, which among the Ancients even in Dancing (as we have feen) was very feldom left out; for paffionate Words give a double Vigour to Harmony, and make for it a furer way to the Heart, than when the Soul is unconcern'd in the bare and folitary Notes. And Vocal Mufic is agreed by all to be the moft noble, and moft touching, that Tone being efteem'd the moft excellent, which comes neareft to *Vocal Sounds.*

Mu-

Mufic therefore ought ftill, as originally it was, to be mingled with the *Drama*, where it is fubfervient to Poetry, and comes into the Relief of the Mind, when that has been long intenfe on fome noble Scene of Paffion, but ought never to be a feparate Entertainment of any Length.

But tho we allow the Vocal the Preheminence of all other forts of Mufic, yet we cannot without the greateft Abfurdities receive even that on Subjects improper for it, or in a manner unnatural, that is, as it is offer'd to us in our *Opera's,* with which of late the Town (I mean the leading part of the Audience) has been perfectly intoxicated, and in that drunken Fit has thrown away more Thoufands of Pounds for their Support, than would have furnifh'd us with the beft Poetry, and the beft Mufic in the World, without declaring againft common Senfe. *Opera's* have been faid to be the Invention of modern *Italy,* e'er the Return of Learning, and in the midft of that barbarous Ignorance, with which the Inundations of *Vandals, Goths, Huns* and *Lombards* had o'er-whelm'd it ; but I think it is pretty plain, that the *Romans* were, before that, funk as far from their ancient Learning and Senfe, as Virtue and Warlike Glory ; and *Lucian* puts it beyond Controverfy, that the Entertainment, which we now call *Opera's,* was in ufe in his Time, when he fays, after he had been ridiculing the Tragedies of his Age———
" And alfo his Clamour from within, he breaks
" open

" open, and unlocks himfelf, and moft *ridicu-*
" *loufly* SINGS his own Sufferings, and renders
" himfelf by the very Tone odious ； yet as
" long, as he perfonates fome *Andromache,* or
" *Hecuba,* his *Singing* is tolerable, *but for a*
" HERCULES *to enter dolefully* SINGING, *and*
to forget himfelf, and neither regard his Lion's
Skin or Club, muft needs to a judging Man appear
a Solecifm.

But this, as I have faid, was in the Corruption of the *Roman* State, under the Empire,
when Learning was almoft again engrofs'd by
the *Greeks,* and fcarce any elfe appear'd in Books
of Note but that Nation, as thofe of *Plutarch,*
Sextus, Lucian, &c. for it was never fo in *Greece,*
as is plain from the *Alceftis* of *Euripides* ； where
the Servants of *Admetus* are fcandaliz'd at the
Singing of *Hercules,* when. *Alceftis* lay dead in
the Palace, and the Family with its Lord were
all in the extremeft Grief and Sorrow ； which
is a plain Argument, that the reft of the Play
was fpoken, and not fung.   Mr. *Barns* indeed,
who is the Author of extraordinary Conjectures,
fancies, that the *Greek* Tragedies were fung like
our *Opera's* ； whereas what we have here in-
ftanced, and the Conftitution of the Chorus in
its Divifion into *Strophe,* *Antiftrophe,* and *E-*
pod, prove the contrary.   But this may pafs
from a Gentleman, who would fain perfuade us, that *Solomon* was the Author of the
Ilias.

What

What infinuated into him this Notion, was the Words he gives us, which imply no more but that Harmony of Speaking, which we have been endeavouring to recommend to the Study of our prefent *Players*. But if this were really true, (whereas it is directly contrary to Truth) yet I cannot imagine, that any Authority can juftifie that, which is abfurd in it felf. But becaufe the Authority of a Man, that is receiv'd in the World, and allow'd to be a Man of a fine Tafte, and admirable Senfe, may be more prevalent with moft Pretenders to Wit, than Reafon it felf, I fhall here tranfcribe what Monfieur St. *Evremont* has deliver'd to the Public on this Head, both in regard of his Reputation, and for the Juftnefs of his Reafoning, which is the beft Confirmation of an Authority ; and tho what he fays be on the *French Opera's*, it will hold ftronger againft the *Italian*. He writes to the late Duke of *Buckingham* in the following manner.

" I have long, my Lord, had a Mind to give " you my Thoughts, and deliver my Senti- " ments on the Difference betwixt the *Italian* " and *French* way of Singing.

" The Difcourfe we had of it at the Dutchefs " of *Mazarine*'s has rather added to, than fa- " tisfy'd that Defire, which I will now wholly " gratify, by thefe few Thoughts I now fend " you upon it. I fhall therefore begin with a- " vowing freely to you, that I am no Admirer " of thofe mufical Plays or Tragedies, which

" we

" we fee in our Time; I own indeed, that
" their Magnificence gives me fome Pleafure,
" that their Machines have fometimes fomething
" furprizing, the Mufic in fome Places may be
" charming, and the whole together feems won-
" derful ; but then you muft grant me on the
" other hand, that thefe Wonders are extreme-
" ly tedious, for where the *Mind* has fo very
" little to do, the Senfes, after the firft Plea-
" fure, which the fhort-liv'd Surprize affords,
" muft languifh and die. The Eyes grow wea-
" ry of being continually fixt upon the glaring
" Objects. In the Beginning of the Conforts,
" the Audience obferve the Juftnefs of the Con-
" cords, and let none of the Varieties efcape
" them, that join in the making up the Sweet-
" nefs of the Harmony; foon after the Inftru-
" ments ftun us, and the Mufic feems no more to
" the Ears, but a confus'd and undiftinguifhable
" Sound. But who can fupport the dull Tedi-
" oufnefs of the *Recitativo*, which has neither
" the Charm of Song, nor the agreeable Force
" of good Speaking ? The Soul tir'd out with
" a long Attention to that, in which it can find
" nothing affecting, retires into it felf to find
" fome fecret Emotion, by which it may be
" touch'd ; and the Mind, having in vain ex-
" pected Impreffions from without, has Recourfe
" to empty Mufings, or grows diffatisfy'd with
" it felf for being fo ufelefs to its own Satisfa-
" ction. In a Word, the Fatigue is fo great
" and fo univerfal, that we only think how to

M " get

" get out ; and all the Pleasure the tir'd Spe-
" ctator can propose to himself, is the Hopes of
" a speedy End to the *Show.*

" * The Reason why generally I soon grow
" weary at an *Opera,* is, *That I never yet saw*
" *any* OPERA, *which did not appear to me most de-*
" *spicable, both in the* † *Disposition of the Subject,*
" *and in the Verses. Now 'tis in vain to charm the*
" *Ear, and flatter the Eye, if the Mind remain*
" *unsatisfy'd, my Soul being in better Intelligence*
" *with my Mind, than with my Senses, struggles*
" *against the Impressions it might receive, or at*
" *least fails in giving an agreeable Consent to*
" *them, without which e'en the most delightful*
" *Objects can never afford me any great Portion*
" *of Pleasure.*

" 'Tis true, a *Foolery* set off, and *hautgout*
" with Music, Dances, Machines, and Decora-
" tions, is a pompous and magnificent *Foolery,*
" but yet it is still but a FOOLERY : 'Tis an ug-
" ly Ground to beautiful Ornament, through
" which I yet discover the Ground with a great
" deal of Dissatisfaction.

" There is another thing in *Opera's* so con-
" trary to Nature, that it always shocks my I-
" magination, and that is, *the singing the whole*
" *from one End to the other, as if the Persons*

---

* *This Reason is worthy our Wits Consideration, who can value them-*
selves on their Understanding, yet bear Nonsense in Music for four Hours
together. nay, and extol it too.

† *This is spoken of the* French Opera's *of* Quinaut, *which as far*
excel all the Italian Opera's, *in Disposition and Verse, as* Dryden *does*
Quarles.

" had

" had ridiculously conspir'd to treat in Music both
" of the most common and most important Affairs
" of human Life.   Can any Man perfuade his
" Imagination, that a Mafter calls his Servant,
" or fends him of an Errand *finging ?* That one
" Friend communicates a Secret to another
" *finging ?* That Politicians deliberate in Coun-
" cil *finging ?* That Orders in Time of Battle
" are given *finging ?* And that Men are *melodi-*
" *oufly kill'd with Sword, Pike or Mufket ?* This
" is to lofe the very Life and Soul of Repre-
" fentation, which no Man of Senfe doubts,
" but is preferable to Harmony.   For Harmo-
" ny ought to be no more, than a bare Atten-
" dant on Poetry ; and the great Mafters of the
" Stage have chofe to add it, not as effential or
" neceffary, but as pleafing, after they have re-
" gulated all that relates to the Subject and Dif-
" courfe.

" In the mean time, by thefe means the Idea
" of the Mafter of Mufick or Compofer takes
" Place of the Heroe of the Opera, and juftles
" him quite out of our Thoughts. *Loüigi,*
" *Cavallo* and *Cefti* are reprefented to our Ima-
" gination ; for the Mind being unable to ap-
" prehend or conceive a *finging Hero,* comes di-
" rectly on him, who made the Mufic ; nor can
" any one deny, but that *Baptifte* in the *Opera's*
" reprefented in the *Palace Royal* is a thoufand
" times more thought on, than *Thefeus* or
" *Cadmus.*

M 2   " I

" I pretend not, by what I have said, to ex-
" clude all manner of Singing from the Stage,
" for it muft be allow'd, that there are some
" things there which ought to be sung, and o-
" thers, which may be sung without sinning a-
" gainft Probability, Decency and Reason. Vows,
" Prayers, Praises, Sacrifices, and generally all,
" that relates to the Service of the Gods, are
" sung in all Nations, and in all Times; ten-
" der and mournful Paffions exprefs themselves
" naturally enough by a kind of Tone; the
" Expreffion of Love *in its Birth*, the Irresolu-
" tion and Doubts of a Soul tofs'd by the seve-
" ral Emotions of that Paffion, are the Subject
" for *Stanzas*, or *Lyric* Poefy, and so is that
" for Music. Every Man knows, that the *Greeks*
" introduc'd the *Chorus* on their Stage, and I'm
" of Opinion, that we have the same Reason to
" follow their Example on ours.

" The Bufinefs of the *Drama*, in my Opinion,
" ought to be diftributed in this manner.
" Whatever relates to Converfation, to the In-
" trigues and Affairs, to Counfel and Action, is
" only proper in the Mouth of the *Actor*, but
" highly ridiculous in that of a *Singer*. The
" *Greeks* made noble *Tragedies*, in which some-
" thing was *sung*; the *Italians* and *French* make
" those, which are deteftable, in which every
" thing is *sung!*

" Would you know what an *Opera* really
" is? I'll tell you, ——— *It is a very* Odd
" Medley *of* Poetry *and* Music, in which
" the

" the Poet and Mafter of Mufic are equally on,
" the Rack for one another, and take a great
" deal of Pains to compofe a very Scurvy-Piece.
" Not but you may fometimes find agreeable *
" Words, and very fine Airs in them, but you
" will find with much more Certainty, before
" any one of them be done, a Diflike of the
" Verfes, where the Poet's Genius has been
" ftinted, and a perfect Satiety of the Singing,
" when too long a Service has jaded the Com-
" pofer.

   " Did I think my felf Mafter of Capacity e-
" nough of advifing thofe Perfons of Confidera-
" tion and good Breeding, who are pleas'd with
" this Entertainment of the Theatre, I would
" counfel them to recover their vitiated Palate,
" and relifh again our good Plays, our *Trage-*
" *dies* and *Comedies,* where Mufic may be in-
" troduc'd without wounding the Reprefenta-
" tion, there they might have a mufical Pro-
" logue, and in the Interludes they might have
" the Mufic animated with † Words, that
" might be the Life of what had been repre-

---

* *This is only in the* French Opera's, *neither the* Italian *nor ours can pretend to them.*

† *He means by this what* Horace *fays of the* Chorus, *thus tranfla-ted by the* Lord Rofcommon,
A Chorus fhould fupply what Action wants,
And has a generous and manly Part ;
Bridles wild Rage, loves rigid Honefty,
And ftrict Obfervance of impartial Laws,
Sobriety, Security, and Peace ;
And begs the Gods to turn blind Fortune's Wheel,
To raife the Wretched, and pull down the Proud, *&c.*

" fented.

" fented. And after the Play is ended, an *E-*
" *pilogue* might be fung, or fome Reflections on
" the fineft things in the Play. This would
" fortify the Idea, and rivet the Impreffions
" they had made in the very Hearts of the Au-
" dience.

" By this means you might fupply enough
" to fatisfy both the Senfes and the Mind ; the
" Charm of Singing relieving the bare *Repre-*
" *fentation,* and the Force of Action the Length
" of the *Mufic.*

Thus far Monfieur St. *Evremont* ; and I forbear giving you his Difcourfe about the mutual
Diflike the *French* and *Italians* have for the *Opera's* of each other, becaufe that Controverfy is
not much to our Purpofe ; and our *Italians*
have not long ago publifh'd a Book, call'd, *The
Comparifon of the* French *and* Italian *Mufic,* in
which the *French* Author gives up the Caufe to
the *Italians,* in return of *Lowigi's* giving it up
formerly to the *French.* Tho if I had any
thing to do with this Controverfy, I fhould very much doubt the Judgment of the *Frenchman*
from one Inftance of many, where he admires
the *Italians* for Singing out of Tune, that they
may give the better Relifh to the fine Harmony,
that fucceeds ; as if a Man fhould admire it as
a Perfection in another to fpeak Nonfenfe firft,
to give the better Tafte to Senfe afterwards.

I confefs, I was a little furpriz'd, to hear of
and fee this Book with Notes by Seignior *H*——
or fome Creature of his ; for I thought they
would

would never have ventur'd so far out of their Depth, as to launch from mere *Sound* into Sense, from pricking musical Notes, to Writing; since that was the only effectual way they could take to convince the World, that we were impos'd on by those, who were not content to bubble us of our Money for Airs and Recitativo's, unless they told us to our Faces, that we knew nothing of the mater, and must, therefore, receive whatever Stuff they would be graciously pleas'd to bestow upon us.

But this Author puts a great Stress on the *Taking* of his Compositions, and the Miscarriage of those of others, when he had before deny'd, that we knew any thing of the Matter. But if he allow that, as a Test of the Excellence of his *Opera*, that will be much stronger for Mr. *Henry Purcel*, whose Music supported a Company of young raw Actors, against the best and most favour'd of that Time, and transported the Town for several Years together, as they do yet all true Lovers of Music. Let any Master compare *Twice ten hundred Deities*, the Music in the *Frost Scene*, several Parts of the *Indian Queen*, and twenty more Pieces of *Henry Purcel*, with all the *Arrieto's*, *Dacapo's*, *Recitativo's* of *Camilla*, *Pyrrhus*, *Clotilda*, &c. and then judge which excels. *Purcel* penetrates the Heart, makes the Blood dance through your Veins, and thrill with the agreeable Violence offer'd by his Heavenly Harmony; the *Arietto's* are pretty light Airs, which tickle the Ear, but reach no farther;

ther ; *Purcel* moves the Paffions as he pleafes, nay, *Paints* in Sounds, and verifies all that is faid of *Timotheus.* Mufic, as well as Verfe, is fubject to that Rule of *Horace* ;

He that would have Spectators fhare his Grief,
Muft write not only well, but * *movingly.*

This was *HenryPurcel's* Talent ; and *his* Music, as known as it is, and as often repeated as it has been, has to this Day the very fame Effect. But all the Airs of thefe *Opera's,* as they touch nothing but the Ear, fo they vanifh as foon, as that is tyr'd with the Repetition ; that is, they live but a Year at moft ; fo that *Purcel's* being compos'd to penetrate the Soul, and make the Blood thrill through the Veins, live for ever ; but thofe foreign Whims, which have coft us above twenty thoufand Pounds, are loft before the Caftratos have fpent the Money they brought them in.

But it has by this very Book been faid, that our Tafte is improv'd, much amended fince the Time of *Henry Purcel,* and that we fhould not now relifh any of his Things. To this I anfwer, that I find the beft Judges of Mufic, thofe who are Mafters of the Compofition, as well as

---

* Non fatis eft pulchra effe Poemata dulcia funto & quocunq; volent animum Auditoris agunto. *It is not enough, that the Poem be beautiful, but it fhould be fweet, and turn the Mind where-ever it pleafes.*

Per-

Performance, prefer what he has done to all the *Opera's* we have had, on our Stage at leaft. I would therefore fain know how our Tafte is mended ? Do the promifcuous Audience know more of the Art of Harmony and Mufic? No— not one in a thoufand underftands one fingle Note. How fhall thefe therefore give the Preference of this new *Mufic*, to that of *Henry Purcel's* ? The Mafters muft decide it, you reply perhaps——— That indeed would bring it into a fmall Com- pafs, to the Decifion of a very few, and yet not to be determin'd ; for the *Englifh* Mafters have ftill a Veneration for *Purcel* ; and the foreign Mafters have too vifible an Intereft to be the Deciders. The only way is by the Rules of Art ; for what goes beyond them is nothing but Extravagance, and no Beauty ; and if the *Itali- ans* fing out of Tune by way of Perfection, they muft enjoy the Advantage, which all Men elfe in the World will condemn as no Harmony, and by Confequence can be no Beauty or Excellence in Mufic, the very Soul of which is *Harmony*.

But to return from this Digreffion, in Vindi- cation of our *Englifh Mufic*, to the Abfurdities of *Opera's* ; I think the Degeneracy of the Age is but too apparent, in the fetting up and encou- raging fo paltry a Diverfion, that has nothing in it either manly or noble.

But, fays a certain Gentleman, the Bufinefs of the Stage is to *pleafe*, and if this Pleafure be found in *Opera's*, what fignifie all the objected Abfurdities ? Tho this be a very ridiculous De- fence,

fence, and will hold of the moſt ſcandalous and dulleſt things in Nature ; yet I have heard it urg'd by Men of allow'd Wit, and indeed, who had more of that, than of Reaſon, and Judgment, which is founded on that. But if this be really a good Argument, *Clinch* of *Barnet*, *Bartholomew-Fair* Drolls, nay a *Jack-pudding* Entertainment in *Moor-Fields* are noble Entertainments, for all theſe pleaſe, and have as good a Title to the Stage, as *Opera's*, nay, from Reaſon a better, as not ſubject to ſo many Abſurdities. But this is conſecrated by the Taſte of Quality.——If the Taſte of Quality ſink to that of the *Canaille*, it is not the Perſons can give it a Reputation, ſince their beloved *Cowley* has told us of a *great Vulgar*, as well as *ſmall*.

Would therefore a Man of Senſe be for a Diverſion, which levels his Underſtanding with that of the Refuſe of the *Mob ?* Yet the following of *Opera's* does this, and inſiſting in their Vindication, that what-ever pleaſes deſerves Encouragement, ſince it is a Scandal to be pleas'd with ſome things, as proving but a weak Capacity, or a very unpoliſh'd Taſte.

There are ſome Pleaſures, which none but Men of fine Senſe, and a Guſt for the Art, can diſtinguiſh, as in Painting, Graving, *&c.* while the Vulgar look with an equal Eye on the beſt and the worſt. A certain Country Squire of my Acquaintance was drinking in a Country Alehouſe, in which ſeeing ſeveral notable Cuts, as of the *Prodigal*, *Robin Hood* and *Little John*,

and

and fome other fcurvy Prints, worfe than ever
Overton fold, he turn'd to the Gentleman, who
fate next him, and faid, ——*Well! this Painting
is a noble Art-——* And indeed a Graving of old
Vanhove's, or worfe, if any worfe can be, would
pleafe the *Vulgar*, as well as one of *Edlinch,
Audrand*, or any of the *Italian* Cuts ; and a
Piece of a mere Sign-Dauber is as valuable in
the Eye of a grofs and common Underftanding,
as one of *Raphael*'s or *Thornhill*'s.   And fo in
Mufic, a *Taber* and *Pipe*, a *Cymbal* or *Horn-pipe*,
will ravifh the Mob, more than the admirable
Mr. *Shoar* with his incomparable *Lute* ; and
the Ballad 'Tune *Lilly Bullero* more, than a fine
Sonato of *Corelli*.   And thus in Poetry, the
Million will prefer *Bunnyan* and *Quarles* to
Milton and *Dryden* ; yet fure no Gentleman of
fine Tafte and Genius in all thefe things, but
would be afham'd to urge fuch an Argument as
Pleafing, fince all thefe, which are fcandalous,
pleafe the moft in Number.

It is therefore as fcandalous to be pleas'd with
any thing irrational and abfurd on the Stage,
in Comparifon of the *Drama*, as with *Jack-
pudding*, or a *Bartholomew Droll* off it ; or to
prefer to *Edlinch*, *Audrand* a *Vanhove*, &c.
or a Confort of Tongs and Keys, or Cymbal
and Bagpipe to Mr. *Shoar*'s Lute, or the Compofitions of *Corelli*.

But, fays another, if All that is abfurd and
irrational fhould be excluded the Theatre, you
muft banifh a great many of the moft celebrated

3   Pieces

Pieces of the Stage ; as, *Othello*, which is compos'd of Parts fhocking to Reafon, and full of
Abfurdities ; the *Maid's Tragedy*, which Mr.
Rhimer has juftly condemn'd, and feveral others,
which no Man has been able to vindicate from
Faults equal to thofe urg'd againft *Opera's*. And
fince our Reafon muft be fhock'd either with
Harmony, or without it, pray let us have *Opera's*, where the Compofer's pleafing Art makes
Amends for the Poet's Fooleries. Nay, fays another, I will undertake to prove, that there is
fcarce one Play, that has met tolerable Succefs,
or is very much efteem'd, and call'd a Stock-
Play, but what is as abfurd, and fhocking to
Reafon, as moft *Opera's* ; and what is worfe,
the Authority, which they have obtain'd with
the *Many* is fo great, that when you attempt to
fpeak againft them, both your *Wits* and *Witlings*
cry out, *That you're paſt Shame.*

If indeed, purfues he, you could advance the
Britiſh Stage to the Excellence of that of *Athens*,
it would want neither *Reafon* nor *Mufic*, but
the happy Mixture would be admirable, and
the Diverfion divine; but as the Stage is, both
in Players and Plays, I cannot difcover fo mighty a Difference in the Merit of the two Diverfions, but that a Man's Senfe is as juftifiable in
the frequenting the one, as the other.

I muft confefs, this laft Objection has too
much Weight in it, but then if the Encouragers
of this Folly had beftow'd half as much in the
Reformation of the Stage, it would have rais'd

it

it to an Equality with, if not above that of *A-thens* it felf, tho that State employ'd immenfe Sums in the Decorations of it, and the fetting out of the Plays; and if any one Man of Power and Intereft would heartily engage on the Part of good Senfe, Poetry, and the Honour of his Country, we fhould foon remove this Objection, and difcard the Dregs of *Italy* with their harmonious Nonfence.

But there are others, who tell us, that it is the Illnefs of our prefent Plays, that excufes their Fondnefs of *Opera's*. But this is without the leaft Shadow of Reafon or Truth; nor can they in any point prove our Plays to be worfe, than thofe of an hundred Years ago, fince it would be too palpable an Inftance of their profound Ignorance or extravagant Prejudice, which is below a Man of Senfe and Judgment, as may eafily be made appear in Tragedy only, of which we are fcarce *yet* arriv'd to a juft Notion. Nor was there much of Comedy known before the Learned *Ben Johnfon*, for no Man can allow any of *Shakefpear*'s Comedies, except the *Merry Wives of* Windfor. There are indeed excellent Humours fcatter'd about, and interwoven in his other Plays; but *Ben Johnfon* was the firft, that ever gave us one entire Comedy. Since him we have had *Etheridge, Wicherly, Shadwel,* and *Crown* in fome of his Plays, with the Reft of King *Charles* the IId's Reign. Add fince the Revolution, Mr. *Congreve* in three Plays has merited great Praife, and very well diftinguifh'd

I his

his Characters and hit true Humour.   Mr. *Vanbrook* too has shewn Abundance of rude, unconducted and unartful Nature ; his Dialogue is generally dramatic and easy.   Nay, after these our very Farce Writers deserve more Esteem, than the taking Plays of an hundred Years ago, as having as much Nature, more Design and Conduct, and much more Wit.

From hence it appears, that this Objection of the Degeneracy of the present Stage, from what it was formerly, as an Excuse for frequenting *Opera's*, is nothing but a mere groundless Pretence ; and that if we met now with as much Encouragement from our dignify'd Audience, as that did from the Vulgar ; or if our Judges could distinguish betwixt *good* and *bad* so far, as to encourage the former, and explode the latter, they would soon have Plays more worthy the *English* Genius, and *Opera's* would retire beyond the *Alps*.

After this Discourse, we took our Leaves of Mr. BETTERTON, and return'd to *London:* I was pleas'd with his Story of the extravagant Actor, since it is a very pleasant Lesson for a great many of our modern Players, and which might it self cure them of Extravagances too much in vogue.

I subjoin here a Catalogue of the Plays, in which Mr. *Betterton* made some considerable Figure.

The Loyal Subject.   *The Wild Goose Chase.*
Maid in the Mill.   *The Spanish Curate.*
                                      The

The Mad Lover.

Pericles *Prince of* Tyre.

A Wife for a Month.

Rule a Wife and have a Wife.

The Tamer tam'd.

The Unfortunate Lovers.

Aglaura,

Changling.

The Bodman.

The Wits.

Hamlet *Prince of* Denmark.

Love and Honour.

Romeo *and* Juliet.

Adventures of Five Hours.

Twelfth Night.

The Villain.

The Rivals.

Henry *VIIIth.*

Love in a Tub.

Cutter of Colemanftreet.

The Dutchefs of Malfey.

Muftapha.

Cambyfes.

The grateful Servant.

The Witty Fair One.

The School of Complements.

The Warrior's a Weather-Cock.

Richard *the IIId.*

Henry *the Vth.*

Sir Solomon *Single.*

The Woman made a Juftice.

Amorous Widow.

The Unjuft Judge.

Epfom *Wells.*

Macbeth.

King Lear.

The Rover.

Don Carlos *Prince of* Spain.

Sir Fopling Flutter.

Circe.

Siege of Troy.

Anna Bulloin.

The Libertine.

Virtuofo.

Spanifh *Fryar.*

Oedipus.

Orphan.

Titus *and* Berenice.

Theodofius.

Plain Dealer.

Mock Aftrologer.

Valentinian.

Amphytrion.

Cleomenes.

Troilus *and* Creffida.

Cæfar Borgia.

Old Batchelor.

Fatal

Fatal Marriage.	*The Way of the World.*
Double Dealer.	*Ambitious Step-Mother.*
Prophetefs.	*Fair Penitent.*
Love for Love.	*All for Love.*
Mourning Bride.	Harry *the IVth.*
Heroic Love.	*The* Britifh *Enchanters.*

And many others too long to infert.

F I N I S.

THE

Amorous Widow:

OR, THE

WANTON WIFE.

A

COMEDY.

As it is Perform'd by

Her MAJESTY's Servants.

Written by the late Famous
Mr. *THOMAS BETTERTON.*

Now first Printed from the Original Copy.

LONDON:

Printed in the Year 1710.

Dramatis Personæ.

SIR *Peter Pride*. A great Boaster of his Honour, his Valour, what a noble Family he is deriv'd from, and of their mighty Courage. } Mr. *Freeman.*

Cuningham. A Gentleman in love with *Philadelphia*, and is much courted by the Widow. } Mr. *Verbruggen.*

Lovemore. His Friend, in love with Mr. *Brittle*'s Wife, and endeavours to have an Intrigue with her ; but the Widow courts him too. } Mr. *Betterton.*

Barnaby Brittle. An old Citizen that keeps a Glass-shop, marry'd to Sir *Peter Pride*'s Daughter. } Mr. *Dogget.*

Jeffrey. Servant to *Cuningham*, in love with *Prudence*. } Mr. *Fieldhouse.*

Clodpole. A simple Country Fellow that *Lovemore* employs in sending Letters to Mrs. *Brittle*. } Mr. *Bright.*

Merryman. A Falconer to *Cuningham*, who takes upon him to represent the Viscount *Sans-Terre*, that is to marry the Widow. } Mr. *Underhill.*

Lady *Laycock*. An amorous old Widow, that courts every one she can for Marriage, fancying her self so engaging, that all that see her must love her. } Mrs. *Leigh.*

Lady *Pride*. Wife to Sir *Peter*, a formal old Lady that boasts much of her Gentility, and of her great Name and Family. } Mrs. *Willis.*

Mrs. *Brittle* Their Daughter, Wife to *Barnaby Brittle* ; a Cunning, Intrieguing Coquet, that always over-reaches her Husband. } Mrs. *Bracegirdle.*

Philadelphia. Niece to the Widow, in love with *Cuningham*. } Mrs. *Porter.*

Prudence. Maid to the Widow. Mrs. *Hunt.*

Damaris. Maid to Mrs. *Brittle*, that assists her in her Intriegues. } Mrs. *Prince.*

THE

THE

Amorous Widow:

OR, THE

WANTON WIFE.

ACT I. SCENE *a Room*.

Enter Philadelphia *with a Letter, follow'd by* Jeffrey.

Phil.  Should believe Mr. *Cuningham* very conftant, if I had Faith enough to credit this Letter, *Jeffry*. What Complaints are here? But 'tis the Stile, that all young Lovers write.

A 2 *Jeff.*

Jeff. Pray, Madam, believe me; you know I am a Man of Integrity : I cannot diffemble. Let him write what he pleafes, If he did not love you, do you think I'd tell you fo?

Phil. When he has Opportunity, I muft confefs, he fays kind things to me.

Jeff. Take my Word, Madam, my Mafter is not like other Men—— Unlefs he loves a Lady, and loves her paffionately too, he never troubles himfelf to compliment her much.

Phil. Never? Yes, *Jeffry*; fometimes, you know, he compliments my Aunt.

Jeff. That's a convincing Proof of his Love to you; you cannot think him reduc'd to the Neceffity of making Love to an antiquated Piece, with defign to know her otherwife, than to obtain the Happinefs of feeing you? But I fhall tell him, Madam——

Phil. Tell him I have receiv'd and read his Letter.

Jeff. Is that all, Madam?

Phil. All! Yes. Are you not content with that?

Jeff. Any indifferent Perfon, that had Hands, and could but read, would have done, as much, as that.

Phil. Well; Tell him then, in time perhaps I may—

Jeff. My Mafter, Madam, can't endure to depend on a perhaps.

Enter Prudence.

Pru. Quick, quick, up to your Chamber, Madam.

Phil. What's the Matter? Is my Aunt coming hither?

Pru. She's at your Heels. Go up the Back-Stairs quickly.

Phil. Farewel, *Jeffry*; Commend me to thy Mafter.   *Exit* Phil.

Jeff. For what, I befeech you? Is not my Mafter bewitc'd, to court a Lady a whole Year, and fhe hardly tell him fhe loves him yet?

                                                    Pru.

Pru. Alas! She's but a Novice. Let me alone with her; I'll order the Bufinefs fo, that if thy Mafter be difcreet and paffionate enough in his Expreffions, he wins her Heart I'll warrant you.

Jeff. He can fay nothing to her, but that damn'd Aunt of hers is harkning to't ftill. What Pleafure can fhe find in Love at Fifty?

Pru. Fie, *Jeffry,* you muft fay Five and twenty.

Jeff. I wonder any Woman can have the Impudence to live, and trouble Mankind after that Age.

Pru. There never was a Woman fo old, but fhe retain'd a good Opinion of her felf.

Jeff. Then fhe dreffes her felf fo fantaftically, that all may fee fhe ftrives to appear Young in defiance of Nature. She is more gawdy in that fhe calls Half-Mourning, than a young Bride is on her Wedding-Night. The Devil's in her if fhe believes any one can love her: 'Tis jeering her, but to be commonly civil to her.

Pru. A little Flattery fires her. She believes all, that is faid to her: And he that does not make love to her, and compliment her, fhall not be twice admitted to her Houfe.

Jeff. O reverend Beauty! on my Confcience, if I would greafe her Chops with a few Compliments, fhe'd mump and fmile upon me.

Pru. No doubt on't.

Jeff. When fhall my Mafter have an Opportunity to fpeak freely to *Philadelphia?*

Pru. Mr. *Lovemore* is thy Mafter's Friend, and is better belov'd here, than he imagines. You muft perfuade him to amufe the Aunt, that Mr. *Cuningham* may have Convenience to court the Niece.

Jeff. Mr. *Lovemore's* tir'd with playing that part fo often; he is cloy'd with the Aunt, and fwears he'll have no more of her.

Pru. I'm fure her Niece and I endure much more.
Tell him, 'twill be Charity in him to relieve us.

Jeff. 'Twill be hard to perfuade him to it.

Pru. This old Lady of mine has languifh'd for a
young Husband ever fince Sir *Oliver Laycock* dy'd :
She cares not what Eftate he has, or what Religion
he's of, fo he be but young and lufty.   Where is the
great Vifcount *Sans Terre*, thy Mafter told her of?
Methinks he's long a coming.

Jeff. Some crofs unlucky Bufinefs hinders him.

Pru. She has lately receiv'd fome Letters, that
have given a full Account of him.

Jeff. So much the worfe.   What is it?

Pru. They fay his Fortune is not very much, but
he is greatly born, and very pleafant ; and that he is
fo great a Lover of Mufick, he has not a Servant but
can Sing or Dance, or Play upon fome Inftrument.
You may know when he's come by the Noife; the
Fiddlers will welcome him to Town ; for all from
Weftminfter to *Wapping* pay him Homage.

Jeff. Wou'd he were but marry'd to her, *Prudence.*

Pru. Whether he marries her or not, is not our
Bufinefs, *Jeffry.*   Let him but fool with us till thy
Mafter has gain'd her Niece, and then our Work is
done.

Jeff. Well, we have had enough of thy old Lady
Laycock. Let us now talk of our own Affairs ; fpeak,
doft thou love me, *Prudence*?

Pru. A pleafant Queftion! Do you doubt it now?

Jeff. If you would have me credit you, fwear it.

Pru. Sure you are jealous *Jeffry*?

Jeff. You're fomewhat near the Matter. I know
your Humour well enough ; you love a bold audacious Fellow, that will fay any thing, and fuch a one
we have come to Town, one *Merryman* our Falconer ;
I fear you'll like him better than you do me.

Pru.

Pru. Oh Fool! why fhould you think fo?

Jeff. I have fome Honour in me; but he's a Fellow that has eaten Shame, and drank after it. He is more impudent than a Court Page, and will take no Denial.

Pru. Hold your Tongue, here's my Lady.

Enter Lady Laycock.

Lady. What Bufinefs has *Jeffry* with you?

Pru. His Mafter fent him to know, whether he might have leave to wait upon your Ladyfhip this Morning.

Lady. Yes; Tell him, I expect him.

Jeff. He durft not come, becaufe Mr. *Lovemore's* with him.

Lady. Go tell 'em, if they pleafe to come, they fhall be welcome both.

Jeff. I fhall, Madam.   (*Exit* Jeffrey.

Pru. You fee what Power your Beauty has. Neither can live a Moment without feeing you.

Lady. No, they have other Bufinefs with me, *Prudence*; they came from *Paris* lately, and brought me a Letter from my Brother; and I believe they come for my Anfwer now.

Pru. But does not one of 'em love you, Madam?

Lady. I have fome Reafon to believe he does; Mr. *Lovemore* has fpar'd no Pains to perfuade me to quit my Widow-hood.

Pru. I have been told, Madam, that Widow-hood is a Gift, Heaven feldom beftows but on its Favourites; you are rich, and know how troublefome Marriage is. For my part, I believe the faireft Hair, the beautiful'ft Curls do not become your Fore-head fo well as *Bando* did; but every one, Madam, knows their own Neceffities.

Lady. I confefs, Widow hood has its Conveniencies; but if Marriage be a Tronble to fome, 'tis a Pleafure to others, *Prudence.*

Pru. You had the Experience of it thirty Years, how did you like it, Madam? They fay, Sir *Oliver Laycock* lov'd your Ladyfhip.

Lady. For all that he was jealous; and, what's worfe, was Old.

Pru. Very well; therefore you refolve to have a young One now, Madam?

Lady You cannot blame me for that? Can you, *Prudence?*

Pru. Oh no, 'tis well known Youth is comfortable. But, methinks, you fhould take one a little nearer your own Age, Madam. A very young Man may be too treacherous for you, Madam.

Lady. Why, is my Age fo vifible?

Pru. No, Madam; with a little Help of Art you have fome Remains of Beauty ftill. You have fomething about your Eyes as pleafant now, as others have at Twenty.

Lady. 'Tis a very malicious World we live in, *Prudence*; they are fo apt to cenfure, and fpeak of any fingle Woman, that one ought to marry to avoid that Scandal.

Pru. Some that are young are forc'd to marry, to avoid Detraction; others wou'd rather all that's Ill fhould be faid of them, than to have no Notice taken of 'em. I knew a young Lady that pin'd to a Confumption, becaufe fhe liv'd three Years about the Court, and never had the Honour to be lampoon'd. The Truth is, none that are Beautiful and Young can avoid Envy, but few are fo malicious, to fpeak againft the Old.

Lady. There is no Age exempt from Scandal, *Prudence.* When we are Young, they fay we fell our felves; when Old, we are forc'd to hire, to buy our Lovers.   *Pru.*

Pru. You know what they fay, Madam, of the old Marchionefs, your Friend, that was fo admir'd, fo courted in her Youth; who, when fhe found fhe was forfook by all, was forc'd to hire a Player by the Quarter: How foon the poor Fellow was tir'd too! How like a Sheep biter he look'd after the firft two Months!

Lady. This *London* is a very wicked Place, 'tis impoffible to live without Scandal here.

Pru. I'm afraid they'll fay as much of you, Madam, if you bargain for a Husband. To covet one, that is both Young and Rich, is too much in Confcience, Madam.

Lady. Thou know'ft, *Prudence*, Wealth is not the thing I feek.

Pru. Then, Madam, the Bufinefs is done; the Vifcount *Sans-Terre* fhall be your Husband, Madam.

Lady. Ah *Prudence*! if he were but as handfome as——

Pru. Ah Madam, that's too much.

Lady. Why may not I wifh for it?

Pru. Confider his Quality, Madam, and 'bate him fomething for that. One thing I muft advife you; be not too prodigal of your Gold at firft; to be liberal fometimes will be convenient, and make him kinder to you.

Lady. For all this, I fhould think my felf very happy, if I were certain of Mr. *Cuningham* or Mr. *Lovemore*.

Pru. A little Jealoufy will inflame 'em. They'll be more preffing when the Vifcount comes.

Lady. But yet methinks, *Cuningham* and my Neice——

Pru. What, Madam?

Lady. Are always whifpering.

Pru. He only compliments her, Madam. She's too young to make Love ferioufly.

Lady.

Lady. With your Favour, there's no trufting to that. To my Knowledge, there are thofe younger, than fhe, that underftand what Love is but too well.

Pru. That's true, Madam ; but *Philadelphia* is fo innocent, that no Man can make Love to her, but to divert himfelf. Here fhe is, Madam.

Enter Philadelphia.

Lady. What does fhe come for? I'll fend her pack-ing quickly.

Pru. Confider what you do, Madam. How can Mr. *Lovemore* entertain your Ladyfhip, unlefs his Friend may divert himfelf the while with rallying with your Niece.

Lady. For all that I could wifh——

Pru. Pray trouble not your felf. Truft me, I'll watch her, Madam.

Phil. Will your Ladyfhip go to *Eaton*'s? The Coach is at the Door.

Lady. No, I'll not go yet.

Phil. If you ftay long, Madam, the beft *Poynt* will be fold before you come.

Lady. No matter. Ha ! what ails the Girl ! How ftrangely fhe looks ! Her Eyes are hardly open yet !

Phil. How, Madam ?

Lady. Then her Head's drefs'd awry. How it dif-guifes her ! Lord ! how frightfully it looks !

Phil. Truly, Aunt, 'tis drefs'd juft as the Fafhion is.

Lady. Fetch her Hood, *Prudence* ; I'll have her put it on till it be mended.

Phil. I drefs'd it to pleafe no body but my felf, Madam.

Lady. I'll have you drefs your felf now to pleafe me : Come, put it on.

Pru.

Pru. My Lady's in the Right. Never was a-ny thing more ridiculous. Here, put on the Hood, I am sure this is much handsomer.

Lady. Why don't you put it on?

Phil. I can't endure it, Madam—

Lady. Do, I say.

Pru. So; Now it is as it should be; all modest Maids should be dres'd so : But here's Mr. *Cuningham* and Mr. *Lovemore.*

Enter Cuningham, Lovemore *and* Jeffry.

Love. Your Servant, Madam ; you see how we love your Company, by giving you this Trouble in a Morning.

Cun. 'Tis a Happiness we are much envy'd for.

Lady. You are welcome, Gentlemen. Pray command this House as freely as your own.

Love. Why does this Lady hide her Face ? Pray, Madam, let us see you.

Lady. Forbear, Sir, I beseech you : She has had the Tooth-Ach lately. If she takes off her Hood, she'll catch cold, and bring the Pain again.

Phil. I thank your Ladyship for your Care of me. But the Pain has been gone so long, I don't fear it now.

Love. Nay then, we must have it off.

Phil. What say you, Madam, Shall I pull it off?

Lady. Yes, Impertinence; I see you have a Mind to shew your self.

Pru. 'Tis the Nature of all young Girls to do what they are forbidden.

Cun. I come not to trouble your Ladyship for your Letter to my Lawyer; your countenancing my Business will be of great Advantage to me.

Lady. This, Sir, is what my Brother commands me: You shall see I take delight to serve his Friends.

Love.

Love. Madam, You promis'd me that Honourable Title.

Lady. Do you pretend to it ?

Love Yes, Madam, more, than any one.

Lady. I have not much Beauty to boaft of; but Virtue, Sir, makes fome amends for the Defects of the other.

Love. Defects ? (Cuningham *Courts* Philadelphia. Pray, Madam, wrong not your felf fo much.

Lady. There are few but know a little their own Value: And tho a Woman be not fam'd for a great Beauty, yet if fhe be agreeable, there are thofe, will like her well enough.

Love. You have that in Perfection, Madam.

Lady. In that, Sir, I know you do not flater. *Phil.*——

Phil. Madam.

Cun. Then, Madam, you like my Choice of this Suit.

Phil. Extremely well : Was it your own Fancy, Sir.

Cun. I am not afham'd to own it, fince you ask it, Madam.

[*They counterfeit to be talking about Fafhions, whilft feemingly* Lovemore *Courts the Aunt.*

Pru. I'll liften to 'em——

He talks to her of nothing but new Fafhions. [*To the* You may, Madam, venture to difcourfe   *Widow.* without difturbance.

Lady. Pray, Sir, tell me freely; how old do you think I am?

Love. Faith, Madam, if you were not a Widow, I fhould think you a Girl fcarce Twenty.

Lady. Now, Sir, you flater me : You might have faid Thirty. I do not love to difguife my Age.

Love. How ! Thirty, Madam ! and look fo youthful: I'll not believe it, 'tis impoffible!

Lady.

Lady. You do not know what Mifery I endur'd whilft my old Husband liv'd. The Griefs I had upon me would have diftracted another Woman. Alas! Sir, 'tis not Age but Sorrow has broke me.

Love. It makes me fad to hear you tell it, Madam, and vexes me to think, an old Man fhould enjoy fuch Happinefs.

Lady. You do not know how many Tears I have fhed.

Love. 'Tis fome Comfort, Madam, to remember he did not live long with you.

Lady. Truly, Sir, Fifteen Years.

Pru. Yes, and Fifteen to that.   (*Afide.*

Lady. Having been fo unfortunate in a Husband, you may believe I have but little Encouragement to venture, Sir, again. For I am very happy now I am a-lone.

Love. You do wifely, Madam ; for fhe deferves not to be pity'd, that rafhly runs into the fame Misfortune ; and therefore you have, Madam——

Lady. Nay, Sir, I have not forfworn Marrying yet.

Love. Pray, Madam, where do you ufe to walk in the Evening ? Into St. *James*'s Park ?

Lady. Not very often, Sir.

Love. Or into the Mulberry Garden ? Is not the Wildernefs very pleafant ?

Lady. If I like my Company, Sir, I never miflike the Place.

Love. Have you feen the new Paradife, Madam ? 'Tis much fuperiour to the former.

Lady. I have heard as much : But, Sir——

Love. Let me have the Honour to wait upon you thither prefently.

Lady. Not yet, Sir ; After Dinner, if you pleafe. But tell me, Sir, do you think me fuch an Enemy to Marriage, that were I fure a young Gentleman lov'd me,

me, and lov'd me truly, I would be fo uncivil to refufe him?

Love. When I confider what you endur'd in Sir *O-
liver Laycock*'s time, I think you ought to do it, Madam; and that Man's unjuft, that urges you to break
your Refolution.

Lady. Pray do not miftake me, Sir; I have made
no fuch Refolution yet.

Love. Nay, Madam, fince you are difpleas'd at
what I faid, we'll change the Difcourfe. Pray, Madam, do you think the young Lord *Lucky* has that Intereft at Court, that Fame reports he has?

Lady. Lord, Sir, this is a ftrange wild Anfwer to
my Queftion. Let me tell you, Sir, if I have any
Merit, Wealth or Beauty, there's one in the World
deferves 'em all.

Pru. Good! How fhe teazes him!   (*Afide.*

Love. But has that one no Fault, Madam?

Lady. You know him very well, Sir.

Love. I know him, Madam!

Lady. Yes, you, Sir. 'Tis your felf.

Love. 'Sdeath! What will become of me now?
                                        (*Afide.*

Enter a Servant.

Serv. Madam———

Lady. What now?

Serv. The Marchionefs is come to vifit you.

Lady. Troublefome Creature. Go one of you and
entertain her quickly.

Pru. Which of us, Madam?

Lady. Go you, *Philadelphia*, and keep her Company till I come.

Phil. I fhall, Madam.   (*Exit* Phil.

Cun. Pray, Madam, what is this Marchionefs?

Lady. Oh, Sir! a moft eternal Talker: Her Tongue
goes like the Larum of a Clock, as faft, and to the

fame

fame Tune ftill. She's almoft Sixty, and yet pretends to Beauty, and loves Courtſhip moſt unreaſonably. Say but a kind thing to her, and you win her Heart. The Truth is, ſhe has not much Reputation ; but the Reſpeſt I give her is to her Quality and to her Perſon. But ſhe's an Original in her kind, Sir.

Love. Oh blind, blind Creature! ſhe draws her own Piſture, and laughs at it.

Cun. Sure, Madam, her Converſation muſt be very pleaſant ?

Lady. She has been much courted in her Youth ; but 'twould make one die to hear her boaſt of her Lovers now. How this Knight ſighs, and that Lord dies for her ; when all the while I know what Neceſſity the poor Creature is reduc'd to. I would have brought her hither, but I know we never ſhould have been rid of her. Excuſe me a Moment, I'll ſend her away, and return preſently. Your Servant, Gen-tlemen, *Exit Lady.*

Cun. How now, Friend——What's the Matter ? Why doſt look ſo ſullenly ?

Love. I play the Aſs here any longer ! No ; if I do, may I turn Pudding to a Rope-Dancer, and ſhew Tricks next *Bartholomew* Fair.

Cun. Nay, but Friend , Dear Friend——

Love. Tell not me of Friendſhip. What Man would endure to be ſo plagued as I have been. I have parry'd with my beſt Skill the dangerous Thruſts that ever were made at me. To tug at an Oar, or dig in a Mine in *Peru*, is Recreation to it. But the firſt time to offer Marriage to me! I ſweat to think on it. It made me tremble twice, for fear ſhe ſhould have forc'd my Neck into her muddy Nooſe of Ma-trimony.

Cun. We have no other way to blind her.

Love. 'Tis all one to me.

Cun.

Cun. If thou lov'ft my Life, Friend, do not forfake me now.

Love. Pray live, if you pleafe, and give me leave to do fo too. Should I again be left alone with her, the beft I can hope for is Diftraction.

Pru. How do you like the Niece?

Cun. She's all Perfection.

Pru. How do you thrive? Do you find her kind, Mr. *Cuningham?*

Cun. She has promis'd me a Meeting this After-noon, if thou canft but remove the Aunt from us.

Pru. I'll try what I can do, but Mr. *Lovemore* is the only Man in her Favour.

Cun. Dear Friend, try but this one.

Love. I'll be hang'd, drawn, and quarter'd for a Traitor firft, and have my Limbs hung up for the Birds to feed upon. No, no, I have my Belly full, I thank you, and fome to fpare.

Pru. But now I think on't, where's this Vifcount all this while? His Arrival wou'd be of great ufe in this Affair.

Love. Prudence advifes well : Methinks he's long a coming.

Cun. Why, you muft know, there is one *Merryman* juft come up out of the Country - He is my Falconer upon occafion, the Fellow is bold, and very apt, and has not been feen much in Town. What think you of him to act awhile, till fome more lucky Occafion prefent it felf?

Love. 'Tis a lucky Thought, and may be of ufe. Where is he?

Jeff. In the Pantry, a ramming down a Wedge of Roaft-Beef to keep out the Town Air, and making Sport with a fimple Country Fellow he has brought out of the Country with him to fee the Town; one *Clodpole*, he calls him.

1

Love.

Love. 'Twould not be amifs to examine him, and inftruct him how to behave himfelf, before he is too much known.

Jeff. No body of the Family has feen him yet, but the Butler ; and he, I know, will be fecret. I'll ftep and call him to you, Sir, if you pleafe ?

Cun. Do fo.　　　　　　　　　　*(Exit* Jeff.

In the mean time, *Prudence,* there's fomething to buy thee a Pair of Gloves.　　　*(Gives her Money.*

Pru. Oh, dear Sir! how long have I deferved this ? Pleafe to command me any thing within my Power, and conclude it done.

Enter Jeffrey *with* Merryman *drefs'd like a Falconer.*

Jeff. Sir, I found him juft paffing by the Door, and have told him part of the Bufinefs.

Love. Well, Friend, doft think thou can'ft act the Part of a Vifcount for a little while ?

Merr. What fort of a Lord is he to be ?

Cun. Oh ! An Amorous Refolute fort of a Perfon, that's much given to love Mufick. You fhall have all things that's fitting for a Man of fuch Quality.

Merr. Well, Sir, let me be once fet out with a good Equipage, and leave the reft to me.

Love. Come with us, Friend, and we'll inftruct thee fully in thy Part.

Merr. Well, give me but my Cue of Entrance, and let me alone to act my Part.

Cun Let's about it then. *(Exit* Lovemore, Cuningham
Jeff. Prudence――　　*and* Merryman.
Pru. What's your Will?
Jeff. One Kifs.
Pru. 'Pfhaw! Is that all ?　　　　*(He kiffes her.*
Jeff. All ! I fay no more, but――
Ah *Prudence, Prudence !*

B　　　　　　　　　　　　*Pru.*

Pru. What damnable whining Tone haſt thou got, ha ?

Jeff. I am afraid of this Viſcount, *Prudence.*

Pru. Away, you Fool ; I have other things to trouble my Head withal—— Farewel.

Jeff. Adieu.　　　　　　　(*Exeunt ſeverally.*

A C T II.

Enter Cuningham *and* Philadelphia.

Cun. WHy, Madam, are you ſo unwilling to credit what my conſtant Paſſion, ſo long in vain, has urg'd ? Do you not believe I love you ? Oh ! Did you but know what I endure, when you refuſe to hear me, you would in Charity have ſome Compaſſion on my wounded Soul.

Phil. I dare not hear this Language from you, Sir.

Cun. What are you afraid of, Madam ?

Phil. All Men ſay the ſame things, Sir, till they have won our eaſy Hearts to pity and believe you ; then ſtraight you ſlight your Conqueſt, and leave us to purſue our Ruin.

Cun. Be not ſo cruel to cenſure all for thoſe Faults, which ſome few commit ; for all, I muſt confeſs, do not ſtand excus'd. But, Madam, you cannot be ſo great a Stranger to my Love, as not to think it real ; or ſo great an Enemy to your own Worth, to believe it has not Power to enſlave a Heart, that's guarded more ſecurely than mine—— But no more ——
Your Aunt——

Enter

Enter Lady Laycock.

Lady. So Niece, I fee your fqueamifh Stomach can digeft all forts of Diet, tho ne'er fo ftrictly charg'd to the contrary. Mr. *Cuningham,* What Bufinefs have you with her? I wonder you are not afham'd to be always following of her at this rate, and endeavouring to take Advantage of her foolifh Youth; for fhe is but a Girl yet, and not fit for the Converfation of a Man, nay, or indeed to be trufted with her felf.

Cun. Madam——

Lady. Go, go, indeed you are much to blame: What will the World judge, think you? Or what Excufe can I make, for fuffering fuch Doings in my Houfe? And you, Hufwife! how dare you difobey my Commands? Is this the Refpect you pay to me, and to my Quality! I believe, in a little time I muft make it my whole Imploy to invite home young Gallants, forfooth, to pleafure you, whilft I, as if I were your Slave, muft retire, and wait till you are ferv'd firft. 'Tis come to a fine pafs indeed; but I'll put an End to it all, and keep you always lock'd up in your Chamber, I will fo.

Phil. I told you, Sir, what would be the Event of your Projects, but you would not be faid nay. I muft be an Inftrument to make your Paffion known, and none fo fit to be trufted with fuch an Affair as I; but henceforward if you can't fpeak for your felf, you may hang or drown, as you pretend, for me, for I'll no more get Anger for you.

Cun. What does fhe mean?

Lady. What's that you fay?

Phil. Mr. *Cuningham* here, Madam, is always urging me to tell your Ladyfhip the Paffion he has for you.

Lady. Saucy Slut!

Phil.

Phil. As if he could not fpeak for himfelf, but muft be ftill plaguing me, and fwearing how long, how well, and how tenderly he loves you ; then fighs and cries, Oh *Philadelphia!* Can I live without her? But fhe, cruel as fhe is, has vow'd to die unmarried.

Cun. Oh the Devil! What will become of me now?

Phil. Then raves worfe, than any one in *Bedlam*, crying, And muft I then lofe her fo? Oh! Death to all my Hopes! I muft not, cannot, will not! and a thoufand fuch like things, which I'm refolv'd never to hear again. So, Sir, don't trouble me any more, but e'en fpeak what you have to fay to her your felf.
(*Exit.*

Lady. Is this true, Mr. *Cuningham?* I did not think there was a Man living, which cou'd love at that rate, and with fuch Conftancy.

Cun. Oh! Madam! what fhall I fay, fince all is ftill in vain! Your Vow, your cruel Vow, has vanquifh'd all my Hopes ; then where fhould I feek for Peace, but in my laft Retreat, the Grave. Farewell ; I cannot bear to ftay, for every Look adds new Poifons to my Soul. (*Is going.*

Lady. Stay, Sir—— I have made no fuch Vow. If your Paffion——

Cun. Oh, Madam! forbear. I know your Goodnefs to be fuch, that rather, than be the Inftrument of what may happen, you would feemingly comply with any thing I can ask. Pardon me, Madam, I have been too much deceiv'd already.

Lady. Pray ftay, Sir, do not miftake——

Enter Philadelphia *with a Piece of* Poynt.

Phil. Oh, Madam, here's the fineft Piece of *Poynt* I ever faw, and the cheapeft; pray, Madam, look at it.

Lady

Lady. Saucy Intrufion. How durſt you come without being call'd ? How often have I told you this, you Minx : Be gone, and leave it in the next Room, till I pleaſe to come and look on't.

Phil. Madam, the Woman, that brought it is in haſte, ſhe bid me tell your Ladyſhip.

Lady. Let her go about her Buſineſs, if ſhe can't wait, for I'll not come yet.   (*Exit* Philadelphia. How horribly unlucky was this to diſturb me, juſt as I was going to tell him of my Intentions, and of my Concern for his Paſſion.   (*Aſide.*

Cun. I believe I am troubleſome, Madam. (*Is going.* Farewel.

Lady. No, pray ſtay, Sir, I have ſomething to ſay to you, but that young Slut interrupted me.

Cun. Oh the Devil !

Lady. But as I was going to ſay, I did indeed reſolve not to marry any more ; and when you have heard me out, you'll ſay I had Reaſon. You muſt know, in my Husband Sir *Oliver*'s Days, I had not that Liberty, perhaps, as other Ladies of Quality took ; for, to ſay Truth, my airy Temper and my Youth, at that time, made my Husband grows jealous, tho' without Cauſe, Heaven knows.

Cun. That I dare ſwear, if all were of my Mind.
                                  (*Aſide.*

Lady. Which made him lead me a very uneaſy Life : So that it made me reſolve on many things at that time, and one was this, That if ever Sir *Oliver* ſhould die, I never would marry again ; but I don't remember that I ſwore to it : Or if I had, you have ſuch a way with you, 'twould be very hard to deny you any thing, Mr. *Cuningham.*

Cun. Oh, Madam ! —— Your Charity comes now too late : I am paſt all Hope.

Lady. Oh, dear Sir, fay not fo ! for fince you fay your Difeafe is grown to that Extremity, that unlefs your Love meet Rewar]————

Cun. Talk not of Impoffibilities. I know how much you pr ze your Honour : And fince you have vow'd never to marry, I have nothing left to hope for elfe.

Lady. 'Tis true, Mr. *Cuningham,* I would not have my Honour fuffer ; but what remains befide that I can do, to fave you from what may be dangerous, fhall not be wanting.

Enter Prudence *and* Philadelphia.

Pru. Oh, Madam ! Madam ! the rareft News———— The Vifcount *Sans Terre,* whom you have fo long expeɛted, is juft arriv'd, and is coming hither with a huge fine ·Equipage, Fiddles, and other Inftruments.

Lady. Oh dear ! how I'm furpriz'd ! I would not have him fee me thus for all the World. *Prudence,* Set my Curls right, and alter my Knots : Quickly, don't ftand fumbling————
Look if the Paint be firm.

Pru. 'Tis pretty well, Madam ; There's here and there a fmall Crack, but 'twill not be difcern'd at diftance.

Lady. Quickly, good *Prudence :* Put me a little better in Order. You'll pardon me, Sir: You fee what a Fright I'm in.

Cun. Pardon, quotha ! the Devil take me, if any thing could be more freely granted.   (*Afide.*

Enter

Enter the Vifcount Sans Terre, *with Mufick, and a good Equipage ; attended by* Lovemore *and feveral Gentlemen. The Vifcount fings as he enters.*

A CATCH.

FRom *the North I came,*
  Where I heard of the Fame
Of the Lady Laycock's *Beauty ;*
  I had pafs'd for an Afs,
  Had I ftay'd where I was,
And not done a Vifcount's Duty.

Vifc. Oh ! are thefe the Ladies?
By your Favour, Sweet Lady.   (*Kiffes* Philadelphia.
A delicate Morfel, by this Hand.
Madam, I fee that Fame has juftly fpoke your Praife.
You are indeed the Wonder of all your Sex.
How fair fhe is !
  Lady. What does he mean ?
  Vifc. Pray, Madam, what young Gentlewoman is that, whofe matchlefs Beauty feems to fill the Place with more, than common Brightnefs ? Sure 'tis fome Goddefs, dropt from Heaven for Men to worfhip !
Fair Angel, pardon this rude Attempt:
The Honour only of your fair Hand.   (*Kiffes it.*
For till I touch it, I cannot think you mortal.
  Lady. Oh, dear Sir ! You make me blufh.
  Vif. [*To Phil.*] Pray, Lady, is this pretty young Gentlewoman your Niece ?
  Phil. [*Afide.*] This Fellow muft be a Fool, or he could ne'er miftake fo grofly.
  Pru. [*To Phil.*] Now we fhall have rare Sport.
Sure he's blind to miftake you for your Aunt.

*ſhew of Proteſtation unto him ; he takes her up,
and declines his Head on her Neck. Lays him
down on a Bed of Flowers ; ſhe ſeeing him aſleep,
leaves him. Anon comes in a Fellow, takes off
his Crown, kiſſes it, and pours Poiſon into the
King's Ear, and exit. The Queen returns, finds
the King dead, and makes paſſionate Aɛtion. The
Poiſoner with two or three Mutes comes in again,
ſeeming to lament with her ; the dead Body is
carry'd away. The Poiſoner woes the Queen with
Gifts ; ſhe ſeems loath and unwilling awhile, but
in the end accepts his Love.*

I only repeat this to ſhew the manner of the
old Time, and what they meant by dumb Shows,
which *Shakeſpear* himſelf condemns in this very
Play, when *Hamlet* ſays to the Players,—" O ! it
" offends me to the Soul to ſee a robuſtuous Per-
" riwig-pated Fellow tear a Paſſion to tatters, to
" very Raggs, to ſplit the Ears of the *Groundlings,*
" who (for the moſt part) are capable of no-
" thing but *inexplicable dumb Shows* and Noiſe---

But the *Pantomimes* or *Roman* Dancers expreſ-
ſed all this in one Perſon, as we have it in Mr.
Mayne's Lucian ; where *Demetrius* the *Cynic* Phi-
loſopher railing againſt Dancing, is invited by
one of them in the Time of *Nero,* to ſee him
perform without either Pipe or Flute, and did ſo ;
" for having impos'd Silence on the Inſtru-
" ments, he by himſelf danc'd the Adultery of
" *Mars* and *Venus,* the *Sun* betraying them, and
" *Vulcan* plotting, and catching them in a Wire
" Net ; then every God, who was ſeverally
                                    " Specta-

Vifc. Well, fince it happens fo, I like it the better; for to fay Truth, I had fix'd my Eye on you at my firft Entrance.

Ah! wou'd 'twere over once.

Methinks I long to have thee in my Arms.

Oh! How I would employ my Faculties,

And furfeit with delight.

What fay you, Lady? Never ftand to confider on't, but fend for a Parfon to fay Grace, that I may fall to. Odds fo, I'm very hungry——— Very fharp fet; I long to be doing.

Lady. Pray, my Lord, walk in, and refrefh your felf after your Journey. I was unmannerly not to ask you before.

Prudence, Come hither, See that all things are in readinefs. Oh, *Prudence!* I am impatient to be alone with him. *Exit* Pru.

My Lord, you will excufe the Diforder you have found me in.

Vifc. Never trouble your felf about it. Join but your Forces with mine, and we'll beget a Race of People, that fhall be immortal. A Race, that fhall create a fecond War with *Jove,* and raife *Olympus* top equal with the Seat of him, that hurls the Thunder.

Lady. No more, my Lord. Pray walk in.

Vifc. All your Commands are abfolute.

[*Exit* Vifcount *leading the Widow, who pufhes out* Phil.

Love. Was there ever fuch a Piece of Fly-Flefh?

Cun. The Rogue acted it to the Life, and came very feafonably to my Refcue.

Had he ftaid a Moment longer, I had been forc'd to have given up the Ghoft.

Love. That ever Nature fhould fuffer fuch a Lump of Rubbifh in the World for Men to ftumble over.

Cun.

Cun. Pox on her old mouldy Chops :
She's for engroffing all to her felf.
How fhe thruft her Niece in before her !
I'll in, and try to beckon her into the Garden, if
you'll interpofe, fhou'd the Aunt mifs her, and fol-
low us.

Love. 'Sdeath ! Would'ft have me run into the
Lion's Den, juft when I have fcap'd his Paw !
No, I have hazarded too much already to venture
more, I thank you. I now have better Game in
Chace.
You know pretty Mrs. *Brittle*, Sir *Peter Pride*'s
Daughter?

Cun. What of her ?

Love. Oh, 'tis the fweeteft little Creature !
So Fair, fo Witty, fo Kind, and fo Promifing !
I'm juft now fending this Letter, in order to appoint
a Meeting with her. But her Husband is fo jealous
(as indeed I hope to give him Caufe for't) his Eye
is hardly ever off her. I am thinking what way it
can be deliver'd without Sufpicion. Let me fee——
(Studies.

Cun. I'll take my Leave ; for I find I interrupt your
Meditations.

Love. Farewel, my Friend ; and may both our
Wifhes profper.   (*Exit* Cuningham.
Jeffrey.

Enter Jeffrey.

Jeff. Sir.

Love. Can'ft thou contrive to carry this Letter to a
young Gentlewoman, and bring an Anfwer, without
being fufpe&ed ? If thou doft, *Jeffrey*, thou fhalt
be well rewarded for thy Pains.

Jeff. Is fhe Widow, Wife, or Maid, pray Sir?

Love. Why doft thou ask ?

Jeff. For a private Reafon I have.

Love.

Love. Well then, to fatisfy thy Curiofity, *Jeffrey,* know fhe's a Wife ; a Young, a Handfome, and a Melting one !

I am all Ecftafy, and impatient till I poffefs her.

Good *Jeffrey,* look on the Superfcription, and about it with all Speed.

Jeff. I dare not touch it: Don't truft me with it.

Love. Why fo, good *Jeffrey ?*

Jeff. I fay again, do not truft me.

Love. Your Reafon, *Jeffrey?*

Jeff. I don't care to meddle in a Caufe, where there's a Procefs of Cuckoldom going forward.

Love. Prithee, why fo ?

Jeff. Why, Sir, I'll tell you. You muft know, Sir, I love *Prudence,* my Lady *Laycock's* Woman, and I believe there's no Love loft between us ; nor do I know how foon we may exchange our Perfons for better and for worfe. Now, Sir, if I fhould be the Inftrument (by carrying this Letter) of your making this honeft Man a Cuckold, who knows but, in return of fuch a monftrous Deed, it may be my own Cafe next ; therefore, Sir, I don't care to meddle in't.

Love. Give me the Letter again ; I did but try thee. Thy Mafter, indeed, has often told me, how fcrupulous thou wert about thefe Matters, but I ne'er believ'd it till now. Stick to thy Principles, and be what thou deferv'ft, thou mayft come to Good at laft. I have no farther Service at prefent. Prithee leave me, I have Bufinefs of Moment. (*Exit* Jeffrey. I had been finely ferv'd if I had fent this confcientious Rogue. What fhall I do ? The Vifcount brought an ignorant Country Fellow up with him, that won't be fufpected in the leaft. 'Tis well thought of ; I'll entruft him, and fend it immediately. Soft——— Who comes here ?——— Oh ! 'tis the Husband.

Enter

Enter Barnaby Brittle.

Your Servant, Mr. *Brittle* ; is the Lady *Laycock* at home, can you tell?

Brit. Yes, yes, I believe fhe is.

Love. I have a little Bufinefs, and muft needs fpeak with her. Sir, your Servant.

Brtt. A little Bufinefs, quotha!
A fine Trade this doating old Widow drives; my Houfe is become as common for all Commers and Goers, as the *Mall* or *Spring-Garden :* But I fhall put a ftop to it in a little time, I believe.

Enter Mrs. Brittle *in bafte, drefs'd very airy* ; *he ftops her.*

Britt. How now—— Whither away in fuch hafte ?

Mrs. Britt. I'm going abroad, Husband. Good bye.

Britt. Hold, hold, by your Leave, I'll know for what, and whither your fweet Ladyfhip is going?

Mrs. Britt. Why, to the Play, fweet Husband.

Brit. Hum! to the Play.

Mrs. Britt. Well, Good bye, Husband——— I fhall be too late, and then there'll be fuch crowding, I fhan't get the firft Row in the Box, for 'tis a new Play; and I had as lief not go, as fit behind.

(Is going.

Britt. Hold, hold, pray ftay, if you pleafe.

Mrs. Britt. Indeed but I can't.

Britt. Indeed but you muft not go, Wife.

Mrs. Britt. Indeed, Husband, but I fhall.

Brit. I fay again, you muft not.

Mrs. Britt. Muft not! Who fhall hinder me ?

Britt. Why, that will I.

Mrs. Britt. I fay, No.

Britt.

Britt. But I fay, Yes.

Mrs. Britt. Don't you pretend to't.

Britt. Don't you provoke me, I fay. Is this the Trade you always intend to drive?

Mrs. Britt. Yes indeed is it.

Britt. I fay, No.

Mrs. Britt. But I fay, Yes. Do you think you fhall keep me always ftifling within Doors, where there's no body to be feen but your old fufty felf? No, I'll to the Play, where there's all forts of Company and Diverfion; where the Actors reprefent all the Brifknefs and Gaiety of Life and Pleafure; where one is entertain'd with airy Beaux, and fine Gallants, which ogle, figh, and talk the prettieft things in the World. Methinks 'tis rare to hear a young brisk Fellow court a handfome young Lafs, and fhe all the while making fuch pretty dumb Signs: firft turns afide to fee who obferves, then fpreads her Fan before her Face, heaves up her Breafts, and fighs——— at which he ftill fwears he loves her above all the World——— and preffes hard his Suit; tells her, what Force her Beauty, her Wit, her Shape, her Mien, all join'd in one, are of. At which fhe blufhing curtefies low, and to her felf replies, What charming Words he fpeaks! his Perfon's Heavenly, and his Voice Divine. By your Leave, Husband, you make me ftay long.

(Is going.

Britt. Not in the leaft——— there will be no great mifs of you, if you don't go. And now you talk of Gallants, blefs us!——— What a Drefs is there! Do you think that fit for a Tradefman's Wife?

Mrs. Britt. No;——— but I think it fit for Sir *Peter Pride's* Daughter, fuch as I am. I warrant you'd have me go abroad like one, that fells Butter and Eggs——— Or like one that cries, Come buy my dainty fine pickled Cucumbers: No, no, I'm refolv'd to drefs——— put on all the Airs I can——— go

abroad

abroad——— fee and be feen——— take my Fill of
Pleafure, and not be fhut up in a Nunnery, to pine
and figh, and wafte my youthful Days in fruitlefs
Wifhes: No, I'm not fo weary of my Life yet, tho'
you do all you can to make me fo. And I would
have you to know, tho you have forc'd me to wed
my felf with old Age and ill Humours, I am not wedded to my Grave!——'tis time enough forty Years
hence to think of that, and I have a great deal to do
before that time comes; therefore I muft, and I will
go abroad.

Britt. Stir one Step if you dare   (*Spits in his Fift.*
If you go to that, I'll try who wears the Breeches,
you or I. You fhall ftay at home, and keep me
Company; I'll fpoil your going to Plays, your Ap-
pointments, and your Intriegues——— I'll make you
know, that I am your Husband, and that you fhall do
what I pleafe. Slife, What's here to do! What,
have you forgot your Marriage Vows already? Pray,
who am I? Am I not your Husband? Are you not
married to me?

Mrs. Britt. No——— You forc'd me; I never gave
you my Confent in Word or in Deed. Could you
think I was in Love with Avarice, with Age and Im-
potence?

Britt. Give me Patience! How! How!

Mrs. Britt. No, you bafely bought me of my Father and Mother.

Britt. Would I could fell thee again.

Mrs. Britt. Like a Slave you bought me, and fo
you intend to ufe me, were I Fool enough, but I'll fee
you hang'd firft.

Britt. Why, what will your fweet Ladyfhip do? I
bought you, you fay?

Mrs. Britt. Yes; Had you my Confent? or did
you once ask it? Or if you had, my Affections were
plac'd elfewhere, and fo they fhall remain.

In

In fpight of all your Threats and boafted Power ! I'll not be us'd at this Rate!

Britt. Good lack !

Mrs. Britt. I that am a Gentlewoman, defcended from the worfhipful Family of the *Pride's* by the Father's fide ————

Britt. Ay, fo 'tis a fign by your Drefs. *Pride's,* quotha !

Mrs. Britt. And a Gentlewoman defcended from the Honourable Family of the *Laycock's* by the Mother's fide. *(She Cries.*

And to be us'd at this Rate by an old nafty Shopkeeper !

I might have married a Merchant, and have kept my Glafs Coach, my tall Footmen in fine Liveries, have gone abroad when I pleas'd without Controul, vifited Quality, nay, took Place of 'em at the Play-houfe, and met with Refpeft from the beft ; and is it come to this ? But I'll to my honourable Father and Mother, and tell 'em all, who, I'm fure, won't fuffer their Daughter to be thus abus'd. *(Cries ftill.*

I cannot, nor will not endure it any longer. *(Exit.*

Britt. This 'tis for a Tradefman to marry a Gentlewoman. A Curfe on fuch Gentility ! What fhall I do ? I fhall be damnably plagu'd with her Father and Mother. Well, next Month I muft take up in *Bedlam* ; a Judgment, which every Citizen deferves, that marries above his Quality. *(Exit.*

ACT

ACT III.

SCENE, *A Street before a Glafs-Shop.*

Enter Brittle *Solus.*

WEll! What a Plague 'tis to be married!
I muſt incorporate with one above my Quality too, and not be content with ſomething in my
own Sphere, like one that had a Mind to live in
Peace and Quietneſs, but nothing would ſerve me
but a Gentlewoman, altho I took her with never a
Tatter to her Back, forſooth ; and now, I think, I'm
fitted with a Vengeance. Would I were but fairly
rid of her, and her Gentility once, the Devil ſhould
take all ſuch Gentility before I'd ever concern my ſelf
with it again. But who have we here ?

Enter Clodpole *as out of* Brittle's *Houſe, looking about*
him as afraid to be ſeen.

Clod. Huſh !—— Softly !—— Mum—— No body
ſees—— Ha, ha, ha—— No body ſees! Softly !—
Ods my Life, who's that ?— Mum ! —— Not a
Word.—— (*Is ſtealing off.*
Britt. Friend, hiſt—— Friend—— Pray ſtay a lit-
tle ; What Buſineſs might you have in that Houſe ?
Clod. Wou'd you know now ? Softly !—— Not a
Word. Ha, ha, ha, you underſtand me.
Britt. But you muſt know———
Clod. Yes, yes, I do know already, but am not
ſuch a Fool to tell you. You ſhan't get a Word out
of me. You underſtand me.

Britt.

Britt. Yes, very well, but————

Clod. Softly!—— not a Word.

Britt. I know that ; but who was you to fpeak with in that Houfe?

Clod. Softly!—— Can no body hear? For you muft know, the old Cuckold of that Houfe, they fay, is damnably given to be jealous ; I would not for ne'er fo much he fhould fee me.

Britt. No, no, I'll warrant you.

Clod. You muft not fay any thing——

Britt. No, no, not a Word.

Clod. His Wife's a main pretty fmirking Rogue, as a Man would wifh to lay his Leg o'er. Softly!—— Is no body coming?

Britt. I'll warrant thee—— Prithee go on.

Clod. What? you want to know all, do you? But I'll not truft you. Mum! not a Word. You underftand me.

Britt. Yes, yes, I underftand you well enough—but you may truft me, I fhan't fay a Word.

Clod. Why luck now!—— Ha, ha, ha, Wou'd you, would you? But you fhall get nothing out of me. I'll warrant you'd have me tell you now, that I brought a Letter to the Gentlewoman of that Houfe—

Britt. Hum!

Clod. And that I deliver'd it to none but her felf—as I was order'd——

Britt. So.

Clod. You underftand me?

Britt. Yes, yes, perfectly well.

Clod. And that I ftay'd for an Anfwer——

Britt. Well, and I hope you got one?

Clod. Mum! not a Syllable! no body muft know!— If it fhould come to the Knowledge of the Cuckold her Husband, 'twill fpoil all.

Britt. Oh never fear.

C

Clod.

Clod. You'll fay nothing of what I have told you?

Britt. No, no, not a Word.

Clod. For you muft know, Mr. *Lovemore* charg'd me, when he fent me, to fay never a Word.

Britt. Is the Gentleman's Name *Lovemore,* fay you?

Clod. Why, do you know him?

Britt. Oh, very well; a tall, proper, handfome Man, and always very generous.

Clod. The fame, the fame.

Britt. And lives juft——

Clod. At the lower end of this Street on t'other fide of the way, over againft the *Golden Ball.* I find you do know him.

Britt. Know him! Why he's my very good Friend. A Pox of all fuch Friendfhip. 　　　　(*Afide.*

Clod. Odd, he's a fine Gentleman as ever I met with in all my Life.

Brit. Yes, yes, he's a very fine Gentleman indeed. I wou'd the Devil Had him. 　　　　(*Afide.*

Clod. He gave me this Piece of Gold to carry a Letter for him, which I deliver'd to the Gentlewoman of that Houfe but now.

Britt. Oh, he's a very civil Gentleman; I have been long acquainted with him. Well, and what Anfwer did you get A very pleafing one, I'll warrant you.

Clod. Softly, you muft not tell a Syllable of this to the Husband, nor that fhe'll fend my Mafter an Anfwer, as foon as ever fhe can get the Cuckold out of the way. But no body muft know. You underftand me.

Britt. Oh, I'll keep your Counfel, never fear.

Clod. She bad me tell him, fhe'd meet him this Evening, if fhe can.

Britt. Ay.

Clod.

Clod. And that she's very sensibly ob—ob—obliged to him, for his Kindness to her.

Britt. Ay, no doubt on't.

Clod. And takes it mighty kind of him.

Britt. She does.

Clod. Odd, she's a pretty Bit ; and then there's a handsome Maid that waits upon her, and is Assistant to her in these Matters, one *Dam—Damaris*, I think they call her.

Britt. Ay, like enough.

Clod. And you must know I like her hugely. She gave me Two or Three such loving Looks, that I am half persuaded she likes me. So that if my Master gets acquainted with the Mistress, I intend to strike in with her Maid.

Britt. Oh, all but Reason.

Clod. But no body must know of it.
You understand me.
Well, good bye to you. My Master will wonder I stay so long. Be sure you say nothing now.
You understand me. (*Exit.*

Britt. Yes, yes, I do so ; farewel.
Well, *Barnaby Brittle*, now thou see'st what comes of marrying of a Gentlewoman. I believe thou wilt be married to something else in a little time, if thou art not so already. (*Points to his Head.*

Enter Sir Peter Pride *and Lady* Pride.

Sir Pet. You seem disorder'd, Son-in-law.

Britt. And I have Reason to be so, if ever any Man had. (*Walks to and fro in a hurry.*

Lady. Good lack! And why so short, Son-in-law ?

Britt. I shall grow taller in a little. time, Good Mother-in-law, if this Trade holds.(*Points to his Head.*

Sir Peter. Explain your Meaning, Son-in-law.

Britt. 'Twill explain it self shortly. (*Walks up and down.*

Lady

Lady. What, is that Hat of yours nail'd on ? Do you know who we are ? And the Refpect due to Perfons of our Quality, good Son-in-law ?

Britt. Ah ! wou'd I did not ; but now I know to my Sorrow, fince you will have me fpeak, good Mother-in-law.

Lady. Will you never leave that faucy Word, of calling me Mother-in-law ?

Britt. Good Lord ! Why what muft I call you then ?

Lady. You ought to fay, Madam and Sir, when you fpeak to us ; or when you fpeak of us, you fhould fay, Sir *Peter*, and her Ladyfhip : For tho' you have married our Daughter, yet there is a great deal of diftinction betwixt you and Perfons of our Rank and Quality.

Sir *Peter.* Go to, it is enough for me to let him know his Duty, without your Inftructions. Sure, I beft know my felf what to do. Son-in-law, you are an impudent Fellow to ufe us at this rate. How often muft we put you in mind of your Duty and Refpect, e'er you'll know it ? Hence-forward learn to behave your felf as you ought, or you fhall hear on't in other fort of Terms. You muft not think becaufe you've married our Daughter, that we will be fatisfied with fuch indifferent Ceremonies and Duty you might have paid, had you married one equal with your felf; nor ought you indeed to fay, your Wife, when you fpeak of our Daughter.

Britt. Good lack !——— Is not your Daughter my Wife ?

Sir *Peter.* She is.——— But you ought not to call her fo.

Britt. I know that too well, now 'tis too late. I'd give a thoufand Pounds fhe were not my Wife.

Sir *Peter.* At it again ? I tell you, tho' you have married her, yet as fhe is our Daughter, you muft not treat her after that familiar way.   *Britt*

Britt. You make me mad —— Is not my Wife my Wife?

Sir *Peter.* I tell you, tho' fhe be your Wife, you muft not call her fo. When you fpeak of her, as being our Daughter, you muft fay, Madam.

Britt. Well, Madam, then fince it muft be Madam, I did not care if fhe were a Dutchefs, fo I were but fairly rid of her.

Here's fuch a ftir about your Gentility, and your Honour: But I believe if I had not married your Daughter, and with my good Money redeem'd your Eftate, your Gentility had been left in the Mud—— for all your great Families, and your nice Honour.

Sir *Peter.* Then do you think it no Honour to be ally'd to the Worfhipful Family of the *Pride's.*

Lady. And to the Honourable Family of the *Laycock's?* Go, Clown. 'Tis a Shame our Daughter fhould be wedded to fuch a Brute. We have been told at what a rate you treat her. What is the Reafon of it, Son-in law?

Britt. Why, you fhall know, good Mother-in law.

Lady. Again at that affronting way! How often have you been told to fay, Madam?

Britt: Well, Madam, then: I always forget thefe fine Words. But, Madam, if you wou'd pleafe, Madam, to hear me fpeak, you fhall know, Madam, whether I have not Caufe to wifh, I never had feen my Wi—— your Daughter, Madam, if I muft call her nothing elfe.

Sir *Peter.* Well, Sir, proceed.

Britt. Why, in the firft Place, I am in a fair way to be made a Cuckold, if I am not one already.

Sir *Peter.* How, Son-in-law? Have a Care what you fay.

Britt. Believe me, what I fay, I can make appear.

Sir *Peter.* Do it then prefently.

C 3 *Britt.*

Britt. Why, fhe has juft now receiv'd a Letter from her Gallant, and made an Appointment to meet him this Evening ; and judge how fmall a time a Pair of Horns are a grafting.

Sir *Peter.* How came you to know this, Son-in-law ?

Britt. Why, juft now——— I caught the Fellow, that brought her the Letter, coming out of my Houfe, and not knowing who I was, I got out of him all the Bufinefs ; and that his Mafter, Mr. *Lovemore*——

Sir *Peter.* Is that the Gentleman's Name ?

Britt. Yes, fo his Man told me. I have often feen him taking a View about my Houfe, and looking up to the Windows ; and 'tis plain what his Defigns were.

Lady. If this be true, I'll tear her Eyes out.

Sir *Peter.* Nay, if it be, this good Sword (never yet drawn in vain) fhall do you Right.
Where is fhe, Son-in-law.

Britt. Within, I'll warrant, ftudying what Excufe to make, to get abroad, and meet her Gallant.

Lady. I'll call her to anfwer for her felf.
Be fure you wrong her not, Son-in-law.   (*Exit Lady.*

Britt. Nay, nay, I make no doubt but fhe is to be believ'd before me ; and fhe ne'er wants Cunning to bring her felf off, I'll fay that for her, tho' the Cafe be ne'er fo plain.

Sir *Peter.* By this good Light, if fhe dares be falfe to her Marriage Vows, fhe dies ; and that bafe Rifler of her Fame fhall bear her Company.

Britt. Oh! Here he comes ; that Spoiler of **my** Honour ; that's he.

Enter Lovemore. *Sir* Peter *meets him. They ftare each other i'th' Face.*

Sir *Peter.* Do you know who I am, Sir ?

Love. I don't well remember I ever had much Ac-quaintance with you.   Sir

Sir *Peter*. I am call'd Sir *Peter Pride*.

Love. It may be fo : I've heard of you, Sir.

Sir *Peter*. My Family, Sir, has ftood thefe many Years with unblemifh'd Fame and Honour.

Love. Very likely, Sir

Sir *Peter*. How far you have endeavour'd to ftain that fpotlefs Fame, be judge your felf.

Love. Pray, Sir, explain this Riddle.

Sir *Peter*. I have a Daughter young, fair, well-bred, has Senfe; fhe is indeed the Wonder of her Sex, and this Man, whom you fee here, has the Honour to be married to her.

Britt. Ah ! 'Tis an Honour, that I cou'd have fpar'd.
(Afide.

Sir *Peter*. Now, Sir, I'm told, that you endeavour to corrupt her Honour, and defile her Marriage-Bed. Sir, I have had the Honour to command abroad, and with Succefs, both to my King and my Country——— As have alfo the Chief Part of all our great Race ; even from *William the Conqueror*, to this prefent Reign, have our unqueftion'd Glories ftood a Pattern to our yet rifing Fame : And he who dares prefume to rob us of that precious Jewel, Honour, muft not think to fcape unpunifh'd, tho' with the Hazard o'th' laft Drop of Blood, that is left, to wafh off the Stain. My Daughter's Honour, Sir, is as dear to me, as this vital Air, by which I breath and live.

Love. Pray Sir, who told you this?

Sir *Peter*. Believe me, Sir, whate'er I fay, I can quote my Author for it.

Love. Then who-ever told you is a Rafcal ; and were he here, I'd ram the Lie down his Throat, or make him eat a Piece of my Sword.

Sir *Peter*. Why he told me——— This Man——— Her Husband here juftified it to my Face, and faid he had Proof.

Love.

Love. How, Sir! Did you frame this abominable Falſhood ? 'Tis well you have the Honour to be ally'd to this worthy Knight, Sir *Peter Pride*, here ; or you ſhould know what it is to father ſuch a Lie upon a Man of my Reputation.

Sir *Peter.* Oh ! Here comes my Daughter.

Enter Lady Pride, *Mrs.* Brittle, *and* Damaris.

Love. Did you, Madam, tell your Husband a ſtrange Story, that I ſhould make Love to you, and endeavour'd to corrupt your Honour ?

Mrs. Britt. I tell him ! Why, when did you make Love to me, Sir ? I aſſure you, had you let me know of your Paſſion, it ſhou'd not have gone unrewarded. Pray, next time you ſend, let it be one that knows how to take more Care. However, you have no great Reaſon to deſpair ; for ſince he complains without any manner of Reaſon, I am reſolv'd he ſhall have Cauſe. Therefore if you do love me, Sir, pray let me know it, and I do aſſure you, you ſhall not want Encouragement. He ſhall not uſe me at this rate for nothing.

Love. Madam, believe me, 'tis all a Riddle to me ; for, till this Hour, I never heard any thing mention'd like it : I am an abſolute Stranger to it.

Lady. Do you hear that, you Clown? Are you not aſham'd to abuſe a Gentlewoman continually, without any Cauſe ?

Sir *Peter.* What is the Meaning of this, Son-in-law ?

Britt. Pray, do but hear me.

Sir *Peter.* Troth, Son-in law, you are a very impudent Fellow.

Britt. Hear me but ſpeak ?

Sir *Peter.* You ſhall not ſpeak. We have heard too much already.

Mrs.

Mrs. Britt. I am sure *Damaris* knows, I never have any body comes near me, but such as himself; nor ever receiv'd any Message, either by Letter, or otherwise——

I never committed any Crime against him, that I know of, unless sitting by my self all Day, and poring over two or three good Books be an Offence. Speak, *Damaris*, did I ever give him any Cause for these Suspicions, and this Usage? Thou know'st all I say or do.

Damaris. Madam, I know no Reason; nor can I bear to see the Hardship you endure! Like a barbarous Man as he is—— To abuse so good a Lady! so Virtuous, so Innocent, and so Pious a Lady! I am sure it makes me weep to think on't—— I am afraid he'll break her Heart in a little time, if——
                                    (*Weeps.*

Britt. Hold your Tongue, you Jade, or I'll make you feel my double Fist. You are not a Gentlewoman——

I may do what I please with you.

Mrs. Britt. Oh, my dear Father!   (*Cries.*
I am not able to endure this any longer.
Never was any Woman abus'd as I am.
I beg you will do me Justice, for I can bear it no longer.   (*Exit crying.*

Lady. *Damaris*, let's follow her, and endeavour to comfort her. Oh, thou Clown, to use a Gentlewoman with so much Cruelty!

Dam. I fear he'll be the Death of her at one time or another.   (*Exeunt Lady* Pride *and* Damaris.

Sir *Peter.* What do you think of all this, Sir? Are not you a very pretty Fellow? Come hither, Son-in-law, ask this Gentleman Pardon, for the Affront you have put upon him in belying of him.

Britt. How! ask his Pardon, that would have made me a Cuckold?

                                            Love

Love. Sir *Peter*, pray——

Sir *Peter.* I fay no more Words : He has wrong'd a Gentleman ; and the leaft he can do, is begging Pardon.

Britt. 'Tis very well ! He offends, and I muft ask Pardon.

Sir *Peter.* No matter for that, you hear he denies it ; and 'tis enough, if a Gentleman unfays what he has faid.

Britt. So that if I catch him making me a Cuckold, and he denies it, I muft not believe it, becaufe a Gentleman faid it.

Sir *Peter.* I fay, you fhall ask Pardon : Therefore no more Words, but do't

Britt. I fhall run mad.
Well, what muft I do ?

Sir *Peter.* Come hither : Take your Hat off——Kneel down, and fay after me.

Britt. Well, fince it muft be fo——   (*Kneels.*
This 'tis to be marry'd to a Gentlewoman, forfooth.

Sir *Peter.* Sir, I ask your Pardon.

Britt. Sir, I ask your Pardon.   (*In the fame Tone.*

Sir *Peter.* For the Affront I have put upon you.

Britt. For the Affront I have put upon you.

Sir *Peter.* By falfly accufing you——

Britt. How ! falfely accufing him !

Sir *Peter.* I fay no more Words.   Say after me.

Britt. Say after me.

Sir *Peter.* Accufing you, of having a Defign to corrupt my Wife's Honour.

Britt. Accufing you of Truth——— And having a Defign to corrupt my Wife's Honour.

Sir *Peter.* For which, knowing my felf in the wrong, I do ask your Pardon.

Britt. For which, knowing my felf not in the wrong, I'm forc'd to ask your Pardon.

Love.

Love. Well, Sir, upon Sir *Peter Pride*'s Account I am content to pafs it by this time : But let me hear no more Complaints. (Brittle *rifes, and runs off*

Sir Peter. Sir, now all is well, I humbly take my Leave. (*Exit Sir* Peter.

Love. Was there ever fuch a lucky Rogue as I? For her to encourage me to make Love to her before her Husband's Face !
Nay, and before her Father and Mother too!
Oh, I am all on Fire till I have her in my Arms!
But foft ! who comes here?

Enter Prudence.

Well, my little Scout, what News ? How fares my Friend ? Is *Philadelphia* kind? Where's thy Lady ?

Pru. Where e'er her Perfon is, I'm fure her beft Thoughts are ftill employ'd on you. And however fhe may pretend a Paffion for Mr. *Cuningham,* fhe loves none but you. Pray, Sir, do but try her.

Love. Oh racking Thought ! I'd rather make Love to a Convocation of Cats at a Witch's Up-fitting, than but fpeak to her. Where's my Friend ? Oh ! here he comes, and his fair Confort.

Enter Cuningham *and* Philadelphia.

Cun. Be not fo cruel to fay, you want the Power: If we negleft this Opportunity, which kindly prefents it felf, the next perhaps may not be ours.

Phil. Would you then have me difpofe of my felf without my Aunt's Confent ? Do not urge me to that, fince I have promifed not to wed without it.

Cun. I ask not her Confent, but yours: Grant me but that, and leave the reft to Time and Chance.

Pru. Madam, how can you deny him that, fince I know you love him?

Cun.

Cun. Ha! Oh, the charming Sound !
And will you not confent to make me happy ?
Or do you not believe I love you ?
By all thofe Fires that burn within my Soul, I
fwear———

Pru. Hold ! Hold, Sir ! You have fworn enough
already to corrupt a whole Nunnery of Sighing,
Praying and Wifhing young Votaries. Why don't you
give him your Hand, fince he has your Heart. I believe you love to hear him fwear and—— Give him
your Hand, or, I'll difcover all.

Phil. Well, there 'tis then ;   (*Gives her Hand to*
                                                         Cuningham.
But I promife nothing elfe. I fear I have given too
much already.

Cun. Oh, never! never! I'll pay thee back fo vaft
a ftore of Love and Conftancy, as fhall weary thee
with ftill receiving.

Pru. Madam, Madam, your Aunt's behind you.

Enter Widow.

Phil. Ha! My 'Aunt ! What fhall I do ?

Cun. Fear nothing, Madam, but give me your
Hand.
I'll bring all off.   (*Pretends to tell her Fortune.*
This Line feems to Point out fome unexpected Crofs :
And this Line thwarting the Line of Life, fignifies a
retir'd Life ; and this joining with it, fhews you'll
be in Danger of ending the latter part of your Days
in a Nunnery.   (*Widow behind them.*

Widow. How, Mr. *Cuningham* ! Can you tell Fortunes ?

Cun. I underftand a little Palmiftry, Madam, and
can give a Ghefs at Phyfiognomy.

Widow. 'Tis very well.
When I enter'd firft, I thought you had been making
                                                              Love

Love to my Neice : I am glad to find it otherwife.
But where's the Vifcount?

Pru. In the next Room, Madam.

Love. I'll wait upon him : I'd feign try whether
his Infide be anfwerable to his outward Appearance.
(*Is going.*

Cun. Nay, prithee ftay; I can affure you, he is
not to be equall'd either in Perfon or Difcourfe.

Pru. He is indeed a fine proper Man, as one would
wifh to fee.

Widow. Why, really his Lordfhip has Parts.

Phil. You and *Prudence* go find him out, and
bear him Company awhile; I'll wait on him immediately, tell him. You, Sir, may go with 'em, if
you pleafe.   (*To* Lovemore.

Love. Madam, moft willingly.

Cun. 'Sdeath! You won't leave me?   (*Afide to*
Lovemore.

Love. Faith, but I will; doft think I'll ftay to en-
dure a fecond Hell? For if there be one upon Earth,
'tis being left alone with her.
Madam, Your Ladyfhip fhall ever command me. (*To*
the Widow.
Come, Lady, if you pleafe, the Honour of your fair
Hand.   (*To* Phil.
(*Exit with* Phil. *and* Pru.

Cun. What will become of me now?   (*Afide.*

Widow. Well, Mr. *Cuningham*, I have long'd for fome
time to be alone with you, that I might fpeak more
freely to you.

Cun. Madam, 'tis too great an Honour.

Widow. I wonder, Sir, you never think of Marrying?

Cun. Madam, as yet I dare not think on't.

Widow. Oh, dear Sir! Pray, why fo?

Cun. Becaufe I have not well confider'd it; and I
have been told, 'tis a dangerous Undertaking, without
having well thought before-hand.   *Widow.*

Widow. Pray, Sir, why should you think so ?
I'll vow 'tis an odd Thought, Sir, for one of your Underſtanding : Why, Sir, I'll tell you.
I have had Three Husbands, and yet I have no great Reaſon to complain : Tho' in my laſt Husband's time, I had not altogether that real Satisfaction, as I had with the other Two; for to deal freely with you, Sir, my Husband Sir *Oliver Laycock*, though he was a very well-bred Man, yet he had his Humours ſometimes, and would be a little given to Jealouſy, ſo that I ſeldom led a quiet Hour when the Fit was upon him. But in my firſt Husband's Days, ſure never Woman liv'd ſo happy! I would not a been unmarried to have had all the Riches of the Earth laid at my Feet : But when I married with Sir *Oliver*, and had once ſeen his Temper, nothing I had in the World but what I would a given to a been free again ; and indeed in my Paſſion I often vow'd never (if pleaſe Heav'n Sir *Oliver* died) to marry any more.

Cun. 'Twas raſhly done.
But no doubt, were there that Man fitting to merit your Favour, and equally deſerving your Perſon and your Eſtate, and one whom your Ladyſhip could like, you might perhaps be perſuaded to break your Vow, and venture once again.

Widow. I'll ſwear I hardly think it, and yet one don't know how one may be tempted ; tho' if I were to be perſuaded, (and I will not forſwear any thing) I know not any one, that can ſo ſoon perſuade me to it as you, Mr. *Cuningham*.

Cun. Death and the Devil ! What have I brought upon my ſelf !   *(Aſide.*
Oh Madam ! You make me bluſh.
But Madam ! How cou'd you with Honour put off the Viſcount, who you know loves you, and is come on purpoſe to marry you ?

Wid.

Wid. Why, I intend him for my Niece you muſt know, who no doubt will be much better pleas'd with the Change. For, to ſay Truth, Mr. *Cuningham,* I have always had more, than a common Eſteem for you, and for your Behaviour ; and have long ſince reſolv'd, that if I do alter my Condition, you are the Man alone I have plac'd my Thoughts upon.

Cun. You make me bluſh, Madam. Wou'd I were a League under-ground, or in any Hell but this. (*Aſide.* You cannot ſure. (*To her.*

Wid. I vow 'tis true, and yet——

Cun. Hear me but ſpeak, Madam ?

Wid. 'Tis odd, that Love ſhou'd over-power People at ſo ſtrange a rate.

Cun. But I ſhould be unjuſt to my Friend, who I know loves you dearer, than his Life.

Wid. Oh dear ! Who's that I beſeech you, Sir ?

Cun. Mr. *Lovemore,* Madam.

Widow. Mr. *Lovemore !* I'll ſwear I don't believe it.

Cun. Oh Madam ! 'tis but too true, as will appear I'm afraid, when he knows you place your Affections on any other Man.

Widow. I'll vow you much ſurprize me, Mr. *Cuningham ;* but how came you to know it ?

Cun. Oft has he begg'd me to bear him Company in ſome lonely Place, where he wou'd ſigh, and tell ſuch things of his diſtreſſed Paſſion, as wou'd have mov'd the moſt obdurate Heart ; and when I ask'd him, why he did not acquaint your Ladyſhip with his Love, he would ſigh, with Arms a-croſs, as if his Heart would force its way through his Breaſt, and cry, Oh that's my Grief, my Friend, I cannot—— dare not tell her ! for ſhould I attempt it once, and meet her ſcorn, (for oh ! thou know'ſt her Vow) I ſhou'd be for ever loſt.

Then

Then ran o'er a thoufand Tales of Love, fo foft, fo moving, and how he priz'd you, that cannot be exprefs'd by any, except one, who loves like him.

Widow. Truly, Sir, if it be fo———

Cun. If it be fo! were your Ladyfhip to obferve his diftracted Throes, you'd pity him.

Widow. But why fhould he not declare it to me?

Cun. That's what I tell him, Madam; Urging that your Ladyfhip——— But mum! who have we here?

Euter Vifcount, Philadelphia *and* Prudence.

Vifc. Ha! Whifpering! And fo clofe! I like it not.

Widow. The Vifcount! this is unlucky. He looks difturb'd! Good Sir, fome other time we'll end this Difcourfe.   (*to* Cuningham.

Vifc. Ha! What are you, Sir? that thus dares to encroach upon my Territories, and invade my Right?

Widow. Nay, pray my Lord, be not difpleas'd. This Gentleman, you muft know, has a Law fuit depending, and is come to entreat a Line of Commendation from me to my Lawyer.

Vifc. Enough; I do believe all you can fay. Ah! thofe Eyes of yours! What Looks are there! they enflame my very Soul.

Widow. Ah, *Prudence*, how I long to be alone with him.

Vifc. I am impatient of this Delay, when fhall we be married?

Widow. Pray moderate your Paffion, Sir.

Vifc. What, you are afraid of that melancholy Gentleman, that ftands fo filently there.

Widow. Speak foftly, I am afraid he hears you, Sir.

Vifc. What care I if he does.

4   *Enter*

Enter a Servant.

Serv. My Lord, the Dancers you fpoke for, wait without.

Vifc. Let 'em enter. Will you pleafe to fit, Ladies?

A DANCE.

Widow. *Prudence*, go tell Mr. *Lovemore*, I'd fpeak with him this Evening.   (*Exit* Prudence.

Phil.— you may take a Turn in the Garden. And, Sir, if you think it no Trouble, you may bear her Company.   (*To* Cuningham.

Cun. Madam, moft willingly.   (*Exit with* Phil.

Widow. Why are you fo melancholy, my Lord?

Vifc. Nothing that's worth the naming. But if you'll walk into the next Room, I'll tell you.

Widow. My Lord, you are a Man of Honour, and I dare truft my felf with you.

Vifc. Madam, if I deferve it not, may you always keep a Whip and a Bell, to fcourge me from you like a Cur.

ACT IV.

Enter Clodpole *and* Damaris: *He gives her a Letter.*

Dam. YOU are a fine Spark, are you not, to difcover all the Bufinefs, and let it come to my Mafter's Hearing?

Clod. Why ay, that's true, as you fay; but who wou'd have thought that he could have known it! But now to our own Bufinefs, *Damaris*——

D   Doft

Doſt thou not love me, *Damaris* ?

Thou know'ſt I love thee with all my Heart.

Good lack! How it beats !— Odd, you may hear it thump all over the Houſe.

Damaris—— How can'ſt thou be ſo hard-hearted?

Dam. Pſhaw! Prithee leave fooling.

Clod. One Kiſs, *Damaris*, to revive me.

(Kiſſes her,

Dam. Pray, *Clodpole*, be civil.

Clod. Damaris! —— Canſt thou not ſpare a little Bit afore-hand?

Dam. Of what, Fool?

Clod. Why, of—— Odd, you know well enough. What, I need not name it to thee.

Dam. I know nothing of the Matter.

Clod. Ay, but you do. Why, I ask but a little tiney, tiney Bit. Do, prithee now do.

Dam. I'll ſee you at the Devil firſt.

Clod. Do, *Damaris*— Spare but a Bit now ; and bate me as much on the Wedding-Night.

Dam. No, I thank you, good *Clodpole :* I have too often been ſnapt that way already. *(Aſide.*

But ſee— yonder comes my Lady and my Maſter — Step with me into the next Room, he muſt not ſee you,

Clod. Ay, any where, any where : Quickly, good *Damaris*. *(Exit,*

Enter Barnaby Brittle *and* Mrs. Brittle.

Britt. I tell you again, that Marriage is a very ſacred Thing, and ought not to be profan'd at this Rate.

Mrs. Britt. What do you tell me of Marriage, I have other things to mind.

Britt. Truly, I do believe as much ; that's the trueſt Word you ever ſpoke : But I think you ought to mind what I ſay. Am I not your Husband? And

are

are not you bound in Duty by that Tye, to be obedient and juft in all your Ways?

Enter Lovemore *on the other fide bowing. She fees him, and Curtefies to him.*

What's that for? What, do you banter me?

Mrs. Britt. Keep your Inftructions for thofe that want 'em, my Thoughts are other ways employ'd.

(She Curtefies, Lovemore *bows.* Brittle *fees him not, and thinks fhe does it in fcorn to him.*

Britt. What, you are practifing your Airs againft you meet your Gallant, are you? And trying how to behave your felf to him? But I fhall fpoil your Defign, I fhall. *(He Bows, fhe Curtefies again.* Leave off your Tricks with a Vengeance, and mind what I fay to you. *(*Lovemore *keeps Bowing to her.* Again, don't provoke me; I fay, don't; if you do, you may chance to repent it. I fay, that Marriage———

Mrs. Britt. I know it, Dear; you need fay no more.

(She takes Brittle *round the Neck, and beckons* Lovemore, *who comes and kiffes her Hand over her Husband's Shoulders all the while.*

You know I love you dearly, by this I do. *(Kiffes him.* Why will you not be fatisfied? Had I the World to give, it cou'd not make me more happy than this Minute. *(*Lovemore *ftill kiffes her Hand.*

Britt. Ah diffembling Crocodile?

What, now you think to wheedle me.

Mrs. Britt. Be fatisfied with this: Hence forward, if you deferve it, I give you my Heart for ever, which, till this Minute, I did not think to do.

(She fpeaks to Lovemore.

Britt. Ah, would 'twere in your Power to keep your Word.

Mrs.

Mrs. Britt. Indeed,I will, let that content you ; and learn to merit that rich Jewel, which this Moment I put within your Power.

(Beckons Lovemore, *who bows, and Exit.*

Britt. If thou would'ft be thus kind always, how happy fhould I be! But that's impoffible! Would you but think fometimes upon the Vow you made in Church, that folemn Vow of Marriage, 'twould put you in Mind of your Duty.

Mrs. Britt. How can I think of any thing, when you will not give me leave fo much as to peep abroad for Air? Do you think a Woman can ever be in a good Humour, that is lock'd up, and kept from what fhe likes? But I'm refolv'd to bear it no longer.

(She walks backward and forward.

Britt. Good lack! What's your Mind chang'd already? I thought 'twas too good to laft long.

Mrs. Britt. But hence-forward you fhan't think to make a Fool of me at this rate. I'll find a way to get out, for all your Spies; and then look to't— I'll ufe you as you deferve.

Britt. Tempt me no farther, I befeech you ; if you do, I fhall ufe you as you deferve. Patience! and I have need enough of it at this time.

Mrs. Britt. I'm refolv'd to encourage every Man, that makes Love to me. I'll kifs and be wanton, fince you provoke me to't. Love, and be belov'd——— and not be fubject to the nafty Humours of an old Jealous—— I can't find a Name bad enough for thee.

(He fpits in his Hand.

Britt. Odd, I've a great Mind to fpoil that handfome Face. The Devil tempts me ftrangely : I muft be gone ; for if I ftay, I fhall certainly be provok'd to do her a Mifchief. *(Runs off.*

4

Enter

Enter Damaris *with a Letter.*

Dam. I waited till my Mafter was gone, to deliver you this Letter ; Madam, Mr. *Lovemore's* Man is within, and waits for an Anfwer.

Mrs. Britt. Give it me, *Damaris,* quickly.

Dam. I need not bid you read it, fince you know from whom it comes.

Mrs. Britt. Oh ! 'tis extremely pretty, *Damaris* I'll in, and write an Anfwer prefently. *(Exit.*

Dam. So fhe has fnapt the Bait at the firft Angling ; how fhe'll get clear of the Hook, I know not. Ha ' he's here himfelf !

Enter Lovemore *and* Clodpole.

Love. Pretty Mrs. *Damaris,* I'm glad to fee you. Is your Lady within ?

Dam. Yes, Sir, writing an Anfwer to your Letter, I fuppofe. You fee, I deliver'd it with Care.

Love. Oh, I underftand you ; there's for thy Pains.
*(Gives her Money, fhe puts her Hand behind her,
and takes it.*

Dam. Oh, dear Sir, by no means. But fince you will have it fo, pray command me.

Love. Can'ft thou contrive to let me fpeak with thy Miftrefs ?

Dam. If you pleafe, Sir, I'll fhew you to her.

Love. Thou wilt oblige me for ever.
(Exit Love. *and* Dam.

Clod. Hift ! *Damaris !——* Odd, I fhall have a rare Wife of her, if fhe gets Money fo faft. Here's a piece of Gold got without the leaft Trouble, as they fay. But foftly !—— Who have we here ?

Enter Brittle.

Oh! are you there, Mr. *Babbler?* You are a pretty
Fellow indeed ; you have made fine Work ! You cannot be told a Secret, but you muſt tell the Husband
preſently.   You underſtand me.

Britt. Who, I tell the Husband, Friend !

Clod. Yes, you ; but I'll ſee you hang'd before you
ſhall get any thing more out of me.   You have made
fine Work ! All's diſcover'd !——— The Cuckold, her
Husband, knows all the Buſineſs.

Britt. Well, but———

Clod. You may as well hold your Tongue, for you
ſhan't get a Word out of me.

No, no, I have found you out, I'faith.

Britt. This Fellow may be uſeful to affirm it to
her Father and Mother. I'll try to bribe him. *(Aſide.*

(Puts his Hand in his Pocket to give him Money.
Why look you, Friend, I'm ſorry this Matter is———

Clod. Mum ! You underſtand me.

I know what you'd ſay now, but 'twill not do. You'd
have me to tell you what I know, but Mum !———
Softly !——— Not a Word. I'll warrant, you'd have
me tell you what Anſwer ſhe gave to the Letter.

Britt. No, no, Friend ; but———

Clod. Softly ! ——— You ſhall get nothing out of
me.   You think I'll tell you now, that the Wife pro.
mis'd to meet him, and that they are together now
in that Room ; but I'm not ſuch a Fool. No, no,
you'll tell the Husband again ; you cannot be ſecret,
and ſo good bye to you. You ſhall get nothing out
of me.   You underſtand me.   *(Exit.*

Britt. I'm ſorry I can't make that uſe of him as I
intended ; but however, he has diſcover'd ſomething
to me, that may do as well. He ſaid her Gallant is
with her now ; I'll liſten.   *(Goes to the Door.*

Oh Sadnefs ! 'tis but too true. Here's fine Doings. But I'll fend for her Parents. Now they fhall fee who's in the wrong, and who's in the right. She can't fcape me now, unlefs the Devil affift her ; and fee where they come in a lucky Hour.

Enter Sir Peter Pride *and Lady* P.

Father-in-law, you're welcome ; and you, Madam. I'm glad you are come, I was juft going to fend for you.

Sir Peter. Why, what's the Matter, Son-in-law ?

Britt. Now you fee what a fine Daughter you have.

Sir Peter. What ! more Complaints? What is the Reafon of all this ?

Britt. Do but hear me, and you fhall know. Here has been her Gallant, and———

Sir Peter. Son-in-law, I'll not believe it. Will you never leave this fooling ? We'll hear no more.

Britt. No, no ; I knew you wou'd never believe a Word I fay ; but fhe can be credited, becaufe fhe's a Gentlewoman, forfooth. Now you fhall fee what a Gentlewoman I have got for a Wife. I have her faft now, faft in that Room with her Gallant, and that I hope will convince you.

Lady. 'Tis falfe, thou bafe Villain. I know fhe fcorns to do fo bafe a thing.

Britt. Pray now don't believe me, but walk in : If you find it not true, never mind any thing I fay, as long as I live.

Sir Peter. Lead, Son-in law. If I find 'em together, by this good Sword they both fhall die.

Lady. But if 'tis not fo, which I do believe 'tis only your Jealoufy again, look to your felf, Son-in-law, I'll fuffer thefe Affronts no longer.

Britt.

Britt. If they are not there now, I am a very Villain.

Come along———— Softly————   (*They all go in.*)

SCENE *Changes to a Chamber, and discovers* Lovemore, *Mrs.* Brittle, *and* Damaris.

Love. You queſtion your own Power, when you miſtruſt my Honour, Madam. Such Charms can never want Force to allay all Thoughts of wronging ſo much Goodneſs.

Mrs. Britt. Well, Sir, I do believe you to be a Man of Honour, and hope you will not wrong my good Opinion.

Enter Sir Peter, *Lady* Pride *and* Brittle, *behind them. They grow enrag'd to ſee 'em together, and make Signs of Revenge. Sir* Peter *lays his Hand upon his Sword.*

Therefore meet me this Evening at the Garden-Door about Nine, and there we'll diſcourſe farther : If I find what you ſay be real, perhaps I may be prevail'd upon to venture farther.

Love. Madam, you b eſs me !   (*Kiſſes her Hand.*)

Britt. Have a little Patience———

Let's draw nearer, and hear what they ſay.
                                    (*They go nearer.*)

Dam. Oh Madam ! Madam ! my Maſter, Sir *Peter,* and my Lady, are juſt behind you.

Mrs. Britt. Ha ! undone for ever !

Love. What will become of me then ?

Mrs. Britt. Let me alone to bring it off.
                                    (*To* Love. *Aſide.*)

Be not you ſurpriz'd at any thing I ſay, but ſeem to humour it.   I'll

I'll hear no more. (*Seems to be angry with* Lovemore. What do you tell me of your being amaz'd ! Did you ever fee any thing in me, that cou'd encourage you to believe I was that Woman you took me for ? I'll warrant you thought, becaufe I feem'd to give you Encouragement before my Husband Yefterday, when he had enrag'd me, that I was in earneft ?

(*They over-hear, feem angry, and to threaten* Brittle, *who pretends by Signs to excufe himfelf.*

Love. What mean you, Madam ?   (*Confufedly.*

Mrs. Britt. But you will find your felf deceiv'd : For tho' my Husband gives me Provocations to ufe him at any rate, yet, Sir, I'd have you to know, I fcorn Revenge ; and will not be brib'd to ftain my Honour, tho' all the Wealth of the whole World were laid at my Feet.

Lady. Do you hear that, Son-in-law ?
          They ftill threaten, he looks fneakingly.

Mrs. Britt. No, Sir, my honourable Parents brought me up with the ftricteft Care ; taught me the nice Paths that lead to Everlafting Fame and Glory : And he, who dares attempt to make me lofe my Way, de-ferves to be us'd thus, thus, and thus, Sir.

(*Gets near Sir* Peter, *fnatches his Cane, and runs at* Lovemore, *who gets behind* Brittle. *She beats* Brittle *unmercifully, while* Lovemore *gets off.*

Britt. Oh, Hold ! Hold ! What, will you murder me ?   (Brittle *rubs his Shoulders.*

Sir *Peter.* Troth, Son-in-law, fhe ferv'd you right.

Lady. You have not half what you deferve ;
And I cou'd find in my Heart to——

Sir *Peter.* Let him alone : I'll correct him. Son-in-law, You are a very impudent Fellow to ufe your Wife thus. What can you fay for your felf ?   (*Feels his Arms and Head.*

Britt. Say for my felf ! Why, I fay, 'tis all a Trick—And a Contrivance to blind the Matter.

Sir

Sir Peter. Is it not plain, you have wrong'd her?
Do you not fee fhe is a virtuous and a good Wife?

Lady. Too good for him, a Clown.

Britt. Well, well, I am over each'd, I fee.

Sir Peter. Son-in-law, I charge you let me hear
no more of this. And inftantly ask your Wife's
Pardon.

Britt. How, Sir!

Mrs. Britt. Oh! let him alone; 'twill be to no
purpofe.
I'm a little out of Order.
Damaris, Lead me to my Chamber.

                (Exeunt with Damaris.

Sir Peter. I fay follow her, and ask her Pardon.

Britt. If I do, the Curfe of Cuckoldom fall upon
me.   *(Runs out another way.*

Lady. Ah, gracelefs Clown.
Come, Sir *Peter,* let's follow, and fee how fhe does.

                  (Are going.

      Enter Prudence.

Pru. Madam, my Lady prefents her Service to
your Ladyfhip and Sir *Peter* ; and would defire your
good Company at a Ball the Vifcount treats her with.

Lady. Our humble Thanks to her Ladyfhip.
We will not fail to wait upon her.

          (Exeunt Sir Peter *and Lady.*

    Enter Widow, meeting Lovemore.

Widow. Oh, Mr. *Lovemore!* I have expeled you;
I am glad you're come.

Love. Madam, Your Ladyfhip does me too much
Honour.
Pray, Madam, when faw you Mr. *Cuningham ?*

Widow. Oh, Sir! He has told me all.
And now you talk of Mr. *Cuningham*—— *Prudence,*

                          go

go find out my Niece, and have an Eye over her.

(*Exit* Pru.

Well, Sir, I am forry you fhou'd make your felf fo great a Stranger to me. In fuch Cafes I am not ungrateful. And where Love is real, there's a double Obligation.

Love. Ha! What does fhe mean by Love and double Obligations? (*Afide.*

Widow. I fee indeed you feem to be in fome Diforder, that I fhould know it; but had you let me known it fooner, I fhou'd perhaps have fav'd you a great many Sighs and Heart-Akings, which your Bafhfulnefs has caus'd.

Love. Sure fhe's mad! [*Afide.*] Madam——

Widow. And yet 'tis never too late to ferve a Friend, and one that loves fo dearly : Nor am I yet fo far engag'd, but I can pity, nay make Return, when Love is fincere, and fo conftant.

Love. Madam, you much amaze me! Nor can I ghefs what you drive at !

Widow. Ah, dear Sir ! I know you are unwilling to let me know it : But fhall I be fincere in asking you one Queftion ?

Love. Moft freely ; fo it be not any thing that leads me farther into the dark.

Widow. Do you not love me, Sir ?

Love. Love you, Madam ! Why truly I hate no body.

Widow. Well, but love me fo, that it much difturbs you, and that you fear I am engag'd to another.

Love. The Devil take me if I ever lov'd you, or can think what you wou'd be at.

Widow. Nay, I was told you would deny it, But pray, Sir, tell me truly ; for indeed, Sir, I am forry you fhould fuffer for my Sake. And fhould you do otherwife than well, I vow it would be a Means of giving me difquiet as long as I live.

Love.

Loue. Pray, Madam, who told you this?

Widow. Your Friend Mr. *Cuningham*, who is much concern'd for you, Sir. And fince you find it is difcover'd, you need not be afham'd to own the Truth.

Enters Prudence, *and liftens.*

Love. Faith, Madam, to deal freely with you, yov're abus'd ; for hang me if ever I had a thought that way, nor do I love you, or ever can.

Widow. You're pleas'd to be merrv, Sir ; but I muft tell you, I have obferv'd it in your Looks; and fince it is fo, own it boldly to the World, and I promife you, I'll not be afham'd, nor difown mine. Come, come, Mr. *Lovemore*, you muft not deny me that ; for fince I dare own it, why fhould you think it ftill amifs ?

Love. Well ! Since all muft out, prepare to hear me.

Mr. *Cuningham* has begun, and I muft make an End.
You muft know, Madam, Mr. *Cuningham* loves you to that degree himfelf, that he's afham'd, knowing how near a-kin he is to you, to let you know it, and fo has form'd this Story upon me, the better to make for him.

Widow. Mr. *Cuningham* a-kin to me, Sir !

Love. Ay, Madam, your Nephew, your Brother's Son, whom he had in *Paris* by Madam *D'Olone*, but for fome Reafon he fince has chang'd his Name.

Widow. Truly, Sir, you furprize me much ! My Brother in *Paris* I heard had a Son, but what became of him I know not.

Love. Madam, this *Cuningham*, my Friend, has the Misfortune (Misfortune I think it, and he thinks fo too, becaufe he loves fo dearly) to be related to you.

Widow. I'm forry, if he does love fo well, that he fhou'd be fo near a-kin.

Pru. Madam, Mr. *Cuningham* is juft come in.

Love. I'll leave you, Madam, for I have a little Bufinefs that I muft difpatch—— Befides, 'twou'd not be convenient for me to interrupt what Difputes you two may have.

Widow. Sir, your Servant.

(*As he goes out, meets* Cuningham *ent'ring.*

Love. Had you no body to put your Tricks on, but me?

But I think I have been even with you. (*Exit* Love.

Cun. What can he mean?

Widow. Mr. *Cuningham*, you do not deal like a Friend by me; you might have trufted me with a Secret of greater weight.

Cun. I do not underftand you, Madam!

What has he been faying to her? (*Afide.*

Widow. You knew one Mrs. *D'Olone*, I fuppofe?

Cun. What fhall I fay now? (*Afide.*

Pru. Was your Brother then Mrs. *D'Olone*'s Husband, Madam, and Mr. *Cuningham*'s Father?

Widow. Who bid you fpeak? Yes he was. What then?

Cun. Oh, I begin to fmoke it. (*Afide.*

Pru. Nothing, Madam, but then Mr. *Cuningham* is your Nephew.

Widow. Indeed, I wifh he were not; but fince it is fo, we muft be fatisfied with our Fate, Mr. *Cuningham* Tho' you are much to blame, Sir, you did not let me know it fooner before Matters went fo far.

Cun. Madam, I confefs my Fault, and do ask your Ladyfhip's Forgivenefs.

Enter

Enter Philadelphia.

Widow. Well, Mr. *Cuningham*, fince you are my
Nephew, we may venture to embrace without a Blufh.
                                (*She embraces him.*

Phil. Is Mr. *Cuningam* your Nephew, Madam ?

Widow. Yes, Miftrefs Pert, what then ?

Phil. Then he's my Coufin, and I may embrace him
too.   (*Runs and embraces each other.*

Cun. Ay, my dear, dear Coufin.

Widow. Why how now faucy, impertinent Slut.
How dare you take this Liberty ?

Phil. Why, is there any Harm in embracing one's
own Coufin ?

Widow. Get you in, Huffy, and dare not to come
but when I call you.

Pru. He's none of your Coufin, Madam.
                          (*Afide to* Phil. *as fhe goes out.*

Phil. I know it. I met Mr. *Lovemore* laughing
by the way, who told me all. Adieu, my dear Coufin
                                            (*Exit.*

Cun. My charming Coufin, farewel.

Widow. I'll fwear, Mr. *Cuningham*, you'll fpoil
that Girl.
Methinks you embrac'd her fomething of the hardeft.
                                (*Seems difturb'd.*
I call her Girl, and yet fhe's near five and twenty—
But as I was going to tell you, Sir, You muft know,
this Brother was not indeed my own Brother, but
fomething a kin afar off : He was my firft Husband's
firft Wife's Brother, and no kin to me. But becaufe
my Husband us'd to call him Brother, I would fometimes do fo too ; and by this Means was thought, by
thofe that knew no other, to be my Brother.

Pru. Then he is not fo near a-kin, but he may
marry your Ladyfhip ?

                                        Cun.

Cun. Oh!———   (*Sighs.*
Widow. Why, truly, Mr. *Cuningham*———.

Enter Jeffrey *in haſte.*

Jeff. Sir, your Lawyer bid me tell you, your Cauſe is juſt now coming on; and if you do not appear, you'll be non ſuited.

Widow. Dear Sir, do not neglect your Buſineſs, nor let your being a kin trouble you.
When next I ſee you.

Cun. Oh, Madam! Wou'd I had never ſeen you, then I'd been happy; but where the Tye of Blood bars our Hopes, there's nothing but Deſpair in view. Madam, farewel.
Find ſome way to excuſe me, you Dog, or I'll cut your Throat.   (*To* Jeffrey *as he goes out.*

Jeff. What ſhall I ſay?   (*Aſide.*
My Maſter has begun a Lie, and I muſt end it.

Widow. Come hither, *Jeffrey.* Doſt think thy Maſter loves me ſo well as he ſays?

Jeff. Faith, Madam, I believe he loves your Ladyſhip but too well! But Mr. *Lovemore* dies, unleſs you take pity on him.

Widow. Doſt think he loves me better, than thy Maſter?

Jeff. Oh, Madam! They ought not to be nam'd together. Mr. *Lovemore*, poor Gentleman, is perfectly beſide himſelf about it.

Widow. Didſt ever hear 'em talk about me?

Jeff. A thouſand times. Mr. *Lovemore* can talk of nothing elſe.

Widow. 'Tis ſtrange he ſhould deny it to me.

Jeff. You muſt know, Madam, my Maſter was in Love elſe-where.

Widow. How *Jeffrey.*

                                        Jeff.

Jeff. If your Ladyſhip will have Patience to hear me out, you ſhall know the whole Story.

Widow. With all my Heart, *Jeffrey*.

Jeff. Why, you muſt know, Madam, my Maſter had the Misfortune to quarrel with a Gentleman, who urg'd him to fight; my Maſter kill'd him: Upon which he was forc'd to change his Habit and his Name—— From *Cuningham* to *Boutefeu*. But thinking it not ſafe to ſtay here, fled; and in his Journey happen'd into a Viſcount's Caſtle, but the Viſcount was gone a Journey. However, this Viſcount had a very beautiful Siſter, that had the Command in her Brother's Abſence; ſhe entertain'd my Maſter very ſplendidly : At laſt he fell in love with her, and ſhe with him.

Widow. Methinks ſhe was very forward, *Jeffrey*.

Jeff. She was ſo indeed, Madam; for before my Maſter left her, ſhe prov'd with Child.

Widow. How ! with Child, and not married, *Jeffrey* !

Jeff. My Maſter had promis'd her Marriage, Madam.

Widow. Oh, the impudent Creature ! And thy Maſter was to blame, not to keep his Word, *Jeffrey*.

Jeff. Not at all, Madam, when you have heard all. You muſt know, my Maſter grew jealous of one of the Servants, as indeed he had Reaſon : And one Day pretended to ride out, and he ſhou'd not return that Night, but left me to let him in, when the Servants were all a bed, which I did. Going up to this Lady's Bed Chamber, and not being expeĉted that Night, found the Servant in Bed with her.

Widow. Unheard of Impudence !
At firſt I was going to condemn thy Maſter, for deceiving a young Creature ; but 'tis likely he was not the firſt, that had to do with her.

Jeff.

Jeff. Very likely fo, Madam. Next Day my Mafter was for packing up his Awls, and for going;
fhe cry'd, and urg'd his ftay, and his Vows to marry
her.

Widow. He had been more to blame to have done
that.

Jeff. In the mean time the Vifcount return'd, found
his Sifter in Tears, wou'd know the Reafon, was told
all. He fwore, if ever he could get hold of him,
he'd hang him at his Caftle Gate, but my Mafter
was got off fafe. What it will come to, if they
fhould ever meet, I know not, but fear the Event.

Pru. A well invented Lye the Rogue has told. (*Afide.*
What was this Vifcount's Name ?

Jeff. The Vifcount *Sans-Terre,* I think he was
call'd.

Pru. The Vifcount *Sans-Terre !*

Widow. Why, he's in this Houfe.

Jeff. What, in this very Houfe ?

Pru. In this very Houfe; in the next Room.

Jeff. Ah, my poor Mafter ! he's but a dead Man,
if he's found; for he'll certainly be hang d.

Pru. Here he comes. Hold your Peace!

Enter Vifcount.

Widow. My Lord, your Servant. I have a Queftion
to ask of you.

Jeff. What fhall I do to make him underftand ?
(*Afide.*
Humour her in all fhe fays, my Lord.

Vifc. Ask what thou wilt, I'll deny thee nothing.

Widow. You had a Sifter.

Vifc. I had fo. Go on.

Widow. And fhe was unfortunately wrong d by a
bafe Fellow,

Vifc. What muft I fay next ?

Pru.

Pru. 'Twas not well done to debauch her, and then to leave her ; but Woe be to him, if your Lordſhip catch him.

Viſc. If ever I do find the Son of a Whore, I'll hang him at my Caſtle Gate.

Widow. He was very much to blame indeed ; but yet, all things conſider'd, he was not in all the Blame neither, counting what a Trick ſhe play'd him. He had reaſon to queſtion, whether the Child was his, or not.

Viſc. I'm quite at a Loſs. Oh! tell me what I muſt ſay next? (*Faints into* Jeffrey's *Arms, who inſtruſts him.*

Jeff. Take it in your Ear, my Lord.   (*Aſide.*

Widow. Help, *Prudence*, my Lord faints.

Pru. Pray, Madam, don't come too near, but give him Air.   (Prudence *and* Jeffrey *tell him what to ſay.*

Widow. Oh! he recovers.

Viſc. Give me a little Air. I beg your Pardon, I never hear my Siſter's Wrongs mention'd, but it puts me in Diſorder ; but if ever I do light upon the Villain, Woe be to him.

Widow. I'll try to get his Pardon.   (*Aſide.* My Lord, methinks her Crime being the greateſt, you might pardon him.

Viſc. What! Pardon him, that has deflower'd my Siſter, got her with Child of a Baſtard, and ſtain'd the Honour of our great Family! No, tho' all the World ſhould plead for him, I'll not forgive it ; he dies.

Widow. Good, my Lord, for my Sake.

Viſc. 'Tis all in vain, Lady. I'm told he's now in this Houſe, and has chang'd his Name. But if I find him———   (*Draws.*

Widow. Oh hold, my Lord, I muſt ſave him. (*Aſide.* My Lord, I have but one Requeſt more.

Viſc. 'Twill be in vain: I'll have Revenge.

Pru.

Pru. Tell him you'll marry him, Madam, and try what that will do.   (*Aſide to the Widow.*

Widow. Give me this Gentleman's Life, and I am content to be your Wife ; otherwiſe——

Viſc. 'Tis a hard Requeſt ; but to ſhew how much I love you, upon that Condition I grant it.
     (*Puts up his Sword.*

Widow. Or, if you think fit, you ſhall have my Niece *Philadelphia,* and with her I'll give you ten thouſand Pounds.

Viſc. Do you think my Love ſo poor, that 'twill be brib'd ? Nay, then I recal my Promiſe. He dies this Hour.   (*Draws and ſearches about.*

Pru. Oh, pray my Lord, forbear ; my Lady did it but to try you ! See, you fright her.

Widow. Well, my Lord, ſince it muſt be ſo, my Chaplain is within, I'm contented he ſhou'd make us one, make good but your Promiſe.

Viſc. I confirm it here.   (*Kiſſes her.*

Pru. My Lord, the Dancers are ready to begin, and all the Company ſtay for you.

Viſc. Let 'em enter, and begin when they pleaſe.

Enter Sir Peter Pride, *Lady* Pride, Lovemore, *Mrs.* Brittle, Cuningham *and* Philadelphia.

Love. Well, Madam, I rely upon your Promiſe.
     (*To Mrs.* Brittle.

Viſc. Come, Gentlemen and Ladies, pray ſit.
     (*They Sit.*

A D A N C E.

After the Dance, Enter Barnaby Brittle, *who runs after his Wife; they get between, he gets hold of her,
and carries her off after Speaking.*

Britt. Here's fine Doings! But I'll fpoil your Sport.
What! my Houfe is become a Mufic-houfe, is it?
But, Gentlewoman, I have fomething to fay to you
within.

Omnes. How now! What's the Meaning of this?

Britt. I fay, my Wife——

Omn. What of your Wife?

Britt. Shall keep me Company, if you pleafe.

Omn. You Company!

Cun. What's the matter with the Fellow? ha!

Britt. Come along, I fay. What's here to do!
Is not a Man's Wife his Wife? And may he not do
what he will with her?   (*Carries her off.*

Sir *Peter.* He's at his old Tricks again.

Widow. Come, let's in, and endeavour to appeafe
him, and then end our Mirth with a Banquet.

Cun. We attend your Ladyfhip.

Widow. Pray, my Lord, do me the favour to lead
my Sifter in.
Come, Gentlemen.

Vifc. Hold there, I will not part with you; I
have two Hands, Madam, and can lead you both.

                          (*Exeunt Omnes.*

ACT

ACT V.

Enter Cuningham, Philadelphia *and* Jeffrey.

Jeff. FEar nothing ; by what I could learn, by this time the old Lady is gone to her Chamber, or near being a-bed.

Cun. Then we may have Time to talk more freely.

Phil. All is not fo fafe as you imagine. I fear another Storm before we yet can land. I know not by what means, but the Vifcount is difcover'd to be a Counterfeit, which I have all along fufpected ; but whether 'tis come to the Knowledge of my Aunt yet, I know not.

Cun. Therefore let's lofe no time, but tye that Knot, which joins our Hearts and Hands for ever : That once over, we have no farther need of the Vifcount.

Enter Lovemore, *and the* Vifcount *enrag'd, with Lights before 'em.*

Vifc. Never perfuade me ; I'll not ftay to be fool'd at this rate any longer.—— Go lead, Sirrah.

(*Exit with Links.*

Cun. What's the Matter now ?

Love. Matter ! Why there's Matter enough in hand. We are all undone ; the March is broke off again, and you are like to lofe your Miftrefs. The Widow will not confent you fhall marry her Niece ; upon which, the Vifcount enrag'd, (as indeed he has Caufe) is refolv'd to ftay no longer.
What 'twill come to, I know not.

E 3 *Cun.*

Cun. This is moſt unlucky.   What's to be thought on next ?

Love. I left *Prudence* reaſoning the Caſe with her ; what will be the Concluſion, is moſt uncertain.   Oh here ſhe comes.

Enter Prudence.

Pru. Oh, Madam ! the ſaddeſt News!

Phil. Why ? What's the Matter?

Pru. All the Buſineſs is over.   Poor Mr. *Cuningham*————

Phil. Ha! What of him ? Speak.

Pru. After a thouſand Arguments, which I us'd to perſuade her, ſhe has at laſt reſolv'd———— I can't ſpeak it.

Phil. On what? Prithee out with it.

Pru. Why, to marry the Viſcount her ſelf, and give you and your ten thouſand Pounds to Mr. *Cuningham.*

Cun. Oh the bleſs'd News ! What ſay you now, Madam ?

Phil. I'll ſwear I was in a Fright at firſt. But art thou ſure ſhe'll hold in this Mind ?

Love. For fear of the worſt, get all things ready, and let it be done this Moment.

Pru. Here ſhe comes. Seem concern'd to part with her, Sir, and try how ſhe ſtands reſolv'd.

Enter Widow.

Cun. And muſt I then loſe her, *Prudence !* Oh, the racking Thought ! Hard ! Hard ! Decree of Fate ! To part with all I hold moſt dear ! I cannot bear it.   *(Walks about.*

Widow. Yes, Mr. *Cuningham,* our Stars will have it ſo.

'Tis

'Tis hard indeed to part: But fince there is no way left to fave your Life, (wnich more than all the World I prize) but this only, I have at laft refolv'd (tho' much againft my Will) to give my felf to the Vifcount.

Cun. Oh! do not name it, Madam, the very Thought is worfe, than Death.

Widow. I'm forry we are fo near a kin, but that's not the chief Reafon ; your Vow to marry another, and yet when I confider fhe was falfe, and had to do with more, than one, and that the Child might as well not be yours, I think you were in the right to part : So I am content (fince my Hopes are loft) that you fhou'd marry with my Niece. But believe me, you do not know how much I'm troubled, to fee another take what I fo much defir'd. But we muft endeavour to be fatisfied.

Cun. Never ! Never! for fince I lofe you, farewel to Love and Joy: The reft of Life I'll wafte in Sorrow.

Enter Clodpole, *whifpers* Lovemore.

Clod. Softly ! *Damaris* bad me tell you, that her Miftrefs ftays for you at the Garden Door.

Love. Oh, very well. I'll go this Moment.

Pru. But what will you do to recal the Vifcount, Madam, who left the Houfe in Anger, nor told any one what his Defigns were ?

Love. I heard him bid the Link-boy lead to the Devil Tavern. If you pleafe, thither we'll go, and conclude upon the Matter. A Glafs or two of Wine may fetch him about again.

Widow. Truly, Mr. *Lovemore*, I'm much oblig'd to you, and fhall endeavour to return your friendly Advice. I hope we fhall live as loving Neighbours ought, but now we lofe time. The Vifcount may perhaps be gone, fhould we ftay longer.

Love.

Love. I'll but give fome Directions to my Man,
and be there almoft as foon as you.

Widow. You will oblige us, Sir.

(*Exit all but* Love. *and* Clod.

Clod. 'Tis main dark, nothing to be feen but the
Sky and Stars. What can this Darknefs portend! The
Almanicks this Year fay, That many things will be
huddled in the dark.

Love. Why, thou art an Aftrologer, *Clodpole*, thou
talk'ft fo learnedly.

Clod. Why, truly I am but a Piece of one; but had
I been a great Schollard, I believe I fhou'd have
thought on things, that never had been thought on
before.

Love. Very likely, truly. But hark! What Noife
is that? There's *Brittle's* Houfe; may be fhe is coming out.

Enter Mrs. Brittle *and* Damaris.

Mrs. Britt. Softly *Damaris*, juft fhut the Door,
we'll not be far from it.

Dam. Is your Husband faft, Madam?

Mrs. Britt. I would not ftir till I faw him afleep,
he's fnoring like one that's drunk.

Love. That's her Voice. Madam, where are you?

Dam. There they are, Madam.

Mrs. Britt. You find, Sir, I am as good as my
Word. I hope you are a Man of Honour, as you fay;
yet were it to do again, I fhould hardly venture fuch
another bold Attempt.

Love. Fear nothing, Madam. Your Perfon and
your Honour both are fafe, whilft I am your Guard.
Can none over hear us?

Mrs. Britt. All the Family, but *Damaris* and I, are
gone to Bed; nor dare we be long from thence, left
my Husband fhould wake, and mifs me.

Love

Love. Talk not of parting e'er we well are met; that were unkind, Madam.
If you pleafe, Madam, to walk a little farther this way, here's a Place more private, than the reft, and will beft befit our Difcourfe.

Mrs. Britt. Well, Sir, I'll not queftion your Honour any more, but truft my felf with you; as you behave your felf now, expect a greater Liberty another time.

Love. I'll warrant you: This way, my Charmer.
(*He leads her out, fhe takes hold of* Damaris, *who follows.*

Mrs. Britt. Damaris!

Dam. I'm here, Madam.

(Clodpole *feels with his Stick for* Damaris.

Clod. Damaris!——— Softly!——— Damaris!———
Damaris!

Enter Brittle, *groping in the dark in a Cap and a Night-Gown.*

Britt. Where can fhe be gone at this time of Night? I heard her fteal down; I'll liften.

Clod. Damaris, Where art thou, *Damaris!*———
Odd, 'tis main dark.

Britt. Who have we here? Here's fomething more than ordinary. But I'll draw nearer.
(*Goes towards him.*

Clod. Damaris, Where art thou?

Britt. Here. (*In a low Voice:* Clodpole *feels him with his Stick, thinks 'tis* Damaris.

Clod. Oh! art thou there?
Well, *Damaris*, muft not thee and I follow the Example of thy Miftrefs, and my Mafter? I'll warrant they'll be hugeous kind to one another; for my Mafter, you muft know, has a mighty Love for her, and fo belike fhe has for him; or elfe fhe wou'd ne'er a left her Husband a bed to a come to him. *Britt.*

Britt. Oh horrid ! 'tis ſo. (*Aſide.*

Clod. How he ſnores now, if a Body were to hear him ! Poor Cuckold ! He little dreams what his Wife and my Maſter are doing. Ha, ha, ha.

Britt. Oh ! this is my Country Chap again. (*Aſide.*

Clod. Poor Cuckold, 'tis good enough for him. For as they ſay, he uſes her mighty ill. But, *Damaris,* muſt thee and I part thus ? One little Bit to ſtay my Stomach, *Damaris :* Tis fit, we ſhou'd follow our Leaders. {*Goes to Kiſs.*

Britt. I can hold no longer. Who goes there ?
(*Hits him a Box.*

Clod. Odd ſo! Oh ! Oh! Who's that ? Oh !
*Puts his Stick a-croſs, and in running out-ſtops a-
gainſt the Scenes ; at laſt gets off.*

Britt. So—— He's gone. Here's a Diſcovery at laſt ! Here's a fine Virtuous Wife for you ! But now all will out in ſpite of her. I'll ſend inſtantly for her Parents ; they ſhall ſee now who's in the right. Oh bleſs us ! What, make her Husband a Cuckold ! Oh! Monſtrous ! (*Goes to the Door, and calls.*
Jeremy ! the Varlet's a-ſleep, I'll warrant. *Jeremy,* I ſay.

(Jer. *above)* Do you call, Sir ?

Britt. Yes, I do call. Come down quickly, I muſt ſend you to my Father-in law's.

Jer. I come, Sir. (*Puts a Rope out, and ſlides down.*

Britt. Make haſte, Sirrah. How long you are co-ming. Ah ! Villain !

(Jeremy *treads upon his Toes, and gets from him,*
You have trod upon my Corns, and lam'd me.
Come hither, and be hang'd.

Jer. I dare not, Sir ; you'll beat me.

Britt. Ah ! 'tis well I ſtand in need of thee.
(*Comes to him.*
Run to my Father and Mother-in-Law, and tell 'em, I intreat to ſpeak with 'em this Moment ; tell 'em I'll
never

never trouble 'em again as long as I live ; beg 'em by all means to come.

Jer. Yes, Sir. *(Exit.*

Britt. Now they fhall fee what a Daughter they have.

Now I fhall fure convince 'em of their Error !

But I hear fome body coming !

May be I fhall make a farther Difcovery. *(Stands afide.*

Enter Lovemore, *Mrs.* Brittle, Damaris, *and* Clodpole.

Mrs. Britt. Nay, Sir, I've ftay'd long enough for one time : Should my Husband wake, and mifs me, I were undone.

I muft be gone.

Love. Stay one Minute longer, I befeech you, Madam.

I have not told you yet———

Mrs. Britt. No more, Sir, if you love me. Farewel.

Love. Oh, ftay ! How can you go, and leave me fo foon ?

You will have time enough to lie by that dull, ftupid Clod, your Husband, e'er the Morning : Methinks I grudge him the leaft Look of you, fince he knows not how to value fo rich a Jewel. Let him live, and pore o'er his Bags, his Drofs, and worldly Gains, whilft we know better how to wafte our youthful Hours in fofteft Kiffes, and everlafting Joys.

Britt. Oh, blafting Sound ! But I have heard enough.

Now to my Poft. *(Exit.*

Mrs. Britt. Good Night, Sir : Now I muft be gone.

Love. When fhall I be thus blefs'd again ?

Mrs.

Mrs. Britt. To Morrow I'll fend for you; and, if poſſible, appoint another Meeting.

Love. Till then, ten thouſand Angels wait on thee. One Kiſs e'er we part.　　　　　*(Kiſſes her.*
Oh, I could dwell for ever on thy Lips!
Sure, there's Enchantment on 'em.

Mrs. Britt. Farewel!

Love. Adieu, my lovely Charmer. *(Exit with* Clod.

Mrs. Britt. Now, *Damaris*, let's ſteal in: Softly! Softly!

Dam. O Lord, Madam! We are undone!
The Door is faſt ſince we have been out.
　　　　　　　　　　　(Puſhes againſt it.

Mrs. Britt. What ſhall we do now, *Damaris?*

Dam. I wiſh my Maſter has not been down.

Mrs. Britt. Let's call *Jeremy* ſoftly.

Both. Jeremy! Jeremy!
　　(They both call up to the Window *in a ſoft Tone.*

Brittle *at the* Window *above.*

Britt. Jeremy! Jeremy!　　　　　　*(In their Tone.*

Dam. Oh, Madam, my Maſter!

Mrs. Britt. Loſt! Undone for ever!

Britt. Ah! Ha! my ſweet Lady! Have I caught you at laſt!
Jeremy! Jeremy!
Where has your ſweet Ladyſhip been, I pray, that you are ſo afraid of being diſcover'd? Come, I know you have a Lie in readineſs: Let's have it.

Mrs. Britt. No where but juſt with *Damaris*, to take a little of the freſh Air; that's all, indeed, ſweet Husband.

Britt. To take the freſh Air, quotha!
Ah, i rather believe 'twas to take a Heat, you Witch you.

Mrs. Britt. Pray, Husband, let the Door be o-pen'd ?

Britt. No : You ſhall ſtay there till your Parents come.
I have ſent for them: They ſhall ſee what Hours you keep. And know of your Gallant you juſt parted from, your vigorous Lover.

Dam. Madam, he over-heard all,
And we are undone.   (*Aſide to her.*

Britt. What, have you no Excuſe ready ?
No Invention ? You and your wicked Inſtrument there, that ſtands like the Serpent at *Eve's* Elbow, to tempt her to Sin.
What, is your Prompter to Wickedneſs dumb ?
I'd fain hear how you intend to excuſe it.

Mrs. Britt. I don't go about to excuſe it, Husband———

Britt. No ; That's becauſe you don't know how.

Mrs. Britt. I do confeſs, I have been to meet a Gentleman, but not alone ; *Damaris* was with me. And ſure there was no Crime in a little harmleſs Chat.

Britt. No, no, not in the leaſt; making me a Cuckold is no harm at all.

Mrs. Britt. Pray, Husband, let me in, and I'll never do the like again, as long as I live ; but you ſhall hence-forward find me the moſt dutiful Wife, that you could wiſh for. Pray, Husband, truſt me but this once.

Britt. No.

Mrs. Britt. Do not diſgrace me to my Parents, by expoſing me at this unſeaſonable Hour, in which I do confeſs I am much to blame ———

Britt. Oh! Do you ſo?

Mrs. Britt. But forgive me now, I'll never do it again.

Britt. Hang them that believes you, I fay.

Mrs. Britt. I am fure I never injur'd you in all my Life ; but am as innocent as the Child unborn, from doing the Ill, which you fufpect.

Britt. It may be fo : 'Twas not your Fault then.

Mrs. Britt. Pray, dear Husband, believe me, and let me in.

Britt. No.

Mrs. Britt. On my Knees I ask your Pardon, do but open the Door.

Britt. No.

Mrs. Britt. If you let me in this time, 'twill work upon me more, than all the Liberty in the World cou'd do befide.

Britt. I care not.

Mrs. Brit . Indeed, Husband, I love you dearly, and love you only : How can you then be fo cruel to refufe me ?

Britt. Ah, cunning Crocodile ?
Now you are caught, 'tis dear Husband, fweet Hus-band, 'tis only you I love : But at another time, 'tis good for nothing old Fool. No, no, I know you well enough, and fo fhall your Parents now.

Mrs. Britt. Pray, Husband, let the Door be open'd.

Britt. No.

Mrs. Britt. Try me but this once.

Britt. I tell you, no.

Mrs. Britt. Not once more ?

Britt. No.

Mrs. Britt. If you provoke me, I may defpair, grow defperate, and do a Deed, which you may re-pent.

Britt. Good lack ! What will your fweet Ladyfhip do?

Mrs. Britt. I'll kill my felf with this Knife here.
                              (*Shews her Fan.*

Britt. Oh, very well !

Mrs. Britt. Nay, 'twill not be fo well as you imagine neither. Every body knows how ill we have
liv'd, and when I'm dead, People will think you murder'd me.

Britt. Ay!

Mrs. Britt. Therefore I'll kill my felf, to have my
Death reveng'd upon you.

Britt. Odd, I'll truft to that.
Befides, killing ones felf has been a great while out
of fafhion. But why don't you difpatch? Methinks
you are long about it.

Mrs. Britt, You may believe me, for I'll certainly
do it, if you perfift.

Britt. Odd, I'll venture it.

Mrs. Britt. Befides, when I am dead, my Ghoft
fhall haunt you.

Britt. Ah, if I cou'd but once get rid of your Perfon here, I fhould not fear your Ghoft hereafter.

Mrs. Britt. Have you no Pity left?
I am juft going to do it.

Britt. And yet you are long about it.

Mrs. Britt. Since nothing but my Death can fatisfy
you——
There and there!

(*Pretends to ftab her felf with her Fan, and falls.*

Dam. Oh, fhe has don't! She has don't!
Oh cruel, barbarous Monfter, to make her kill her
felf!

Mrs. Britt. Now, *Damaris,* you find too late I did
not jeft——
I know thou'lt fee my Death reveng'd upon my
cruel Husband, who has accus'd me falfly; for I af-
firm with my dying Breath, I never wrong'd him.
Farewel!
Death beckons me into a dark and gloomy Vale, where
I muft follow.

Dam.

Dam. She's gone ! She's gone !
Oh, thou worfe than Savage ! To murder fo fweet a
Lady, fo innocent and fo good : Nay, I'll fwear you
did it.   *(Cries over her.*
   Britt. I hear no Noife !   *(Looks frighten'd.*
Is't poffible the Devil fhou'd be fo great with her,
that fhe cou'd kill her felf to be reveng'd on me !
But I'll light a Candle, and go fee.
      (Goes from the Window.
  Mrs. Britt. **Now,** *Damaris,* ftand clofe in this
Corner :
Clofe, Clofe.   *(They ftand afide.*

Enter Brittle *with a Light* ; *they flip by him, go in,
and lock the Door : He looks about.*

  Britt. Ha, ha, ha ! I thought indeed how well fhe'd
do it : Here's none of her ! She made me believe fhe
kill'd her felf, and the mean while ran away. Well,
e'en let her go; I fhall have this Satisfaction, her Parents fhall be Witnefs of her Hours. I'll in, and
wait their coming.
    (Goes to the Door, and finds it lock'd. Knocks.

Mrs. Brittle *and* Damaris *above at the Window,
where he was.*

  Mrs. Britt. Away, you idle Sot ; is this a time of
Night for an honeft Man to come home in?
  Dam. Go, go, you may be afham'd !
  Britt. Why, have you the Impudence———
      (Looks up, and fees 'em above.
  Mrs. Britt. How many Nights am I forc'd to fit
up to wait for his coming in ? And he tells the
World, 'tis I am to blame. But now it fhall be feen
who's to blame, and who not. My Father and Mo
ther are coming, they fhall fee what Hours you
kcep———   *Britt.*

Britt. I confefs, I ftand amaz'd at this Impudence.

Mrs. Britt. They fhall know all.

Britt. Why, have you the Face to deny——

Mrs. Britt. Go, go, I'll hear none of your impudent Excufes; you are drunk, you Sot, you Swine. But here comes my honourable Father and Mother.

Enter Sir Peter *and Lady* Pride.

I'm glad you are come to be Witnefs of what I ftill fuffer, by this ungrateful Ufage of a cruel Husband. You fee what Hours he keeps; every Nighe at the Tavern roaring with his Companions, whilft I am forc'd to fit at home alone, waiting for his coming; and when he does come, he ftrait raves and abufes me at fuch a rate, that I am not able to endure it.

Britt. Why, was there ever fuch Impudence! I wifh this Candle were in my Belly, if——

Mrs. Britt. I know what he'll fay now, if you'll believe him; he'll tell you, that I am ftill in the wrong, and 'tis I that have been out at this late Hour, and as for his part, he has been within all this Evening, and knows nothing of all this Matter, not he: But I'll leave your felves to judge, if this is an Hour for an honeft Husband to come home at.

Britt. Why then may I never——

Mrs. Britt. You fee he's fo drunk, he can hardly ftand.

Lady. Faugh!—— I fmell him hither. He ftinks of Liquors and Tobacco like a Tarpaulin, that has not been fober whilft his Twelve Months Pay wou'd laft.

Britt. I tell you, that I am not drunk, nor have I been out of my Houfe.

Sir Peter. Stand farther off, I cannot bear the Scent of a Drunkard.

F *Mrs.*

Mrs. Britt. I told you he wou'd deny it.

Britt. I fay, that 'tis fhe that has been out juft now, and with her Gallant, and therefore I fent for you ; and that I have not been out of my Doors.

Mrs. Britt. Do you hear him ? But *Damaris* can juftify, I have not fet my Foot over the Threfhold fince Day-light.

Dam. If fhe has, never believe me more.

I can affure your Honours 'tis true ; for I have not been out of her Company fince he went out to the Tavern.

Mrs. Britt. Therefore I do befeech you, good Father and Mother, to revenge my Caufe, for I am not able to endure it any longer : If I do, you'll never fee me alive another Week.

Britt. 'Tis a ftrange thing, that fhe muft be believed, and I not.

I tell you——

Lady. Stand farther off.

Faugh ! What a Smell there's about him.

(She goes crofs the Stage.

Britt. Well then ; I'll ftand farther off, if you will but hear me fpeak.   *(Goes backward.*

I fhall fay nothing but the Truth, and what I can prove.

Sir *Peter.* Again at your Proofs, and your idle Jealoufies !

Be dumb, Coxcomb ; it were a good deed to break your Head, for fending thus for us out of our Beds, and making Fools of us ftill. If you ever dare to do the like again, we'll find a Means to handle you——

If there be no Law (but cutting of Throats) to revenge thefe Affronts—— I fay no more—— But remember you are warn'd.

Britt. If you wou'd but let me tell why I fent for you——

Sir

Sir *Peter.* We have heard and feen too much already.

Therefore dare not to fpeak a Word more.

Mrs. Britt. And is this all his Punifhment?

Sir *Peter.* No; Come down, and he fhall ask your Pardon. 'Tis the leaft he can do.

Mrs. Britt. 'Twill be to no purpofe; when your Backs are turn'd, he'll be as bad again.

Sir *Peter.* I fay no more Difputes, but do as I command. *(They come down from the Window.* Now, Son-in-law, kneel down, and ask your Wife Forgivenefs.

Mrs. Britt. Shall I forgive him; no, I defire to be divorc'd.

Lady. Come, Daughter, I fay you muft pardon him.

Mrs. Britt. Well, Madam, I'll endeavour to obey you.

Sir *Peter.* Why don't you kneel, and do as I command?

Britt. Well, I find there's no Remedy, fhe has over-reach'd me again, and I muft fubmit: But I am refolv'd I'll get rid of this Nooze, tho' I tuck my felf up in another.

(Sir Peter *makes him kneel to his Wife.*

Sir *Peter.* Come, fay after me. Madam, I ask your Pardon.

Britt. Madam, I ask your Pardon.

Sir *Peter.* For the Folly I have committed——

Britt. For the Folly I have committed in marrying you.

Sir *Peter.* In my wild Sufpicions.

Britt. In my wild Sufpicions.

Sir *Peter.* Which I do declare were utterly falfe.

Britt. Which I do declare were utterly falfe.

Sir

Sir *Peter*. And that I fwear never to do the like again.

Britt. And that I fwear never to do the like again, if I were once unmarried.

Mrs. Britt. Here——Kifs the Book. (*Gives her Hand.* But if ever you do't again————
You fee 'tis to no purpofe to turn Hagard; it you do, I'll tame you. (*Afide to him.*

Lady. Look if the Noife has not brought all the Company hither.

Enter Vifcount, Widow, Lovemore, Cuningam, Phi-ladelphia, Prudence, Clodpole, *and* Jeffrey, *with Lights before 'em.*

Love. Your Servant, Sir *Peter*. Sir, I hope you will not take it ill; we faw a Light in your Houfe, and fo made bold : We are refolv'd to fpend an Hour or two in Mirth, and hope you will all join with us. (*To* Brittle.

Widow. Your Ladyfhip I know will pardon it upon this Occafion. (*To Lady* Pride.

Lady Pride. Is your Ladyfhip marry'd? May we give you Joy?

Widow. My Niece and Mr. *Cuningham* are.

Mrs. Britt. Give you Joy then.

Cun. and *Phil*. We thank you, Madam.

Phil. Now, Sir, fince our Hands are join'd, and all is reconcil'd, I have a Boon to ask.

Cun. Whate'er it be, conclude it done.

Phil. I have obferv'd fome Sparks of Love between *Jeffrey* and *Prudence*; and I believe they wou'd be glad to follow our Example.

Cun. What fay'ft thou, *Jeffrey*? If thou haft a Mind to marry, fpeak freely.

Jeff.

Jeff. Sir, I have debated much about the Matter, and am at laft refolv'd to venture.

Cun. Then if you, Madam, give your Confent, and *Prudence* be willing, we'll put 'em together.

(To the Widow.

Widow. With all my Heart; *Prudence* has been always a good Servant, I'll fay that for her.

Jeff. There's my Hand then; the reft of my Body fhall be forth coming.

Pru. A Match.

Love. Then let me fpeak. *Clodpole* loves *Damaris,* and I believe wou'd be glad to make up the Chorus; now if Mrs. *Brittle* pleafe to part with her——

Britt. You fhall have my Confent with all my Heart; and I'll give a Sum of Money to be rid of her.

Love. And I'll give *Clodpole* fomething to fet him up in a little Farm in the Country.

Clod. Damaris!—— Doft hear that?

Mrs. Britt. What fay you, *Damaris?*

Dam. If I thought he'd make a good Husband, and not be jealous——

Love. That I dare anfwer for him.

Clod. Well, then 'tis agreed, and there's my Hand.

Dam. For better for worfe.

Clod. To have and to hold; a Tenement for Life.

Cun. And now all things being thus happily concluded——

Widow. No, Mr. *Cuningham,* not while your Friend is unprovided. Methinks 'twere pity he fhou'd be no Actor in this Comedy.

Love. Oh, Madam, my Thoughts are not yet fix'd fo much upon any Object, but the next I encounter can retrieve the paft.

Cun.

Cun. My Friend never wants a Miſtreſs (I'll ſay that for him) in any Place, if he has but an Opportunity, which he ſeldom wants.   I have often wonder'd at his Luck.

Mrs. Britt. Say you ſo ?   I find he makes it his Buſineſs to enſnare and deceive Women at this rate.

(*Aſide.*

I'm glad I know it in time, whilſt I have Power to make my Retreat. I had like to have been finely caught.   Well, Husband, ſeeing ſo many join'd in Happineſs, if you'll promiſe never to be jealous, I'll promiſe from this Moment never to give you Cauſe, and endeavour to make you as happy as I can.

Britt. Wou'd you'd give me Cauſe once to believe you.

Viſc. Well then, if you are all agreed, the Parſon that marry'd Mr. *Cuningham* is but juſt by ; e'en ſend for him, and let him end the Work he has begun.

For my part, I intend to put off mine for ſome time longer.

Widow. How ! My Lord ! Have you ſerv'd me thus ? Did I forſake all for you, and do you pretend to———

Viſc. No Words now, 'twill ſpoil Company ; another time we'll diſcourſe it farther. Come, let's have a Dance, and then to Bed.

Omn. With all our Hearts.

A DANCE.

Viſc.

Vifc. 'Tis well : So now, you that are ready to
tafte the Sweets of Matrimony, fall to ; for my part,
I have no great Stomach to it yet.

And none I hope will blame me if I tarry,
Since thofe that wed in hafte, as faft mifcarry.

(*Exeunt Omnes.*

F I N I S.

Variant
to Page *viii*

that *Harmony*, *Decorum*, and *Or-der*, which ought perpetually to ſhine in ſuch PUBLIC REPRESEN-TATIONS.

I am, *S I R*,

Your Sincere Friend,

and *Humble Servant*,

Charles Gildon.

THE

EIGHTEENTH CENTURY SHAKESPEARE

During the one hundred and seven years covered by this series, the reputation of William Shakespeare as poet and dramatist rose from a controversial and highly qualified acceptance by post-Restoration critics and "improvers" to the almost idolatrous admiration of the early Romantics and their immediate precursors. Imposing its own standards and interpretations upon Shakespeare, the Eighteenth Century scrutinized his work in various lights. Certain qualities of the plays were isolated and discussed by a parade of learned, cantankerous, and above all self-assured commentators.

Thirty-five of the most important and representative books and pamphlets are here presented in twenty-six volumes; many of the works, through the very fact of their limited circulation have become extremely scarce, and when obtainable, expensive and fragile. The series will be useful not only for the student of Shakespeare's reputation in the period, but for all those interested in eighteenth century taste, taste-making, scholarship, and theatre. Within the series we may follow the arguments and counter-arguments as they appeared to contemporary playgoers and readers, and the shifting critical emphases characteristic of the whole era.

In an effort to provide responsible texts of these works, strict editorial principles have been established and followed. All relevant editions have been compared, the best selected, and the reasons for the choice given. Furthermore, at least one other copy, frequently three or more, have been collated with the copy actually reproduced, and the collations recorded. In cases where variants or cancels exist, every attempt has been made to provide both earlier and later or indifferently varying texts, as appendices. Each volume is preceded by a short preface discussing the text, the publication history, and, when necessary, critical and biographical considerations not readily available.

1. 1692　**Thomas Rymer**
A Short View of Tragedy (1693)
xvi, 184p.　　　　　　　　　　　　　　　　　　75s.

2. 1693　**John Dennis**
The Impartial Critick: or, some observations upon a late
book, entitled, A Short View of Tragedy, written by
Mr. Rymer, and dedicated to the Right Honourable Charles
Earl of Dorset, etc. (1693)
xvi, 52p.
　1712　**John Dennis**
An Essay on the Genius and Writings of Shakespear: with
some Letters of Criticism to the Spectator (1712)
xxii, 68p.　　　　　　　　　　　　　　　　　　70s.

3. 1694　**Charles Gildon [ed.]**
Miscellaneous Letters and Essays, on Several Subjects. Philo-
sophical, Moral, Historical, Critical, Amorous, etc. in Prose
and Verse (1694)
xvi, 132p.　　　　　　　　　　　　　　　　　　55s.

4. 1710　**Charles Gildon**
The Life of Mr. Thomas Betterton, the late Eminent Tragedian. Wherein The Action and Utterance of the Stage, Bar,
and Pulpit, are distinctly consider'd . . . To which is added,
The Amorous Widow, or the Wanton Wife . . . Written by
Mr. Betterton. Now first printed from the Original Copy
(1710)
xvi, 176, 87p.　　　　　　　　　　　　　　　　84s.

5. 1726　**Lewis Theobald**
Shakespeare restored: or, A Specimen of the Many Errors,
As well Committed, as Unamended, by Mr. Pope in his Late
Edition of this Poet (1726)
xiii, 194p. 4°　　　　　　　　　　　　　　　£5 5s.

6. 1747　**William Guthrie**
An Essay upon English Tragedy with Remarks upon the
Abbe de Blanc's Observations on the English Stage (?1747)
34p.
　1749　**John Holt**
An Attempte to Rescue that Aunciente, English Poet, and

Play-wrighte, Maister Williaume Shakespere, from the Maney Errours, faulsely charged on him, by Certaine New-fangled Wittes and to let him speak for Himself, as right well he wotteth, when Freede from the many Careless Mistakeings, of the Heedless first Imprinters, of his Workes (1749)
94p.   55s.

7.   1748   **Thomas Edwards**
The Canons of Criticism and Glossary. Being a Supplement to Mr. Warburton's Edition of Shakespear. Collected from the Notes in that celebrated Work, and proper to be bound up with it. To which are added, The Trial of the Letter Υ alias Y; and Sonnets (Seventh Edition, with Additions 1765)
368p.   £5 5s.

8.   1748   **Peter Whalley**
An Enquiry into the Learning of Shakespeare (1748)
84p.
      1767   **Richard Farmer**
As Essay on the Learning of Shakespeare ... the Second Edition, with Large Additions (1767)
viii, 96p.   70s.

9.   1752   **William Dodd**
The Beauties of Shakespeare: Regularly selected from each Play, With a General Index, Digesting them under Proper Heads. Illustrated with Explanatory Notes and Similar Passages from Ancient and Modern Authors (1752)
2v., xxiv, 264; iv, 258p.   £10 10s.

10.   1753   **Charlotte Ramsay Lennox**
Shakespear Illustrated ... with Critical Remarks (1753-4)
3v., xiv, 292; iv, 276; iv, 312p.   £15

11.   1765   **William Kenrick**
A Review of Doctor Johnson's New Edition of Shakespeare: In which the Ignorance, or Inattention of That Editor is exposed, and the Poet Defended from the Persecution of his Commentators (1765)
xvi, 136p.
      1766   **Thomas Tyrwhitt**
Observations and Conjectures upon some Passages of

Shakespeare (1766)
ii, 56p.   75s.

12. 1769   **Elizabeth Montagu**
An Essay on the Writings and Genius of Shakespear, compared with the Greek and French dramatic Poets. With some
remarks upon the misrepresentations of Mons. de Voltaire
(1769)
iv, 288p.   90s.

13. 1774   **William Richardson**
     1784   Essays on Shakespeare's Dramatic Characters: With an
     1789   Illustration of Shakespeare's Representation of National
            Character, in that of Fluellen (sixth edition 1812)
            xii, 448p.   £6 6s.

14. 1775   **Elizabeth Griffith**
The Morality of Shakespeare's Drama Illustrated (1775)
xvi, 528p.   £9 9s.

15. 1777   **Maurice Morgann**
An Essay on the Dramatic Character of Sir John Falstaff
(1777)
xii, 186p.   63s.

16. 1783   **Joseph Ritson**
Remarks Critical and Illustrative of the last Edition of
Shakespeare [by George Steevens, 1778], (1783)
viii, 240p.
     1788   **Joseph Ritson**
The Quip Modest; A few Words by way of Supplement to
Remarks, Critical and Illustrative on the Text and Notes of
the Last Edition of Shakespeare: occasioned by a Republi-
cation of that Edition (1788, first issue)
viii, 32p.
With the preface (revised) to the second issue of *The Quip
Modest* (1788)
viii p.   84s.

17. 1785   **Thomas Whately**
Remarks on some of the Characters of Shakespere, Edited

by Richard Whately (Third edition 1839)
128p.   55s.

18. **1785**   **John Monck Mason**
    1797   Comments on the Several Editions of Shakespeare's Plays,
    1798   Extended to those of Malone and Steevens (1807)
          xvi, 608p.   £9 9s.

19. **1786**   **John Philip Kemble**
          Macbeth and King Richard the Third: An Essay, in answer to
          Remarks on some of the Characters of Shakespeare [by
          Thomas Whately] (1817)
          xii, 172p.   63s.

20. **1792**   **Joseph Ritson**
          Cursory Criticisms on the Edition of Shakespeare published
          by Edmond Malone (1792)
          x, 104p.
          Edmond Malone
          A Letter to the Rev. Richard Farmer, D.D. Master of
          Emanuel College, Cambridge; Relative to the Edition of
          Shakespeare, published in 1790. And Some Late Criticisms
          on that work (1792)
          ii, 40p.   60s.

21. **1796**   **William Henry Ireland**
          An Authentic Account of the Shakespeare Manuscripts (1796)
          ii, 44p.
    1799   **William Henry Ireland**
          Vortigern, An Historical Tragedy, In five Acts; Represented
          at the Theatre Royal, Drury Lane. And Henry the Second,
          An Historical Drama. Supposed to be written by the Author
          of Vortigern (1799)
          80, iv, 79p.   75s.

22. **1796**   **Edmond Malone**
          An Inquiry into the Authenticity of Certain Miscellaneous
          Papers and Legal Instruments, published Dec. 24, 1795. And
          Attributed to Shakespeare, Queen Elizabeth, and Henry
          Earl of Southampton (1796)
          vii, 424p.   £7

For Product Safety Concerns and Information please contact our EU
representative GPSR@taylorandfrancis.com
Taylor & Francis Verlag GmbH, Kaufingerstraße 24, 80331 München, Germany